The
COMPREHENSIVE GUIDE
to *YOUTH*
MINISTRY
COUNSELING

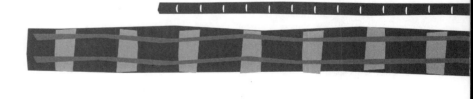

Group
Loveland, Colorado

Group's R.E.A.L. Guarantee to you:

This Group resource incorporates our R.E.A.L. approach to ministry—one that encourages long-term retention and life transformation. It's ministry that's:

Relational
Because learner-to-learner interaction enhances learning and builds Christian friendships.

Experiential
Because what learners experience through discussion and action sticks with them up to 9 times longer than what they simply hear or read.

Applicable
Because the aim of Christian education is to equip learners to be both hearers and doers of God's Word.

Learner-based
Because learners understand and retain more when the learning process takes into consideration how they learn best.

The Comprehensive Guide to Youth Ministry Counseling
Copyright © 2002 Group Publishing, Inc.

Visit our Web site: **www.grouppublishing.com**

Credits
Contributing Authors: Colleen J. Alden, Roy E. Barsness, Sally Schwer Canning, James D. Frost, Scott Gibson, D. Patrick Hopp, Cynthia Lindquist, Larry Lindquist, Julie A. Odell, Kyle D. Pontius, Trevor Simpson, Robert A. Watson, and Terri S. Watson
Editor: Kelli B. Trujillo
Creative Development Editor: Amy Simpson
Chief Creative Officer: Joani Schultz
Copy Editor: Pam Klein
Art Director: Kari K. Monson
Designer/Computer Graphic Artist: Andrea Boven
Illustrator: Matt Wood
Cover Art Director/Designer: Jeff A. Storm
Cover Illustrator: Nicholas Wilton
Production Manager: Dodie Tipton

Library of Congress Cataloging-in-Publication Data
The comprehensive guide to youth ministry counseling.
    p. cm.
Includes bibliographical references and index.
ISBN 0-7644-2356-8 (pbk. : alk. paper)
   1. Youth—Pastoral counseling of. 2. Church work with youth. I. Group Publishing.

BV4447 .C575 2002
259'.233--dc21

2002004253

10 9 8 7 6 5 4 3 2 1   11 10 09 08 07 06 05 04 03 02
Printed in the United States of America.

CONTENTS

FOREWORD

BY DR. LES PARROTT III

I'm encouraged by the very fact that you have picked up this book and are reading these words. More than ever, your help is desperately needed. Far too many people have all but given up on today's teenagers. Many potential helpers do their best to simply stay out of this generation's way. Maybe I shouldn't be surprised. Teenagers have long been considered hostile, moody, withdrawn, whiny, narcissistic, aggressive, rebellious, and unpredictable. Even Anna Freud, who specialized in treating young people, considered adolescent behavior to be so close to neurotic and psychotic disorders that differentiating between normal adolescents and those who had pathological problems was a very "difficult task"![1]

As I have traveled across North America speaking at dozens of churches and conferences for youth workers, I have sadly observed that some people are reluctant to get personally involved, focusing instead on the upfront parts of ministry. But truth be told, if you are a youth worker, you cannot avoid the compelling need to get personally involved and help hurting teenagers. Their problems are our problems, and we can no longer sidestep their painful issues or simply refer them to someone who's "more qualified."

A study that was published in the Child and Adolescent Social Work Journal found this disturbing fact: Parents of teenagers expressed a deep disappointment about the ineffectiveness, inaccessibility, and general shortage of people given to personally helping adolescents. The study surveyed parents who had received help from professionals. Almost 60 percent of those parents indicated that they weren't satisfied with that help. They said that the helping process turned out to be unhelpful, and in some cases seemed to make things worse. The parents most frequently complained that counselors did not understand what was happening to them, to their families, and to their teenagers. Because of this lack of understanding, the professionals could not help them.[2]

There is a charge to all of us who strive to help young people today: We must collaborate with parents and their teenagers. We must "encourage the timid, help the weak, be patient with everyone" (1 Thessalonians 5:14b). As youth workers, we can never replace teenagers' families as the single most important factor in helping young people make progress with their difficulties. Even today, moms and dads rank higher than peers, relatives, pastors, teachers, and counselors as resources for advice and help. But parents today, more than ever, need help in helping. I have found that about half of all parents don't feel that they're as good at parenting as they should be. The good news is that a growing body of evidence indicates that parents—with guidance from people like you—can successfully help resolve a number of struggles for their adolescents. And the book that you hold in your hands is dedicated to doing just that. This book touches on many of the common flash points of adolescence and zeroes in on what you can do to counsel youth and their families with care and competency.

Which brings me to an important point: Maybe you don't feel equipped to help this unique generation of adolescents, let alone their parents. Join the club. Many of us do not feel competent to counsel. But, believe me, you are better than you think—if you realize that the most important instrument you have in helping teenagers is yourself. Why? Because *who you are* as a person is more important than *what you do.* This understanding does not diminish the importance of the Holy Spirit, of course. The point is that your attitudes and behaviors either help or hinder the healing work that the Holy Spirit is prepared to do through you. And once you understand this critical point, you are ready to acquire the necessary tools to do the work he has called you to.

Before you rush into the chapters that make up this book, I feel compelled to help you focus on the personal qualities you'll want to cultivate. These qualities serve as a foundation that every youth worker must tend to. I sometimes ask a group of youth workers at a seminar, "What are the essential ingredients when it comes to helping teenagers?" Responses usually include ideas such as sensitivity, hope, compassion, awareness, and knowledge. The list goes go on and on. We all have theories about what is most important. However, psychological studies have shown that people—especially young people—are more likely to find help when they are with someone who is *warm, genuine,* and *empathic.* Regardless of other skills a youth worker may possess, these three traits seem to be most important. So before you turn to the chapters in this book that catch your interest, let me say a few words about each of these three traits.

Personal Warmth

The key to personal warmth is acceptance. It is an attitude that does not evaluate a person or require change; it is simple acceptance of the thoughts, feelings, and actions of a young person. This warmth allows a teenager to develop a base of self-worth—"If my youth worker accepts me, then maybe I *am* valuable." This does not necessarily mean *approving* of everything a teenager does, however. Jesus showed warmth to the woman at the well, but he certainly never condoned her sinful behavior. Jesus respected the woman and treated her as a person of worth, in spite of her lifestyle.

Genuineness

Adolescents have a built-in radar that spots phoniness even at a distance. They are experts at detecting fabricated feelings and insincere intentions. They give their own polygraph test to every overture of help. That's why genuineness is so important. Honest thoughts and authentic feelings are expressed in subtle ways—in our eyes and posture, for example. Authenticity, in other words, is something you *are,* not something you *do.* Genuineness has been described as a lure to the heart. Jesus said, "Blessed are the pure in heart" (Matthew 5:8a). Or, to say it another way, "Consider the youth minister in whom there is no guile." When genuineness is present, a hesitant and skeptical adolescent is far more likely to invest energy in the helping process.

Empathy

Empathy, the third of these essential traits, occurs when you put yourself in a young person's shoes and accurately understand his or her world. Two important distinctions about empathy are helpful. First, empathy is not identification. You don't need to blare rap music from your car radio to enter the adolescent's world. In fact, teenagers want to be seen as unique and complex.

They resent blatant attempts by adults to identify with them. Second, empathy is deeper and stronger than sympathy. Sympathy is standing on the shore and throwing out a lifeline; empathy is jumping into the water and risking your own safety to help. And the risk is real. Truly understanding the aching heart of a struggling adolescent *will* change you. Yet when you have the courage to enter the pain of a hurting teenager, you begin to build a relationship in which healing can occur.

Unfortunately, there are no universal or simple formulas for resolving the complex problems of today's youth. But if we, as youth workers, are to make a difference in the lives of teenagers, it will be because we practice proven principles of counseling, rely on biblically based theology, and seek the ultimate counsel of the Holy Spirit in our efforts to help hurting adolescents and their parents. And this book is effectively designed to help you do just that.

> Les Parrott III, Ph.D.
> Seattle Pacific University
> Author of *Helping the Struggling Adolescent*[3]

---

[1] Anna Freud, "Adolescence," in *Adolescence and Psychoanalysis: The Story and the History,* edited by Maja Perret-Catipovic and François Ladame (London: Karnac Books, 1998), 56.

[2] Rod K. Tomlinson, "Unacceptable Adolescent Behavior and Parent-Adolescent Conflict," Child and Adolescent Social Work Journal (vol. 8, no. 1, February 1991), 34.

[3] Les Parrott III, *Helping the Struggling Adolescent: A Guide to Thirty-Six Common Problems for Counselors, Pastors, and Youth Workers* (Grand Rapids, MI: Zondervan Publishing House, 1993, 2000).

From college and career decisions, faith development, and blended family issues to anger, depression, and eating disorders, the teenagers you work with are dealing with a multitude of concerns and problems. As a youth worker, you've no doubt found yourself face to face with some of these issues. Whether you're trained in counseling or are just a rookie, it's never easy knowing what to say (or what *not* to say) when you're ministering to a student who's dealing with what seems like an insurmountable challenge.

The Comprehensive Guide to Youth Ministry Counseling will equip you to come alongside your students as they ride the waves of adolescence. Within the twenty-five chapters of this book, you'll...

- discover basic counseling principles from expert Christian psychologists, counselors, and therapists;
- learn the basics of many problems and disorders that are common among adolescents;
- become aware of "red flags" that let you know when you need to refer a student to a professional counselor;
- find out about resources that you can check out to delve further into a specific problem or disorder; and
- help your students explore issues by using the photocopiable student pages at the end of each chapter.

Use the first chapter, "Counseling Principles for Youth Ministry," to develop a strategy for the way you minister to hurting students. Look through the chapters in this book to get ideas of counseling strategies for specific problems and challenges that your teenagers face. When a specific problem comes up, use the topical index (pp. 187-188) to find counseling principles related to that issue.

The next time you're sitting in your office with a distraught teenager, remember that you don't have to go it alone! Use this resource to get expert advice from Christian counselors, therapists, and psychologists to help you minister more effectively to your students.

CHAPTER 1

Counseling Principles for Youth Ministry

ROBERT A. WATSON, Psy.D., **AND TERRI S. WATSON,** Psy.D.

What a privilege it is to be called by God to minister to the needs of teenagers during this critical time in their lives. As a youth leader, it is likely that you will be one of the first people a student confides in regarding problems and concerns. While many youth workers may not feel fully equipped to deal with complicated mental health issues or family problems, the presence of a caring individual with basic listening skills who is involved in teenagers' lives can make a *huge* difference in decreasing, and even preventing, many types of adolescent problems. When a student opens up to you about spiritual, emotional, or relational problems, it can often feel like "holy ground" as you become the loving presence of Christ in the teenager's life. It's also a huge responsibility and, at times, can feel burdensome. In the following pages, we hope to provide some general principles and specific techniques for counseling adolescents that will increase the effectiveness of your own pastoral counseling ministry.

The Role of Counseling in Youth Ministry

What is the role of counseling in youth ministry? How can youth leaders attend to the growing emotional and psychological needs of their students and yet still maintain a primary focus on Jesus' call to make disciples of all nations?

We struggled with these same questions when we were new college grads working as youth ministers in a cross-cultural setting. We found ourselves alarmed by the number of emotional and relational problems our students presented that seemed to interfere with the development of an intimate relationship with Christ. It's very difficult for a teenager who has experienced abuse or neglect, for example, to believe that God is trustworthy, faithful, and loving. More and more, we found ourselves drawn to addressing the barriers that made it difficult for teenagers to embrace the gospel and to trust God with their lives. Twenty years later, as psychologists, we are still committed to using our skills to address psychological problems as barriers to spiritual growth.

Addressing the barriers that interfere with a student's spiritual development is a crucial part of ministry. Counseling teenagers on personal or emotional difficulties can go hand in hand with attending to their spiritual needs. We've found the parable of the sower to be helpful in conceptualizing the role of counseling in ministry. In Matthew 13:3-23, Jesus uses the language of soil and seeds to illustrate different responses to God's message. Jesus compares shallow, rocky, and thorny soils to the hearts of individuals in which the message of the kingdom cannot take firm root, in contrast to good soil, which bears a bountiful crop. Emotional and relational problems can contribute to hardness or shallowness of the heart and create a barrier to receiving God's truth.

By engaging in pastoral counseling, we allow God to use us to address the "rocky soil" of teenagers' hearts by exploring the barriers that interfere with the students' spiritual growth and development. Difficulties with trust, rebellion against authority (including God), distorted views of God, defensiveness, fear, perfectionism, and self-hatred can all be barriers to teenagers' growth in Christ and can impede the development of a healthy community of believers. It is important not to ignore these common emotional and psychological barriers to spiritual growth, and addressing them honestly and directly is a crucial component of ministry. On the other hand, we must be careful not to focus too much on the emotional and psychological concerns to the neglect of teenagers' spiritual development. Keeping these in balance is the art of counseling in youth ministry!

COUNSELING TEENAGERS 101: EIGHT BASIC PRINCIPLES FOR YOUTH LEADERS

Here we'll suggest eight guiding principles to keep in mind as you counsel teenagers and their families as part of your youth ministry. While this section is not designed to enable you to "hang out your shingle" as a professional psychotherapist, it will provide you with some important things to consider and may increase your confidence and competence in providing support to the students you are shepherding. Most important, our intent is to help you avoid many common pitfalls that can occur when counseling youth.

1. Distinguish Between Normal Developmental Struggles and Problems

Most youth ministers have a pretty good sense of when a student has a serious problem such as drug use, promiscuity, angry outbursts, or bingeing and purging. Often the behaviors in the gray area between "normal" and "problematic" are the ones that are confusing to parents, youth ministers, and even professional counselors. These behaviors often draw the attention and concern of adults in a young person's life. Let's look at four areas of development and identify common "gray area" behaviors associated with each:

- *Launching:* Healthy development involves letting go of old ways of relating to parents and is essential for teenagers as they leave childhood and enter adulthood. But the behaviors associated with launching into adulthood can sometimes create storms in a young person's family. Some acts of challenging authority, breaking the rules, keeping secrets from parents, and so on, are actually normal ways of declaring independence from the roles and emotional attachments of childhood. This kind of "healthy" problem behavior is more likely to occur in families that tend to apply excessive external pressure on their children to conform behaviorally.

- *Internal vs. External Guidance Systems:* As kids develop, we hope that they'll begin to shift from a primary reliance on external guidance systems (such as their parents' rules and values or their teachers' priorities and plans) to a reliance on internal guidance systems (such as their own values and morals and a capacity to plan and prioritize what to do next).

Some teenagers who are people pleasers may be a joy to be around because they are so accommodating, but they also run the risk of becoming too reliant on others for guidance and direction. They rarely draw attention to the fact that they're struggling or having problems because they imagine that others would be disappointed in them. To prevent the development of more serious problems as they enter adulthood, these students need to be helped to focus less on what other people think and more on what *they* think, believe, and value—especially, of course, in relation to Jesus.

- *Identity and Sense of Self:* You could think of a person's identity or sense of self like concrete: it gradually hardens or cures over time. By the time a young person reaches adolescence, his or her sense of self and character is beginning to set. It is not too hard yet, you can observe its basic shape, and it can be molded to some extent by external forces. But it has only a little time before it becomes very hard.

  Teenagers are intensely interested in identity. They try on different "selves" like clothes; they want others to tell them who they are, and then they reject such offerings as intrusive; and they are drawn to music and literature that explores variations on the question, "Who am I?" Sometimes the transition from one self to another can leave others astonished and alarmed. If a teenager is not putting himself or herself or others at risk, these dramatic shifts should be met with curiosity and even with a sense of playfulness. Think of this as the adolescent version of a child who's playing dress up.

- *Peers and Peer Culture:* It is clear that their peers exert an enormous influence on the development of teenagers and young adults. In fact, you could think of a young person's peer group as the healthy adolescent version of a toddler's special blanket—both offer comfort, security, and a sense of safety as a person journeys from the familiar life in the family to explore the outside world. But both will also eventually be given up in exchange for a real relationship with a significant other or a healthy level of independence. The issue isn't *whether* peers and peer culture will serve this role—the issue is *which* peers and peer culture will serve it. Common problems associated with this issue might involve parental disapproval of the choice of friends or parental dismay at their waning influence on their teenager's life.

2. Seek to Understand the Student's Problems in Context

Responding effectively to the psychological problems of teenagers and their families includes seeking to understand the context and causes of particular problems. For example, all of the skilled counseling in the world will not be sufficient for a teenager whose psychological problems stem primarily from biological causes. On the other hand, seeking only medical treatment will be ineffective for problems that are rooted in a teenager's family. As you work with students and their families, keep in mind that many common adolescent problems are multidetermined—that is, the problems may have biological, psychological, sociocultural, and spiritual dimensions. Consequently, the more complex the problem, the more likely it will require a multidimensional solution.

Many psychological problems have genetic and biological components, and in those cases, it's important to encourage a family to consult with the family physician or a psychiatrist. Such disorders include some forms of anxiety and depression, psychosis, attention-deficit hyperactivity disorder, and addictive disorders. Don't forget to consider the family's culture and socioeconomic status in understanding problems and coming up with solutions. Allow the teenager and the teenager's family to educate you about their culture and what can be considered normal or dysfunctional.

3. Adopt a Family Approach to Your Counseling

Without a doubt, the most important resource in understanding and addressing a teenager's problem is his or her family. A *systemic* approach to counseling views the teenager's concerns in the context of the entire family. Adolescent problems can often be symptoms of larger difficulties in the family—a lack of structure and discipline, too much structure, communication problems, marital problems, or more serious problems such as family violence, substance abuse, or incest.

As you begin to counsel a student, be sure to introduce yourself to his or her parents or guardian. If possible, meet with the teenager periodically in his or her home to begin to develop a relationship with the family. Ask the parents about their concerns or perceptions of their teenager's well-being. Find family strengths and resources that can help a teenager through his or her difficulties. More likely than not, your ministry to a student will develop into a ministry to the family.

4. Counsel Confidentially

Teenagers and their families need to know that they can trust you to protect their privacy by keeping the content of your conversations with them confidential. Confidentiality is a legal right that belongs to clients in professional counseling relationships, and counseling experiences in ministry should also reflect this important ethical principle. This means that before discussing a student or family with others (including church leadership), you must ask the student or family for permission.

Several important exceptions exist to this principle of confidentiality. When a teenager discloses information that leads you to have a reasonable suspicion that he or she is a victim of sexual or physical abuse or that he or she is in danger of harming himself or herself or someone else, confidentiality is secondary to ensuring the safety of the student by informing the proper authorities. We'll talk more about this later in the chapter.

What is your obligation if parents want to know what their teenager is talking to you about? This potentially tricky situation can be avoided if issues of privacy are discussed with parents upfront. We've found it helpful to let parents know at the beginning of our work with their son or daughter that counseling is most effective if it is private; and we ask for the parents' cooperation in allowing their teenager to have a confidential relationship in which to discuss his or her concerns. We assure parents that we will provide them with regular summaries of how their teenager is progressing and that we will inform them if anything comes up to suggest that their son or daughter is experiencing serious problems which place the teenager at risk. We tell parents and teenagers that, in addition to suicidal or homicidal thoughts, this also includes substance abuse and promiscuity—behaviors that can compromise a student's safety. With these assurances ahead of time, parents and teenagers are better able to trust and respect the privacy of the counseling relationship.

5. Know When to Refer, How to Refer, and Who to Refer To

Knowing when to refer a teenager or his or her family for professional help is a necessity to safeguard your important ministry. While counseling can be a rewarding and meaningful component of ministry, providing for all of a teenager's mental health needs is not realistic. Utilizing the gifts of others, such as mental health professionals, can safeguard your energy and sanity.

Consider the following guidelines for knowing when to make a referral:

- when you begin to notice that one teenager or family is consuming most of your time, energy, and thoughts
- when you encounter a teenager with multiple and complex individual or family problems and you feel yourself being drawn into the storm
- when a student or family has a history of involvement with counseling services
- when you suspect a teenager's problems may stem from medical or biological causes or significant family stress
- when a teenager's behaviors are interfering with his or her functioning at school, church, and home
- whenever there is suspected substance abuse, suicidal thoughts, physical or sexual abuse, or the threat of harm to others
- when you've done all you can to help a teenager without results

It's also important to consider how to make a referral. Connecting a teenager or a family with the needed services is not always an easy task. Families may resist seeking professional help due to real financial difficulties, lack of understanding of what professional help entails, or cultural differences. Sometimes families may want to stay in a state of denial about their problems or may tend to overspiritualize them.

Gently and firmly communicate your concerns to the family and your reasons for referring the student for professional help. Provide the family with the names of *at least three* mental health professionals, including those with low-fee or sliding-scale options. If possible, try to match the family with a professional who shares their cultural background. Offer to go with the family to the first meeting or to contact the professional ahead of time if the family gives you permission. Be active in following up with the family to ensure that a connection has been made.

Knowing who to refer teenagers and their families to is the final challenge. Develop a list of potential referrals, and get to know each counselor personally so that you can match your students and families with the appropriate professionals. A good match between a teenager and professional counselor is essential. In fact, one of the best predictors of a positive counseling experience is the "goodness of fit" in the relationship between a counselor and client. You'll want to refer to mental health professionals who are licensed in your state; who specialize in working with children, adolescents, or families; and who are Christians that integrate their faith with their practice of professional counseling. Contact the youth and family services organizations in your community to find out about various services, programs, and fees.

6. Know and Use Community Resources

In addition to mental health professionals, communities possess a number of other important resources for teenagers and their families that can provide critical support and help during times of need. Many counties publish human services directories that list programs and services for a variety of problems such as bereavement, divorce, chronic mental illness, substance abuse, and single-parent support. As you network in your community, ask others who work with students, such as school personnel, probation officers, and pediatricians, about good programs that are available. Your teenagers and their families will benefit greatly from having a wide "safety net" of services and programs to assist them through their difficulties.

7. Know Your Legal and Ethical Obligations

Even though you are not a professional counselor, as an individual who works with young people you have an obligation to report any physical abuse, neglect, or sexual abuse that you observe, reasonably suspect, or hear about from a teenager or parent. This reporting involves calling the child abuse hotline in your state and providing them with the necessary information. If you're unsure whether to make a report in a particular instance, call the hotline and inquire. While reporting suspected abuse is never easy, it is the first step to ensuring the safety of the teenagers you work with and initiating needed services.

It is also important from a legal (and ethical) standpoint to inform the appropriate authorities in situations where an individual is at risk to harm himself or herself or someone else. Should a teenager disclose such thoughts, immediate action is required. This can include informing the parents, making an agreement with the teenager that he or she will not act on these thoughts, or even calling law enforcement officials, if necessary, to escort the teenager to an emergency room.

Other general guidelines to protect yourself legally include the following:

- Avoid counseling a student alone in the church or in his or her home where no one else is around—particularly if the student is of the opposite sex. Instead select a meeting place where you can maintain privacy but where others are nearby.
- Keep written notes about your counseling with a student if you make a child abuse report or if he or she threatens to harm himself or herself or others. Be sure to document any action that was taken on your part to ensure the teenager's safety.
- When in doubt about whether or not to act, consult a professional. Don't try to make a difficult judgment call on your own!

8. Know Yourself

One of the major pitfalls for a professional counselor involves acting on one's own feelings toward a client or family without adequate self-examination and self-understanding. Entering into a helping relationship with a hurting teenager is bound to stir up all kinds of feelings in the helper. It is not uncommon to feel annoyed, helpless, attracted, or repulsed—sometimes all in the same conversation! It is essential for all counselors, professional and pastoral alike, to pay attention to these feelings rather than to bury them. Pretending that the feelings are not there is the shortest route to acting on those feelings without conscious understanding and intention.

We encourage you to seek out regular consultation, support, and accountability for your counseling work with a supervisor or mentor. It's easy to lose perspective and objectivity when you're actively involved in helping others with their problems and with their spiritual development. Weekly meetings with a wise mentor or supervisor can help you maintain a helpful perspective, avoid ethical pitfalls, recognize your limitations, and remain balanced in attending to spiritual and psychological needs. Exposing yourself and your work to another person can be anxiety-provoking, but the benefits far outweigh the risks. Not only will you become a more effective counselor, but you will also grow in your own level of self-awareness.

SPECIFIC TECHNIQUES TO ENHANCE YOUR COUNSELING EFFECTIVENESS

The Importance of the Relationship

The most powerful tool that the counselor has to promote trust, growth, and healing is the relationship that he or she develops with the student. Research has shown that the quality of this relationship is the key variable in predicting success in counseling. It is imperative to remember that techniques, knowledge, and interventions are secondary to the development of a trusting, collaborative, honest relationship in which the teenager feels understood, respected, and valued. Trying to help a troubled adolescent without the development of this relationship is difficult, if not impossible.

The primacy of relationship is modeled for us in Scripture. In Matthew 22:34-40, Jesus emphasized the importance of relationships—loving God and loving others is the foundation for all the law and prophets. Empathy can help equip us for the hard work of understanding and loving a person, not as we would like them to be, but as they really are. This is an essential aspect of Christian *agape*.

Research on the effectiveness of counseling suggests that it does not necessarily take a professional counselor to provide support and relief to a person for emotional or psychological problems. As discussed earlier, there are times when it's important to make a referral to a professional, for the sake of both the youth worker and the teenager. However, a young person can receive tremendous benefit from the development of a caring, supportive relationship in which he or she can explore emotional, relational, and spiritual concerns. Specific techniques that enhance the development of this relationship are discussed next.

Listening and Empathy: The Relationship Cornerstones

Most of us think that we're better listeners than we really are. But truly listening to another—suspending our own needs, thoughts, and mental wanderings enough to put ourselves in someone else's shoes for a time—poses one of the greatest challenges to the counselor and youth minister. Effective counseling, however, cannot take place without active and empathetic listening.

Active listening involves hearing the concerns expressed by the teenager and reflecting back to him or her in your own words what you've heard—capturing both the content *and* the emotions of the student's concerns. Empathy involves putting yourself in the teenager's shoes, trying to understand the problem from the other person's perspective, and laying aside your own biases and assumptions. This can be especially challenging because of age differences between you and the student, as well as differences in gender, cultural background, and socioeconomic status.

Remember that Jesus, in what was the ultimate act of empathy and sacrifice, became one of us first before he saved us. We need to do our best to understand a teenager's world before we offer advice or solutions. Empathy is often the springboard for compassion; when we understand what it's like to be in the shoes of even the most difficult member of the youth group, we begin to experience compassion and love and to look past the problem to see the hurting person.

Seeking Strengths

Another important technique in counseling teenagers and their families is to be constantly on the lookout for individual and family strengths and areas of competency that can be important assets in the process of overcoming difficulties. In the midst of pain and suffering, people often lose sight of what they do well, and they may need a caring youth worker to remind them. Pointing out successes can be an important component of this. For example, you could talk with a socially isolated teenager in the youth group about how he was able to get up the courage to attend three meetings in a row; or you could discuss with a limits-testing student what she did differently that led to good behavior at a youth retreat.

Challenging Students to Be Responsible

Once you have established a trusting relationship with the student, listened carefully and thoroughly to the student's concerns, and empathized or provided support, it's important to gently and lovingly help the teenager explore his or her contributions to the problem. For example, you could empathize with a teenager regarding the difficulties of having strict parents who ground her for breaking curfew, but still ask her why she sets herself up for the consequences by breaking curfew in the first place. This encourages the student to accept responsibility and to begin to examine her own behavior. Effective counseling encourages responsibility, which combats feelings of helplessness and lays the groundwork for developing a plan of action. Honest challenges are easier for teenagers to digest when they are sandwiched between expressions of empathy and support.

Pulling It All Together: A Three-Step Approach

One simple and effective approach to counseling involves three steps: *examining* the problem, promoting *understanding* of the problem, and developing specific *response* strategies. This approach works in the following manner. A student opens up to you about his discomfort in social situations, particularly around girls. You help him examine the problem in more detail: How does he feel in social situations? What has he tried to do to make friends? What are his worries and concerns about what might happen? As you focus on building a relationship with the student and examining the problem, he feels comfortable opening up to you about some of his difficulties at home.

Together you begin to make connections and come up with insights into his problems. He discovers that his negative expectations of others often keep him from even trying to talk with people. This understanding leads to ideas about specific actions that he can take.

As part of the response plan, you give him some pointers on social skills. He practices social conversations by role-playing with you. You help him find several verses of Scripture that he can meditate on to soothe his anxiety. You pray together. In subsequent sessions, you continue to examine his problems, promote understanding, and help him develop a response plan.

Stopping Problems Before They Start: Prevention and Education

The church is an ideal place to have the types of supportive and educational activities that can prevent or decrease the incidence of a number of common adolescent and family problems.

Examples of effective prevention activities include parenting classes, marital support or restoration retreats, and workshops for children and parents on sexual health and values. Church-based self-help groups are another important source of support for teenagers and families. A "mentor family" program or small-group ministry for families with teenagers can provide students with adults other than their parents to mentor and counsel them. Consider planning several prevention activities per year for your congregation. Working to prevent psychological and relational problems before they start is one of the best uses of your counseling resources.

Attending to Spiritual Needs: Spiritual Formation and Counseling

When Joseph was seventeen years old, his envious brothers sold him to slave traders. The slave traders sold him to Potiphar, the captain of Pharaoh's guard, and Potiphar's wife falsely accused Joseph of rape. After several years of imprisonment, Joseph ascended to a position of great authority and power in Egypt and eventually faced the brothers who had sold him years earlier. Joseph's response to his brothers who had wished him dead reveals how God had used painful life events to transform Joseph: "You intended to harm me, but God intended it for good to accomplish what is now being done, the saving of many lives" (Genesis 50:20).

There are many ways that your ministry to teenagers promotes spiritual development and growth. Helping students see that God is up to something in them *in spite of* their brokenness is essential to the process of drawing meaning from suffering. Through your compassionate and wise counsel, young Christians can see that God turns into good what others meant for evil. Like Joseph, they can allow their own suffering to be used in powerful ways for the furthering of Christ's kingdom.

EXERCISES TO IMPROVE YOUR COUNSELING SKILLS

- Be mindful of your listening skills in your relationships with others. Do you take the time to really listen to people before responding? Are you able to allow the focus to be on the speaker without turning the conversation back to yourself? Can you resist the urge to give advice or fix the problem, and instead, offer support as the person draws conclusions and develops action steps?
- Practice listening skills with a friend. Ask the person to talk about a problem with you. Work on actively listening and reflecting back what you hear your friend say. Help the person explore the problem, without trying to solve it or offer advice. Then ask for feedback on your listening skills.
- Consider videotaping one of these practice sessions and evaluating it. Observe your body language as well as your spoken responses. Work on providing a warm, receptive presence. It may be difficult to watch yourself on videotape when you first start, but it will become easier over time.
- Periodically ask your students for feedback on how well they feel understood by you.
- Consider reading *The Lost Art of Listening* (New York, NY: The Guilford Press, 1995) by Michael P. Nichols to increase your understanding of this important counseling skill.

CHAPTER 2

Victimized—
Overcoming Abuse

SCOTT GIBSON, M.S.W., L.C.S.W

THE BASICS

The statistics are too high. Of all of the sexual assaults handled by law enforcement agencies, 67 percent of those crimes are committed against juveniles.[1] And this doesn't take into account the fact that most sexual assaults are not reported. A study released in September 2001 revealed that "between 300,000 and 400,000 U.S. children—many from middle-class homes—are victims of some type of sexual exploitation every year."[2] The amount of physical and emotional abuse in this country is also alarming. Despite federal, state, and local programs that are geared toward stopping these crimes, far too many children are abused each year. And the impact on the victims can be severe. Long after the physical trauma and bruises go away, emotional and psychological wounds remain that need to be healed and attended to.

It is common for the emotional damage of abused children to surface in adolescence. As youth workers, we must be equipped to help these survivors in their journey of healing. As leaders, we must take responsibility for providing a safe place within the church where teenagers can find help and healing. There is much hope today for survivors of abuse.

I once worked with an organization that did street intervention with male and female prostitutes. Most of these young men and women had been sexually or physically abused as children. These individuals taught me a lot about the impact that abuse can have on people. Abused individuals are at high risk for anxiety, depression, substance abuse, physical illnesses, and problems at school or work. It is very important that teenagers who are survivors of abuse are identified as soon as possible to minimize the potential long-term consequences of abuse. By providing a healing environment, you can help a victim build a strong sense of self and trust.

Many youth workers, too, have histories of being abused. I've known many youth workers who, through a career in youth ministry, are trying to right the wrongs they suffered. This can be good, but make sure that *you* get the attention and care that you need. When you've attended to your personal issues, you're able to provide a healthy environment for the students in your youth ministry.

There are probably teenagers in your ministry who are currently being abused. Some of the abuse may even be from family members who attend your church. The emotional nature of this problem can be extremely challenging, and it's important that you have the support of your church leaders as you walk with families who are facing this issue. If your pastor or church leaders are unfamiliar or uncomfortable with these types of situations, you will need to involve other professionals to help you with the difficult decisions you'll face.

The church has too long been a place where sexuality has been shamed, and often individuals who are struggling with sexual abuse can sense this. Make sure that you do plenty of proactive education and outreach with your students to help them understand how God feels about them. Let teenagers know that God loves us and sees our tears. As Psalm 56:8 says, "Record my lament; list my tears on your scroll—are they not in your record?" God is *not* embarrassed by or ashamed of our wounds.

WHEN TO REFER

Early detection of abuse is *very* important. Some or all of the following symptoms might indicate that a student is being abused or has been abused:

- a poor self-image
- unusual interest in or avoidance of things of a sexual nature
- sexually acting out
- depression or withdrawal from peers and family
- anger and rage or unusual aggressiveness
- self-destructive behaviors or suicidal thoughts
- anxiety and fears or problems with sleeping
- fear of entering into new relationships or activities
- problems in school
- flashbacks or nightmares
- drug or alcohol abuse
- physical signs of mistreatment (such as bruises, scratches, or other marks)

When a student discloses that he or she has been or is being sexually, physically, or emotionally abused, assure the student that he or she did the right thing by talking to you about it. Take seriously what the teenager is saying. The initial response that a student receives when disclosing a situation of abuse is critical to that person's ability to work through and heal from the traumatic experiences. However, don't try to deal with this serious issue alone—immediately contact a professional Christian counselor.

COUNSELING IDEAS

Counseling a student who has been sexually or physically abused is complex. Because of the intense nature of the issue, it's essential that you refer the abused student to a qualified Christian counselor. The following section is designed to aid you, as a youth worker, in understanding how you can be a part of the healing process along with the professional counselor. Your role in walking with the students in your ministry is vital.

Your Initial Response

You may be the first one to hear about the abuse. It's important that you take seriously what the student is saying, and commend the student for coming forward and talking to you about it. Survivors of abuse often keep secrets in order to get through it all. Telling an adult takes a tremendous amount of courage. If the student has been or is being abused by someone in his or her family, the student may feel guilty about telling someone. The student may also fear that the abuser will further abuse him or her for exposing the secret.

There will be times when you may suspect that a student is not telling you the truth. You might sense that things don't add up—either there's more to the story (and you're not hearing about it), or there's too much to the story. Whenever I have these types of feelings, I talk to the student about how the story is coming across to me (the student will sense that you don't buy it) and admit that I might be off base. I *always* make sure that I involve other people prior to questioning someone's story. If you have to err on one side or the other, it's better to be gullible than to question the student's story. Usually the truth comes out over time.

"It's Not Your Fault"

One of the most important things you can do is to assure the student that the abuse is not his or her fault. This idea can be challenging for teenagers to accept since their sexuality is becoming more apparent at this age. A number of years ago I worked with a young man who had been raped by an older man. This young man was going through puberty and believed that his new sexual body had been responsible for the abuse. He had been repeatedly asking for forgiveness from God for what he believed was his sin. First, I let him know that I understood, and I validated why he had drawn that conclusion; but we also dealt with the truth about the situation. It was important for him to understand that he had done no wrong in God's eyes. Once he came to understand this, he began to experience restoration in his relationship with God.

Secure Protection

During the initial conversation, you'll want to offer the student your help in securing protection so that any ongoing abuse stops. Counselors are required to report child abuse, and in most states, so are clergy. As a youth worker, it is in the best interest of the student for you to *immediately* act on and report any suspicion of abuse.

Your church should have a strategy to handle abuse cases consistently and effectively. If your church currently does not have such policies, bring together a group to work on the issues, ask Christian counselors for assistance, or talk with other churches, and develop policies that protect your students. Get these policies in place as soon as possible.

I know of situations in which the teenager tried to tell his or her youth leader about abuse, but the youth leader didn't know how to handle it, so the abuse went unattended. This created a further abuse by the church—an abuse that can be extremely faith-shaking for a student. When a student tells you that someone is abusing him or her, ask specific questions so you'll understand exactly what's happening. Take notes so that you'll have accurate information to report to the proper authorities. If you are uncomfortable dealing with these situations, schedule an appointment for yourself with a professional counselor to debrief and learn how to handle similar situations in the future.

If, as you are talking with the student, you discover that the abuse happened in the past and is not currently taking place, you will still want to affirm the student for talking about it. This first step of talking about the abuse is often the biggest one to take. Encourage the student to journal his or her thoughts and feelings about the abuse. Let the student know that you are there to provide support.

In these initial conversations, it's essential to instill hope. Many people who have worked through their abuse go on to live productive, happy lives. There is great hope offered in Scripture. In Romans 8:37-39 Paul says, "In all these things we are more than conquerors through him who loved us. For I am convinced that neither death nor life, neither angels nor demons, neither the present nor the future, nor any powers, neither height nor depth, nor anything else in all creation, will be able to separate us from the love of God that is in Christ Jesus our Lord."

Acknowledge and Explore Feelings

Jesus is more powerful than any abuse or abuser in a student's life. But be sure that the teenager understands that this victory is a process, not an overnight answer to prayer. God certainly can heal in many ways, but for most people the healing process involves professional help and talking with others about their experiences. Ask abused students about their feelings: "How did you feel?" or "How are you feeling now?" An important part of the healing process is for victims to have their feelings validated by another person. Survivors of abuse often feel very abnormal. To the extent that their feelings make sense to you (even though the abuse may not), let them know. Pray with them and express any feelings you might have that will comfort them.

Sharing the Story

At some point, you may want to consider encouraging the student to tell his or her story to others in a safe environment, such as in a small-group setting or other safe meeting. The decision to do so should be done in consultation with the student's counselor and parents. The potential for healing is powerful as the teenager lets go of some of the burden of shame about what happened. If you know of a person (college-age or older) who experienced abuse as a teenager or young child, consider having that person share his or her story with your youth group. This can help struggling students have greater hope in our powerful God, and it can encourage them to work through healing their own wounds.

Date Rape

Anyone who works with teenagers will have to deal with the issue of date rape. Depending on the circumstances, young women (and even young men) can become confused about whether they were abused or whether they "asked for it." One student I worked with who had been date raped felt that she was responsible for giving her date signals that she wanted to have sex. But if a teenager does not want to be sexually intimate and is made to do so, that's sexual abuse. You may need to support the student in reporting the date rape to the proper authorities.

Paul says in 1 Corinthians 3:16-17, "Don't you know that you yourselves are God's temple and that God's Spirit lives in you?...God's temple is sacred, and you are that temple." God has given us the responsibility to manage our bodies; empower young men and women to see that their bodies are their own and precious to God.

Bullying

In your ministry, you may also encounter situations in which teenagers are being abused by their peers. Bullying, harassment, and assaults are running rampant within our society and schools today. This harassment and abuse can lead to depression and low self-esteem. Often, once a teenager begins to be bullied, the other students will avoid him or her; students fear that any association with the teenager who's being bullied might impact their own social status, and they don't want to increase the likelihood of being bullied themselves.

Bullying ranges from teasing to serious harassment and physical violence. Bullying can be either verbal or physical. In general, males use physical threats (although I have seen young women do this), and females tend to be more verbal. One thirteen-year-old I worked with had five of her female peers come to her after class and tell her, "We've decided that you don't fit in. You aren't allowed to be seen with any of us in the future." This young woman was devastated. It impacted her already fragile self-esteem and she began using self-injurious behaviors to manage her pain.

If you suspect that a student is being bullied, seek help for him or her as soon as possible. Ask the student to tell you exactly what's going on. At first he or she may be uncomfortable talking about it. I usually tell the student that it's not necessary to mention any names, but we can still talk about the situation and try to figure out what to do.

When you ask a student specific questions about the nature of the abuse, also ask what he or she has tried to do to stop it. Find out what things worked, and what didn't. Assure the teenager that the situation is not his or her fault, and work together to come up with positive next steps. Ask the student what he or she has learned from these trials, and strategize other coping skills. Your most important role will be to empower the teenager.

You'll also want to obtain help from the appropriate school authorities. Bullying is a problem in many schools, and there are many programs for training administrators and teachers how to address this problem. The authorities at the student's school have a responsibility to work toward protecting the rights of each student.

Never encourage the bullied student to fight back or retaliate. In my counseling sessions with students, we practice options that the victim can use the next time that he or she is bullied. In situations where the individual is isolated socially, we work on helping him or her develop friendships. Bullying doesn't take place as easily in a crowd. Encourage and empower the student to be assertive. For those students who are withdrawn and depressed as a result of a bully's abuse, help the teenager and his or her family seek a Christian counselor for further help.

I have also counseled bullies. Many of these students are survivors of abuse themselves and are often depressed and angry about what's going on in their lives. They often choose victims who are passive, fearful, and lonely, and their targets usually have difficulty defending themselves.

Bullying is often a symptom of underlying problems. If you suspect that one of the students in your youth group may be involved in bullying, sit down with the person and ask him or her what's going on in his or her life. Ask how the teenager feels about himself or herself. In working with some of these students, I have found that they are often hurting, and their bullying is just a cry for help and attention. These students will usually be resistant to your efforts to help. A bully has often developed a strong, protective outer shell that can be frustrating to break through. I have sometimes worked for months with bullies who have stayed very closed. It takes time, and the walls they have built are there for a good reason. If you think you are going to go in and bulldoze the barriers down, get ready for a battle. Work with these students in understanding why the walls are there.

Further Study

Do further study to improve your effectiveness in working with abused students. Consider taking additional coursework if you find yourself dealing frequently with situations of abuse. If you're not hearing abuse stories at all, look closer at what you may be overlooking, because abuse *is* out there—even in the church.

Recommended Resources

Books

- *Caring for Sexually Abused Children: A Handbook for Families and Churches,* R. Timothy Kearney. Downers Grove, IL: InterVarsity Press, 2001.

- *The Mosaic Mind: Empowering the Tormented Selves of Child Abuse Survivors,* Regina A. Goulding and Richard C. Schwartz. New York, NY: W.W. Norton & Company, Inc., 1995.

- *Sexual Abuse in Christian Homes and Churches,* Carolyn Holderread Heggen. Scottdale, PA: Herald Press, 1993.

- *Survivor Prayers: Talking With God About Childhood Sexual Abuse,* Catherine J. Foote. Louisville, KY: Westminster John Knox Press, 1994.

- *The Wounded Heart: Hope for Adult Victims of Childhood Sexual Abuse,* Dan B. Allender. Colorado Springs, CO: NavPress, 1990.

- *The Wounded Spirit,* Frank Peretti. Nashville, TN: W Publishing Group, 2000.

Your Own Well-Being

You have the great privilege of helping students in the process of healing from abuse. This can be exciting and very rewarding. But there will also be times when you face great discouragement because of the intense nature of these issues. Don't become a statistic and allow these tough issues to pull you out of the game; continue to attend to your own emotional well-being. Your ministry is essential to students who desperately need a caring adult to understand what they're going through.

When a student is abused, he or she can often be depressed and have low self-esteem. At an age when a teenager is making some important life decisions, this abuse can significantly impact a person's future. The role your youth group can play in supporting and reaching out to abused students can be powerful. Rely on God's strength as you minister to your students.

---

[1] Howard N. Snyder, "Sexual Assault of Young Children as Reported to Law Enforcement: Victim, Incident, and Offender Characteristics," in a report by the U.S. Department of Justice, Bureau of Justice Statistics (July 2000), 12.

[2] From a report at the CNN.com/Law Center, "Study: Child Sex Abuse 'Epidemic' in U.S." (posted September 11, 2001), www.cnn.com.

STUDENT PAGE Use the photocopiable worksheet on page 25 to help teenagers who've been abused begin to understand God's love for them. Use the handout to facilitate discussion during a counseling session. Allow the teenager to complete the page, and then discuss his or her responses; or work with the student to complete the page together.

Dealing With Abuse

In the space below, draw a picture to describe what you feel as you remember when you were abused.

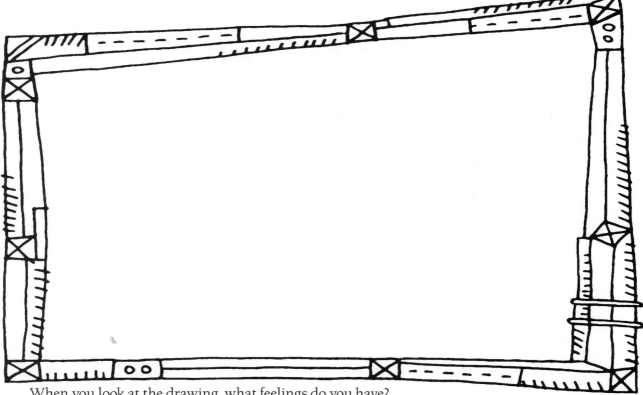

When you look at the drawing, what feelings do you have?

Read Psalm 34:17-18.

Think about this Scripture passage. When God looks at your drawing, how does God feel about you? Explain.

Read Psalm 147:3.

What does God want to do with your wounds? How does that make you feel?

Read Luke 4:18.

If one of Jesus' missions is to "release the oppressed," what steps can you take to heal?
- Talk to someone (such as your youth pastor, a counselor, parent, teacher, or close friend).
- Pray.
-
-

CHAPTER 3

Bad Grades Again?–
Assisting Students With Academic Struggles

D. PATRICK HOPP, Ph.D.

THE BASICS

We all know what it's like to occasionally lack motivation in some area of our lives. We've sat at our desks and stared at a computer screen or walked by a pile of laundry, waiting for a better time to get started on it. But for some students, procrastination and apathy go beyond these momentary motivational dry spells into a desert in which any attempt to get started seems to end in a disappointing mirage. These students are often bright and capable—their academic struggles do not stem from a lack of intelligence or ambition—but they cannot seem to break free from the burdens that weigh them down and keep them from reaching their academic potential. There are many different kinds of external burdens that come to mind, such as family problems, depression, or relationship struggles, but perhaps the most common obstacles come from within.

Self-Perception

Many students struggle academically *not* because of some external distraction or problem, but from obstacles that they've placed in their own minds. Research shows that how we think and feel about things has a great deal to do with our level of success and motivation in those areas. Academic performance is no exception. Students who believe that they're not good at math perform at a lower level than students who believe that they'll excel. When students start to think of themselves as not just poor in math but as poor students, they may soon expect to fail in all areas of academics. All too often these negative predictions become self-fulfilling prophecies.

I'll never forget the most important moment in my own academic career. It did not occur when I was in college, seminary, graduate school, or while I was teaching at a university—it happened in the fourth grade. My fourth-grade class at Hamblen Elementary School was divided into three groups of students: the Piglets, the Eeyores, and the Poohs. Although these were euphemistic terms meant to disguise our true identities, no one was fooled. We all knew that the Eeyores were the average students, while the Poohs were the bright kids who were doing advanced work in a special area of the room. And I was a lowly Piglet—one of those kids who needed a little extra help, who just couldn't quite keep up with the rest of the class. In short, we were the "dummies." My transformative experience happened on a Wednesday afternoon during a spelling lesson. I was very busy in the back of the class playing practical jokes with a friend when, all of a sudden, I was very rudely interrupted by the fearsome Ms. Giezzel.

Ms. Giezzel was one of those teachers that could turn a young boy to stone with a disapproving glance. She was notorious for her strict discipline and heavy hand. I can still remember the look on her face when she walked up to my desk that day and said, "Young man, you're coming with me." I wasn't sure what I had done, but I *was* sure that it wasn't going to earn me any gold stars. Much to my surprise, Ms. Giezzel did not march me to the principal's office, but right to the front of the class where she sat me down in the middle of the esteemed Poohs. Apparently she had recognized some potential in me that was hidden even to myself. I had always thought of myself as a Piglet—what right did I have to be with the advanced students? Although I felt out of place, I quickly acclimated to my new environment and learned to perform at a level worthy of the Poohs.

Once I began to think of myself as a good student, my academic identity changed. I eventually went on to excel in high school and college, and I even earned a Ph.D. I've often wondered how my life might have been different if not for Ms. Giezzel's actions that day. By recognizing my potential and acting on it, she helped me to change not only how I thought about school, but also how I perceived myself. Anyone who works with young people is in a similar position to change students' lives.

Fear of Failure

Another common problem that hinders academic performance is when students are motivated more by a fear of failure than by a desire to succeed. It is well documented that when people act to avoid punishment rather than to gain rewards, their work is less creative and they don't perform as well. This is true for all kinds of tasks, including academic work. Students who study because they're afraid of getting bad grades or afraid of disappointing their parents are bound to do worse than if they were motivated by a desire to do well. When students are motivated by these negative incentives, they learn to associate studying with the possibility of failure. As a result, they tend to procrastinate more, which causes them to fall behind and makes it all the more difficult to generate the necessary motivation to complete tasks.

One of the best illustrations of this phenomenon that I've encountered occurred while I was teaching a large introductory psychology class comprised mostly of college freshmen and sophomores. After the second midterm exam, a young man approached me to talk about his grade. He was obviously quite upset and wanted to see if there was anything he could do to raise his grade. When I agreed to meet with him during my office hours, I was shocked to find that he did not ask a single question about any of the items on the exam and did not even offer to do extra credit. His only plea was that he needed to maintain a high grade-point average so that he could be admitted to law school. He was convinced that this one grade, a B+, on this one exam was going to ruin his life. Talk about pressure! He was motivated by a fear of failure, not by a desire to succeed.

Internal Incentives

We also know that students tend to do better work when they are motivated by internal incentives (the desire to learn or an interest in the subject matter) vs. external ones (the desire for good grades or approval). As a professor, I see this difference played out in the classroom every quarter. There are always a few students in each course who are genuinely fascinated by the material. They ask questions both during and after class. They take the time to apply the material to their own lives and to the lives of those around them. For them, studying is not a chore but is something that comes naturally as a result of their interest.

Then there are those students who are motivated only by external incentives, usually grades. You can see the anxiety on their faces when exams are given out. When they raise their hands in class, I can usually predict the question—it's inevitably some variation of "Is this going to be on the exam?" Although some of these students earn high marks, I know that they have *not* enjoyed the process.

WHEN TO REFER

Although the previous section applies to the majority of students dealing with academic struggles, anyone who counsels young people should also be aware that there are more serious problems that can inhibit students' academic performance. Learning disabilities, attention-deficit disorder, depression, anxiety disorders, and substance abuse are all common barriers to academic success. If you suspect that a young person may be suffering from one of these problems, refer the student to a psychologist or other mental health professional who can assess the situation and make appropriate treatment recommendations. The following section gives a brief description of some of these problems and their symptoms.

Learning Disabilities

Learning disabilities affect a person's capacity to interpret either auditory or visual information and may relate to difficulties in coordinating information from different parts of the brain. A person is said to have a learning disability when his or her level of academic achievement in a specific area (such as mathematics, reading comprehension, or spelling) is significantly below what is predicted by his or her cognitive ability (intelligence). People who do quite well in most areas of academics can still have a learning disability that prevents them from effectively processing information in one or more specific areas. It should also be noted that bright students with learning disabilities can achieve average or even above-average grades in the areas of their disability, but they still may not be reaching their potential. Here are some common indicators that a young person may have a learning disability:

- The student finds it difficult to follow directions or understand instructions.
- The student makes frequent reversals of letters or numbers.
- The student has difficulty learning new concepts or making connections between the new concepts and previously learned information.
- The student makes consistent reading or spelling errors despite having been corrected.
- The student has difficulty with eye-hand coordination.

Please note, however, that the only way to accurately diagnose a learning disability is for a student to be tested by a professional.

Attention-Deficit Disorder

Perhaps no other condition has received more attention in the past few years than ADD (or ADHD), and many people have been convinced that they or their children have this disorder when, in fact, they do not. Attention-deficit disorder can occur either with or without symptoms of hyperactivity. Some of the more common symptoms include distractibility, forgetfulness, disorganization, restlessness, and impulsivity. Students with ADD can be helped with medication as well as psychotherapy. Parents of ADD students can also receive assistance and training to help them deal with their child's unique needs. The first step in effective ADD treatment, however, begins with a proper diagnosis. (For more information about working with students who have been diagnosed with ADD or ADHD, see Chapter 6.)

Depression

One of the defining characteristics of depression is apathy that affects most areas of a person's life. Other symptoms include social withdrawal, lack of energy, change in appetite, change in sleep patterns, poor concentration, and pessimistic thoughts. (See Chapter 10 for more information about depression.)

Anxiety Disorders

Anxiety disorders can be debilitating and may interfere with several areas of functioning, including academic performance. Symptoms include chronic worry, muscle tension, shortness of breath, insomnia, intense fear of specific things or situations, an excessive need for order or rituals, and panic attacks. (For more information about ministering to students with anxiety disorders, see Chapter 5.)

Substance Abuse

Serious substance abuse or addiction often interferes with a person's work or academic performance. Lack of motivation is a common symptom of substance abuse, especially when the person uses sedatives. Other symptoms may include a change in the student's circle of friends, financial problems, and deceptive or manipulative behavior. (See Chapter 12 for a more detailed discussion of substance abuse.)

COUNSELING IDEAS

As a youth worker, you're in a good position to identify possible problems in students' lives. Teenagers may be more comfortable talking to you than they would be to their parents or other authority figures.

If it appears that a student is having problems, don't be afraid to ask. One of the biggest mistakes that youth leaders make is not asking questions. Too often we're afraid to ask probing questions because we don't want to make students feel uncomfortable; but in reality, it's often because asking the questions would make *us* feel uncomfortable. If you suspect that any of the problems that have been mentioned in this chapter might be interfering with a student's schoolwork, the best way to find out is to ask simple, direct, and matter-of-fact questions. You might want to lead into the questions by stating that you care about the student and want to know what's happening in his or her life, but you shouldn't "beat around the bush." Once you have assessed the situation and are reasonably confident that you don't need to refer the student to a mental health professional, there are several things that you can do to help.

Don't Minimize the Problem

The student has probably already been told that he or she just needs to work harder or isn't really applying himself or herself. This approach usually just makes the teenager feel worse and creates even more pressure that might lead to an increase in anxiety or procrastination. A better approach is to sit down with the student and find out how he or she sees the problem. Ask the teenager what he or she thinks about school. Find out how the student goes about studying. Look for indications that the student might have one of the problems discussed earlier in the chapter. Is the student concerned more about failure than success? Does his or her motivation stem mostly from internal or external sources? How does the teenager's academic performance fit with his or her view of himself or herself?

Help Create a Positive Academic Self-Image

Find the subjects that the student enjoys or excels at and build on them. The teenager needs to begin to see himself or herself as a person who is capable of academic success. Find out what the student did to succeed in other courses. What did it feel like to succeed? What specific actions did he or she take to make this success happen? Reinforce the teenager's efforts and past successes to help him or her visualize future success. Encourage the teenager to draw or journal about what academic accomplishment might look like or feel like. Next ask the student how he or she imagines bringing about this future success. What specific and concrete goals would need to be achieved? What is the first step toward meeting each of these goals?

Scripture can help teenagers visualize success and begin to change how they think and feel about themselves and their potential. God told us through his Word that he loves us and that through him all things are possible—this includes academic improvement! The following are just a few references that might be incorporated into a student's prayer and meditation life:
- Mark 10:27
- Romans 8:38-39
- Romans 12:2
- 2 Corinthians 5:17
- Hebrews 12:1
- 1 John 3:1a

Discover the Student's Interests

Rather than focusing on what things in school don't spark the student's interest, find out what the student *is* interested in. This will help you build rapport with the teenager and show that you're interested in getting to know him or her. When you know what a student is interested in, you can come up with creative ways to incorporate those interests into the student's academic life. For example, if a teenager who is studying biology is mainly interested in sports, you could link these two areas by asking questions such as, "What are the biological principles behind optimal muscle performance in an athlete's body?" or "What chemicals are released into the bloodstream during aerobic activity?" The goal is to make the "irrelevant" information become relevant to the teenager's life.

Provide Study Tips

Sometimes teenagers need help in developing good study skills. If the opportunity arises, share with the student the techniques that worked for you in school. It will probably be reassuring for the student to learn that you had to work at it too. We all have little tricks we've developed to make things easier. The "Study Tips" handout (p. 33) provides helpful tips that you can offer to students who are having academic problems. These tips can decrease procrastination and increase the effectiveness of the time the student spends studying.

Recommended Resources

Books

- *Study Power: Study Skills to Improve Your Learning and Your Grades*, William R. Luckie and Wood Smethurst. Cambridge, MA: Brookline Books, 1998.

Web Resources

- www.chadd.org (Web site of CHADD–Children and Adults With Attention-Deficit/Hyperactivity Disorder)

- www.ldanatl.org (Web site of the Learning Disabilities Association of America)

- www.ldonline.org (Web site of LD OnLine, resources and information about learning disabilities)

Other Resources

- Talk to learning professionals at your local high school, or seek out advice from professional learning centers or tutors.

STUDENT PAGES Use the photocopiable handouts on pages 32 and 33 to help teenagers understand their attitudes about studying and to help them learn effective study tips. Use "Study Struggles" (p. 32) in a counseling session with a student who is having academic difficulty or experiencing apathy. The student can answer the questions and then go over the answers with you, or you can work with the student and complete the page together. Use the student's responses to help you discuss possible obstacles to academic success. Use the "Study Tips" handout (p. 33) to start a discussion about positive study habits.

Academic Struggles

Study Struggles

Answer the following questions and go over your answers with your youth pastor or counselor.

1. When I try to study I am often distracted by _____.

2. When it comes to grades, my biggest concern is _____.

3. The place and time I usually study is

    _____.

    Other things I sometimes do at the same place or during this time are

    _____.

4. My main motivation for studying is _____.

5. If I were a better student then I would _____.

6. The person who is most frustrated with my academic performance is

    _____.

7. The things I am most interested in are _____.

8. My favorite subject in school is _____ because _____.

9. My least favorite subject is school is _____ because _____.

10. Circle the letter that corresponds to the sentence that best fits your attitude about studying.

    a. "I don't know why I study...I don't know what good it does me."

    b. "I study because I don't want my teachers or parents to be disappointed in me."

    c. "I study because I feel guilty when I don't."

    d. "I study because it is important to me."

    e. Other: _____.

Study Tips

If you're having a hard time with some areas of your schoolwork, try these tips to help you manage your time and do your best!

- Make an academic calendar. As soon as papers, tests, and other assignments are given to you, write down the due date in your calendar.
- Create a daily homework schedule that includes the estimated chunks of time you'll need to complete specific assignments.
- Break large assignments into smaller, more manageable tasks, and work on one piece at a time.
- Find a place to study that's free from distractions. Study there consistently, and try to use this place only for studying. This will help to reduce distractions because you'll associate the place only with studying.
- Review notes and reading materials often throughout the semester rather than waiting until right before exams to cram everything into your memory.
- Try to mentally associate new material with personal experiences and things you know well. For example, what might a historical figure you're learning about have in common with the lead singer of your favorite band?
- Find creative ways to make studying more fun. Make up your own version of games such as Jeopardy! or Trivial Pursuit to learn the material for your classes.
- After you've studied the material on your own, review it with a classmate to compare your perspectives and share your thoughts.
- For information that you have to memorize, try these two tricks.
    1. Make flashcards with questions on one side and answers on the other.
    2. Use a mnemonic device to help you remember. A mnemonic device is something that helps you encode information in your brain so that the information is easier to retrieve. Common methods include using the first letter of each word in a list to make a sentence, or picturing each thing that you need to remember in a particular location of your house.

CHAPTER 4

Anger and Angst—
Understanding Teenage Hostility

ROY E. BARSNESS, Ph.D.

THE BASICS

It was the summer before our son turned thirteen. We were sitting on the deck with a group of friends, enjoying the beauty and tranquility of the Puget Sound, naïve to the years ahead—and all seemed well. But as the conversation progressed and our friends, who were veteran parents of teenagers, began to share their stories, our parental reverie was broken. One parent remarked that the day her child turned thirteen, events in the family changed so dramatically that she didn't stop crying until her child reached the age of twenty. Another couple shared that when their son reached adolescence, he went into his room, shut the door, and they weren't sure if he would ever come out again. One of our other friends said that her child, too, had chosen to go mute as a teenager, and he finally found his voice again as a sophomore in college. We were, to say the least, discouraged.

Then, as if on cue, our own charming and agreeable child introduced us to those tumultuous years of adolescence, and we came to know firsthand the intensity of a young man's mind and heart. As the shadow of adolescence descended across our lives, we entered into the struggle for power, meaning, influence, safety, and integrity that's normal during the teenage years—and we were never quite certain *who* might be the first to leave home!

Adolescence is a time of considerable upheaval, both physiologically and emotionally. Do you remember what it was like? Hormones run wild and are full of demands, but teenagers don't have the fully formed values that are necessary to inform those desires. They're children in adult bodies, looking for purpose, power, freedom, and their place in the world. Adolescents are separating from their parents, yet they still need them. They're trying to belong somewhere or to someone, but they're at the mercy of their desire for acceptance. They're tempted by drugs, alcohol, sex, and violence as they look for meaning in their lives. It is a wild thing, this time of adolescence. No wonder teenagers become angry!

It doesn't help that we live in a violent society. In 2000, more than six million violent crimes (such as rape, robbery, and assault) were committed in the United States.[1] Approximately 12 percent of murder victims are teenagers or children, and studies have shown that teenagers are raped or sexually assaulted at a much higher rate than older adults.[2] Four out of ten teenage girls have either been abused by a boyfriend or have a friend who has been abused.[3] Physical attack and theft are the most common crimes committed at schools.[4] Violent teenagers most often choose other teenagers as their victims.[5] We live in a society whose attitudes toward violence unwittingly promote expressions of anger by teenagers that are harmful to themselves and others.

Healthy vs. Harmful Expressions of Anger

Anger is a given. It is a common and normal emotion, not a sin. Anger is, in fact, an automatic response that produces both physiological and psychological reactions, as well as interpersonal difficulties. When we're mad, we're fully engaged—mind, body, and soul! Anger is disruptive and can be a precursor to change; it is in the *expression* of anger that it becomes either harmful or healthy.

Harmful expressions of anger can lead to a vile hatred that can be a predecessor to physical harm. Negative manifestations of anger include prejudice, gossip, addictions, depression, anxiety, and physiological problems—these can become destructive to oneself or to others.

Healthy expressions of anger can lead to change. Essentially anger is communication. Anger is designed to declare—often very boldly—that something is wrong or that something needs to be changed. The expression of anger can provide an opportunity for unmet needs to be fulfilled. As a reaction to frustration, anger can release feelings of entrapment and reduce feelings of hopelessness that one does not have the ability to create change.

Identity Development and the Search for Meaning

Teenagers face many emotional issues during this period of their lives. In Erik Erickson's "womb to the tomb" model of psychosocial development, adolescence is the period when a person is actively forging his or her identity and seeking to announce, with resounding confidence, "I am!" This time of young people's lives is a struggle between dependence and independence, and others around them often have no warning of when these two needs may conflict.

Adolescents are faced with questions about identity, separation, and relationships as they strive to fulfill their potential. When teenagers fail to answer the question "Who am I?" it leads to confusion, and ultimately it can lead to self-contempt or contempt of others.

In working with young people, it's important to remember that this is a tumultuous time in their lives. Keep in mind how intense a teenager's feelings and reactions can be, and keep things in perspective as you work together to examine what's happening in the young person's struggle toward adulthood. I try to approach adolescents at the existential level of *finding meaning* in their lives rather than at the behavioral level. Seeking to understand the need or the meaning behind a teenager's actions will help you develop the necessary bond with the student that's critical to his or her further personal and spiritual development. Almost invariably, when you approach issues with the focus on behavior, it only exacerbates the intensity of those issues. Instead, view teenage behavior as language—as an attempt to express some fear or need. Using this approach will do more to assist young people in reaching a better understanding of themselves than focusing on fixing their undesirable behaviors. There is only one exception to this rule: If the student's behavior becomes harmful to himself or herself or to others, the behavior must be immediately addressed and the student should be referred to a professional counselor.

Five Unmet Needs

Anger is usually the result of unmet needs in one or all of these five areas:

- *Belonging:* Although belonging is a universal need, it is of supreme importance during adolescence. Young girls tie up the family bathroom for an hour as they get ready for school, hoping that they'll be pretty enough and cool enough to fit in. Boys wear their pants at half-mast, asking a similar question, "Is there a place for me?" It matters little if teenagers are loved at home; the prevailing concern is that they are accepted in the real world—the world of their peers. Imagine, then, the agony of the adolescent who does *not* fit in. Adolescents are looking for a place to belong, and they face many rejections, offering ample opportunity for hurt and anger to result.

- *Dignity:* Adolescents need to have a sense of accomplishment. They need to achieve, be productive, and feel that they matter. By experiencing moments of pride when they do well at sports, or when they receive an honor, they know that they are worth something and that they are making a difference in their world. But when their dignity is assaulted, they are vulnerable to outbursts of anger.

- *Influence:* Adolescents struggle with the need for power and control. They need to know that they are capable of making good decisions and are able to successfully follow through with their choices. They want to know that their opinions matter. It is in this arena of power and influence that most conflicts occur between teenagers and their parents or other adults.

- *Safety:* Young people require secure relationships and safe environments in which to test their emerging identity. In their struggles, they need to know that someone will be there if they fail.

  The primary place of safety should be the home. The home must be a safe refuge from the struggles of the day—and free from physical, verbal, or sexual abuse. Any young person who lives in an unsafe home will never be able to understand and process his or her emotional life. The school and the community are also places where safety is important. If the adolescent doesn't feel that he or she is able to trust the environment, he or she is vulnerable to many emotional problems, not the least of which is anger.

- *Self-Esteem:* Teenagers need to know in their hearts that they're OK, and they need to like themselves—at least most of the time. They need to have confidence that they'll be able to overcome the obstacles in their lives. Teenagers must also have the sense that they're of value and are important.

These five fundamental needs—belonging, dignity, influence, safety, and self-esteem—are crucial in the development of an adolescent's sense of self. When these needs are not met, anger is often the result. Keeping these five basic needs in mind can be helpful as you work to understand teenagers' angry behaviors.

WHEN TO REFER

Anger is a normal emotion, but teenagers who express their anger in harmful ways need help. If a student you're working with fits into any of the following categories, refer him or her to a professional Christian counselor.

- He or she may cause harm to self or others.

- The teenager has little or no support from his or her family.
- The student's anger is chronic (persists over time).
- Working with the student limits your time for ministry and community involvement.

COUNSELING IDEAS

Offer Authentic Compassion

One of the most important things that we can offer to our students is authentic compassion. If you can view a struggling teenager as a person who is created in the image of God, and can walk with the student through his or her hurt and confusion, you will help the student effectively express himself or herself. If you treat a young person with dignity and respect, you help him or her understand the importance of offering the same to others.

Listen

Over many years of providing psychotherapy, I have learned that the willingness to listen is a great gift that I can give to a person. We often are heard, but we are rarely listened to. If you offer an open and willing ear and suspend your need to blame, accuse, or offer advice, you will provide an environment in which a teenager can develop more productive ways to work through his or her anger.

Explore Unmet Needs

Be willing to look at the five basic needs behind a teenager's anger rather than trying to solve a problem. By focusing solely on the behavior, you will fail in helping the student to positively express that need. An angry adolescent is most likely trying to reveal some fear or need to you, and this will almost always involve one of the following areas:

- the teenager's insecurities about belonging
- his or her feelings of powerlessness
- an attack on his or her self-esteem or dignity
- a concern for safety

When the need is identified, explore with the teenager realistic ways in which the need can be met. To adequately address anger in a teenager's life, you must also talk about a teenager's relationships with family and friends, and assist the student in communicating his or her fears and needs more effectively to others.

Keep a "Community" Perspective

Try not to isolate the problem or the person. Consider with the student the impact of his or her anger on you, on his or her family, and on his or her social group. If possible, encourage the student to bring his or her concerns and feelings before the youth group (or others affected by the behavior) to help the teenager better understand the issue. If the situation is handled well, the community will become a more caring and loving place for all.

The importance of using the group as a healing agent was apparent in my own life when my son wanted to quit his youth group. As his parents, we told him that, although he was free to make the decision to leave the group, he had two obligations that he would need to fulfill. First, he would need to find another youth group to attend that he felt would better nurture his spiritual life. Second, he would need to process his desire to leave the group with the youth leader and with the other members of the group. As my son shared his intentions, the group members were all awakened to his hopes and dreams in ways that they hadn't considered before. Not only did my son decide to remain in the youth group, but the group became a more meaningful experience for everyone involved.

Whenever there is a difficulty with one person, it's very likely that there is also difficulty for others. When a student voices his or her concerns, a renewed sense of community can be born. It's important to note, however, that before the group can be used as a healing agent, trusting relationships must have already been developed between the youth worker, the troubled teenager, and the group itself. Students must be willing to enter into a group process that may not always produce immediate results, and group members must agree that they will work together for the good of all.

Get the Parents Involved

It is well known that young people whose parents are supportive are more likely to succeed in life than people whose parents aren't supportive. Evaluate the support system that the parents provide, and call upon the parents to assist you as you counsel their son or daughter. Look at the following areas:

- the level of supervision in the home
- the family's attitudes toward anger
- the techniques used by the family for conflict resolution
- how anger resolution is modeled within the family
- the consistency of love that's demonstrated
- the consistency of rules and discipline
- the attitudes toward violence on television or the types of video games played
- the general communication style of the family

If you are working with a student who has a chronic anger problem, insist on working with the family as well—it's very likely that some of the issues that come up were birthed in the parent-child relationship. Working with the family will also help to positively reinforce any intervention that you may offer.

Assess the Peer Group

As you work with a student, never underestimate the power of his or her peer group. During adolescence, the peer group is the single most important relational context that a teenager has. Suspend your judgment of the teenager's peer group until you understand the student's need for those friends. Consider the following areas as you evaluate the peer group with the teenager:

- Clarify whether or not it's a constructive group that helps the teenager grow.
- Find out if the student is able to voice differences of opinion with his or her friends or if the student is "punished" for doing so.
- Talk about whether or not it's an open group that allows for diversity.
- Clarify with the student the group's views on drugs, alcohol, and sex.
- Have the teenager explain how his or her values are similar to, or different from, the values of the group.

- Discuss with the student his or her role in the peer group. Is he or she an empowered member? Or is the teenager essentially a victim to the rules established by the group?

After talking about these issues, explore with the teenager how he or she might be more influential for the good in his or her peer group—or explore if the teenager might want to re-evaluate the situation and begin to develop more productive peer relations.

Be a Role Model

Research has shown that a close, nurturing, and trusting relationship with an adult outside of the family is important to the well-being of an adolescent. How you model conflict resolution and the expression of anger is important as the teenager attempts to work through his or her difficulties. How you demonstrate kindness, how you work out conflict, how inclusive you are, and how you express your feelings all will impact how a young person relates to you and how he or she will learn to relate to others.

You are being watched. What you do will speak volumes and affect how much you are trusted and respected by the teenager you're working with. Ask the student how he or she perceives you. Find out if he or she trusts you. Does the student see you as someone that he or she can learn from? As a role model, you can work with the student in the following areas:

- Help the student see that he or she can be a problem solver.
- Help the student focus on the problem, rather than focusing on the people involved.
- Work together with the student to find solutions.
- Teach the student that reconciliation is more rewarding than winning.
- Help the teenager look for options.
- Talk about your feelings so that the student becomes comfortable talking about his or her feelings. This is not to suggest full self-disclosure; rather, offer your authentic reactions and responses as they emerge relationally.
- Teach the fundamental communication skill of "I" statements. Have the student practice statements such as "I feel angry," rather than "You make me angry." Let the teenager know that using "I" statements encourages nondefensive communication.

Recommended Resources

Books

- *The Angry Teenager: Why Teens Get So Angry, and How Parents Can Help Them Grow Through It,* William Lee Carter. Nashville, TN: Thomas Nelson Publishers, 1995.

- *At Risk: Bringing Hope to Hurting Teenagers,* Scott Larson. Loveland, CO: Group Publishing, 1999.

- *Control Your Anger,* Charles R. Swindoll. Plano, TX: Insight for Living, 1995.

- *In Control: A Skill-Building Program for Teaching Young Adolescents to Manage Anger,* Millicent H. Kellner. Champaign, IL: Research Press, 2001.

- *Make Anger Your Ally,* Third Edition, Neil Clark Warren. Wheaton, IL: Tyndale House Publishers, 1990.

- *Risk in Our Midst: Empowering Teenagers to Love the Unlovable,* Scott Larson. Loveland, CO: Group Publishing, 2000.

Web Resources

- www.apa.org (Web site of the American Psychological Association)

- www.focusas.com (Web site of Focus Adolescent Services, information and resources for working with troubled teens)

- Teach the student the art of negotiation and the importance of compromise.

---

[1] "Firearms and Crime Statistics," summary findings from the U.S. Department of Justice, Bureau of Justice Statistics at www.ojp.usdoj.gov/bjs/guns.htm.

[2] "Victim Characteristics," violent crime victim statistics from 1999 and 2000, from the U.S. Department of Justice, Bureau of Justice Statistics at www.ojp.usdoj.gov/bjs/cvict_v.htm.

[3] "Fast Crime Facts" from the National Crime Prevention Council at www.ncpc.org.

[4] "Incidents of Crime and Violence in Public Schools" in Violence and Discipline Problems in U.S. Public Schools: 1996-97. Report NCES 98-030 from the National Center for Education Statistics at http://nces.ed.gov/pubs98/violence.

[5] "Fast Crime Facts" from the National Crime Prevention Council at www.ncpc.org. For more information see the Bureau of Justice Statistics National Crime Victimization Survey (through www.ojp.usdoj.gov/bjs). See also the FBI's Uniform Crime Reports (www.fbi.gov/ucr/ucr.htm).

STUDENT PAGES Use the photocopiable worksheets on pages 41 and 42 as counseling tools. Use the "Five Basic Needs" handout (p. 41) to help a teenager think about possible unmet needs and consider how these needs may be related to his or her problem with anger. Go over the responses with the student, and talk about why the student marked each statement as he or she did. Let the student work on the "Understanding My Anger" handout (p. 42) at home, then discuss the responses with the student at your next meeting.

Five Basic Needs

Take a look at each of the statements in these five areas of need. Do you feel that the statement is true about your life? Mark each statement as true or false, then discuss your answers with your youth worker.

Belonging

_____ I feel as though I have a few good friends who understand me.

_____ My family understands me and encourages me.

_____ My parents are proud of me.

Dignity and Self-Respect

_____ I take pride in what I can accomplish.

_____ My teachers, coaches, or leaders recognize my contributions.

_____ My friends notice my _____.

Power

_____ I feel as though I can make decisions and that they will be respected.

_____ I feel that I can make changes in my life if I need to.

_____ My opinion is heard and valued in my home.

_____ My opinion is heard and valued within my peer group.

Safety

_____ I feel safe in my home.

_____ I would be able to tell my parents if someone did something wrong to me.

_____ I would be able to tell another adult if someone had harmed me.

Self-Esteem

_____ I feel good about myself.

_____ I think that I'll be able to accomplish goals that I set for myself.

_____ I think I'm a good friend.

_____ I think I'm a good son/daughter.

_____ Life is generally pretty good.

Understanding My Anger

To understand your own anger patterns, take a piece of paper and spend some time writing down short answers to these questions:

Who or what makes you angry?

When do you get angry?

What are your typical reactions?

What situations make you the most angry?

How long do you stay angry? Do you have an outburst and then forget about it? Do you harbor anger for a long time?

Is there anyone or anything that helps you resolve your feelings?

How useful is your anger in expressing what you need? How does it produce change?

CHAPTER 5

Not Just Worried–
Understanding Students With Anxiety Disorders

JAMES D. FROST, M.A.

THE BASICS

Anxiety is the feeling we have when we sense that our safety or some aspect of our well-being (such as our self-esteem, acceptance by others, or sense of meaning and purpose in life) is endangered. We have all experienced anxiety at some point as a normal reaction to something that threatens our well-being. Anxiety can prompt us to take appropriate action to avoid a bad outcome, such as studying harder to avoid getting a bad grade on a test. Mild anxiety can even improve performance in some situations.

Anxiety becomes a problem, however, when we feel unable to deal effectively with the challenges before us. When we believe something important to us is at risk and we feel powerless to do anything, anxiety can become a distressing, even paralyzing, force. Many people will go through some event during their lives that will be accompanied by intense anxiety of this sort. A loved one may be hospitalized with a life-threatening illness, a student may worry that he or she is going to fail an important class, or a person may face layoffs at work. When such a crisis has passed, however, the anxiety typically fades. For individuals with an anxiety disorder, however, feelings of apprehension and powerlessness are a part of everyday life.

Anxiety Disorders

An anxiety disorder is distinguished from normal anxiety in part by the intensity and frequency of the anxiety, the severity of impairment it causes, and how long it has been a problem. A number of different disorders have anxiety as the primary feature. All are alike in some respects, and yet each is distinctive. A clinical diagnosis of any mental disorder is based on a number of symptoms and should only be made by a licensed professional. The brief descriptions that follow, however, can be helpful in learning to recognize the most common anxiety disorders.

- *Panic Disorder*: characterized by recurrent episodes of very intense fear that come on suddenly and rapidly build to a peak. Panic is associated with dramatic physical symptoms such as chest pain, increased heart rate, difficulty breathing, feeling dizzy, and chills or hot flashes. During a full-blown panic attack, a person feels totally out of control and may fear that he or she is going to die or have a heart attack.

- *Phobias*: characterized by intense and excessive fear that occurs in specific situations. The most common fears are of certain animals or insects; weather or environmental factors, such as storms or water; blood, injections, or injuries; and other situations such as being in an elevator, riding in a car, or flying. In many cases, the phobia may involve panic symptoms as described previously.

- *Agoraphobia*: the fear that a person will humiliate himself or herself or become embarrassed in public, often triggered in situations where it would be difficult to get away if anxiety symptoms occurred. Panic attacks are often a part of the disorder. Agoraphobics avoid being away from home and avoid crowded places, such as supermarkets. When a person does have to go out in public, the slightest anxiety can trigger an urge to flee.

- *Social Phobia*: intense anxiety about being embarrassed or otherwise viewed critically by others in social or performance situations.

- *Obsessive-Compulsive Disorder (OCD)*: characterized by obsessions (thoughts, ideas, impulses, or images that one cannot stop thinking about) and compulsions (repetitive behaviors that a person feels unable to prevent himself or herself from doing, used to ward off anxiety or prevent some bad thing from happening). Common obsessions include a fear of being contaminated by germs, worries about having done some terrible thing or having left some important thing undone, an excessive need for orderliness or symmetry, and impulses or images of a violent, blasphemous, or sexual nature. Devout Christians may experience vulgar or profane obsessions that stand in marked contrast to their values and are therefore both very distressing and particularly puzzling to them. Common compulsions involve excessive repetition of certain behaviors, such as hand washing, putting things in order, or repeated checking; maintaining symmetry, such as performing an act a prescribed number of times or making sure that both shoes are tied with exactly the same tension; and performing mental acts, such as counting or repeating words to oneself. In some cases even prayer can become a compulsion when a person feels driven to repeat a prayer to achieve a brief respite from anxiety.

- *Separation Anxiety Disorder*: the fear in a child or teenager of separation from the home or from his or her family. A child may worry about something happening to separate him or her from parents (such as becoming lost or getting kidnapped), or a teenager may worry that harm will come to someone to whom he or she is closely attached. The fear exceeds what would be normal given the person's age and situation. Teenagers may have nightmares involving their fears of separation or complain of physical symptoms such as headaches, stomachaches, nausea, or vomiting at the anticipation of being separated from their parents.

- *Post-Traumatic Stress Disorder (PTSD)*: persistent and distressing re-experiencing of a traumatic event through nightmares, flashbacks, intrusive memories, or mental images of the event. A student with PTSD may experience intense distress whenever anything reminds him or her of the trauma (for example, if a person rides in a car after he or she has been in a car accident). The teenager will often go to great lengths to avoid situations that he or she associates with the trauma.

- *Generalized Anxiety:* excessive worry about a variety of things, such as family, social acceptance, health, finances, school, or work, including physical symptoms of anxiety.

Anxiety disorders all seem to involve some degree of irrational thinking, uncomfortable or distressing physiological symptoms, and behaviors that are centered around avoiding situations that could trigger the anxiety.

WHEN TO REFER

Refer a student to a professional Christian counselor or psychologist in any of the following situations:

- when the teenager's anxiety is a result of a trauma (such as a physical or sexual assault or a car accident)
- when the student's anxiety has persisted for at least six months
- when the student's anxiety significantly interferes with school or other major responsibilities
- when obsessions or compulsions are present
- when a person has thoughts of suicide

When a student exhibits physical symptoms, it's a good idea for the student to see a physician to rule out medical causes.

COUNSELING IDEAS

Take the Problem Seriously

Because the distress of an anxiety disorder is irrational, people often think that just explaining this to the student should do the trick. This not only doesn't work (students with anxiety disorders usually realize that their anxiety is unrealistic), but it undermines one of the most critical functions of being a helper—namely, providing support. It's important for the teenager to know that you understand the seriousness of his or her trouble and that you empathize with him or her. Remember that while this student may not have a "real" reason for his or her anxiety, the anxiety is real nonetheless. In a panic attack, for example, a person's body reacts just as it would if that person's life were really in danger, because that's what the person's brain believes.

Encourage Education

One of the best ways to begin to deal with any psychological problem is to learn about it. Encourage the teenager to visit the library, check out self-help books, or search the Internet for information to gain an understanding of anxiety, its effects, and how to fight it.

Teach Relaxation and Calming Skills

There are a number of techniques that people can use to relax and calm themselves if they are willing to put forth a diligent effort to master the techniques. Learning to manage and reduce the physical distress provides great relief. These exercises are helpful with most anxiety disorders as well as with normal anxiety and everyday stress.

- *Visualization*: Lead a student in visualization exercises like this one: "Close your eyes and imagine yourself in a peaceful place—on a tropical island, for example. Make your image more vivid by involving as many senses as possible. See the palm trees gently swaying in the breeze, feel the warmth of the sun on your skin, smell the salt of the ocean, and hear the sounds of sea gulls crying and the waves crashing on the beach." The more the student's mind is occupied with this fantasy, the more his or her body will react to its calming effects.

- *Distraction*: Encourage the teenager to engage in some simple physical activity to occupy his or her mind and take attention away from the physical tension or panic that he or she feels. A former client of mine reported that paying close attention to the second hand of his watch as it ticked around the dial would distract him from the panic and help the symptoms pass more quickly. Breathing slowly into a bag during a panic attack also helps in this way, and it reduces the risk of hyperventilation. Anxiety feeds off itself, so diverting attention away from it is helpful.

- *Deep Breathing*: Anxiety (especially panic) is often associated with a tendency toward rapid, shallow breathing. This actually makes the feelings of anxiety worse and can lead to hyperventilation. Learning to change one's breathing can be a great help in reducing the body's anxiety reactions, especially during a flood of anxiety. To practice deep breathing, the student should sit or lie comfortably and place a hand lightly on his or her abdomen. Tell the teenager to take deep, slow breaths that fill the lungs fully. The student should breathe from the abdomen, so that when his or her hand is placed on the abdomen, it will rise and fall with each breath. Breathing through the nose also tends to facilitate the process and reduces the risk of hyperventilation. The teenager should practice abdominal breathing for at least fifteen minutes twice a day until it becomes easy and natural. When a person makes himself or herself use such deep breathing during a panic attack, it can quickly reduce the distressing symptoms and the feeling of losing control.

- *Muscle Relaxation*: There are many different relaxation exercises. The method I like best was first developed by Dr. Edmund Jacobson more than fifty years ago but has been modified by other therapists. (For a more thorough description of this technique, see *The Anxiety and Phobia Workbook* by Edmund Bourne.[1]) A short version of this technique is provided on the student page at the end of this chapter (p. 50). In this exercise, a panicked person will alternately tense and release various muscle groups, studying the sensations as he or she does so. Concentrating on the sensations of tension and relaxation is important so that the student will quickly learn to recognize muscle tension when it occurs and be able to relax it away. I recommend that a student practice these exercises daily for at least three weeks so that this relaxation response will be deeply ingrained.

Through diligent practice, these techniques will become almost automatic. Students who have regularly practiced the muscle relaxation exercises, for example, have reported significant benefits, and I have even had some students who were able to successfully terminate therapy shortly after mastering this skill.

Encourage Journaling

Research has shown that expressing feelings in writing is an effective way to help people deal psychologically with many different types of problems. Even chronic physical illnesses have been shown to improve through structured writing exercises similar to keeping a journal. There seems to be something about translating emotions into language that is very healing. It is important that a person's deepest feelings are expressed freely in the writing process and that journal entries are made regularly.

Encourage Prayer

People with anxiety problems need to know that God is listening and is able to deliver them from any problem. Although God doesn't always deliver them in the way they had in mind, the process of prayer still has many benefits as an avenue of expression, and it can be very calming.

Encourage a Daily "Serenity Check"

As a diabetic, I've learned to check my blood sugar frequently to keep it in balance. The trick is to catch deviations before they become big, so that only small adjustments are needed to bring the level back to normal. In a similar way, I encourage many of my students to take a "serenity check" at least once a day. I instruct them to take a few minutes for calm and honest reflection on how they've been feeling. Is their serenity or inner peace dropping? If so, why? What adjustments need to be made to restore it?

Recognize Unrealistic Thinking and Expectations

Upsetting emotions are caused not so much by the events in our lives, but by how we think about those events. One person accepts that a traffic jam, while frustrating, is beyond his control; another person, seeing the same traffic jam as an outrage, yells, curses, and gets his blood pressure up. All of us have, at some point, blown things out of proportion or jumped to conclusions. The thinking of individuals suffering from anxiety disorders, however, is very frequently characterized by these and other forms of thought distortion.

The anxiety-prone person is likely to take a view of things that magnifies the seriousness of a situation and minimizes the person's awareness of his or her resources for dealing with the challenge. For example, a student might hold himself or herself to unrealistically high standards, such as regarding it as unacceptable if he or she doesn't make all A's on a report card. The teenager may also ask a series of "What if..." questions and predict some dire outcome to a situation in the absence of any reason for such pessimism.

The Feeling Good Handbook by David Burns[2] is an excellent self-help book for learning to change the thought processes that lead to upsetting emotions such as anxiety and depression. This book will help you recognize common forms of what Burns calls "twisted thinking" and understand how this affects emotions. The book will also help you encourage the student to honestly look at a situation. For example, you might ask the student, "Do you really *have* to make all A's? What would be the worst thing about getting a B?"

When a teenager worries that a bad thing is going to happen, challenge the student to think like a detective and objectively consider the evidence both for and against the predicted calamity.

Anxiety Disorders

Then challenge him or her to begin thinking according to a more realistic view: "I really want to get all A's, but I know that it may not be possible. It's more important that I do my best and learn as much as I can." These are statements that express the truth without twisting it.

Break the Cycle of Avoidance

Anxious people become very good at avoiding whatever makes them anxious. An agoraphobic avoids being away from home, and someone who is afraid of heights stays away from ladders and balconies. When a person avoids the situation, he or she feels less anxious; this avoidant behavior is rewarded and is thus strengthened. An anxious person cannot be talked out of a strongly conditioned response of avoidance. The person has to make himself or herself endure the anxiety-producing situation to learn that there is nothing to be afraid of and that he or she can survive the anxiety.

First a student needs to master the relaxation and breathing skills described earlier to manage the distress he or she will feel in the situation. Then break the process of "facing the fear" into small, manageable steps. A person with a fear of heights, for example, could start with a very mild height (a stepladder) and gradually move up to greater heights after the anxiety has been mastered at each successive level. The steps can be as small as needed to facilitate progress (such as merely imagining stepping onto a ladder). Success at each level should be practiced repeatedly until the anxious responses are extinguished or easily mastered.

Encourage a Healthy Lifestyle

A person's lifestyle can either enhance or diminish his or her physical and emotional health. Unhealthy habits add unnecessary stress that affects a person psychologically and physically. Help an anxious teenager examine health habits including diet, exercise, and the use of caffeine, alcohol, nicotine, and drugs. Look closely at the pace of a student's life, the amount of sleep he or she gets, other forms of rest and rejuvenation, and the number of responsibilities the student takes on.

Recommended Resources

Books

- *The Anxiety and Phobia Workbook,* Edmund J. Bourne. Oakland, CA: New Harbinger Publications, Inc., 1990.

- *Don't Panic: Taking Control of Anxiety Attacks,* R. Reid Wilson. New York, NY: Harper & Row Publishers, Inc., 1986.

- *The Feeling Good Handbook,* Revised Edition, David D. Burns. New York, NY: Plume, 1990, 1999.

- *The Prism Workbook: A Program for Innovative Self-Management,* David B. Wexler. New York, NY: W.W. Norton & Company, Inc., 1991.

Explore Life Circumstances

Think of anxiety as a psychological alarm system. A blaring smoke detector signals that something is on fire. In the same way, anxiety should prompt us to examine our lives to see what's wrong. Sometimes the problem may be obvious to everyone except the person who is affected. Help the anxious person identify life circumstances, such as problems at work or illness in the family, that could be contributing to his or her anxiety.

Tackle It or Turn It Over

Problems that cause stress can usually be divided into those things the person can do something about and those things that are beyond a person's control. If there's something a teenager can

Anxiety Disorders

do to affect a problem, encourage the anxious student to turn his or her worry into action and tackle the problem. If the situation is beyond the teenager's control, help him or her turn it over to God and try to truly let go of it. Getting worked up over what a person cannot change is useless, as Jesus expressed when he asked, "Who of you by worrying can add a single hour to his life?" (Matthew 6:27).

Find Spiritual Meaning and Purpose in the Problem

I often ask teenagers some variation of the following question: "If God was trying to speak to you through your problem, what do you think he might be trying to say?"

Mark, a sixteen-year-old with whom I worked, responded to this question by recognizing that his social anxiety caused him to stay isolated and depressed. He felt that his suffering was God's way of telling him to reach out and make connections with others. As Mark did this, he began to make friendships, started a spiritual formation group with two other teenagers, and exerted some spiritual leadership in his church youth group and at his school. His treatment also included medication and relaxation exercises to decrease anxiety and depression; but his sense of a spiritual purpose to his problem formed the framework for a change that went much deeper than the mere reduction of symptoms.

Use Scripture to Encourage

God has provided many words of comfort in Scripture that address the cares and concerns of this world. When you use the Bible to comfort, however, keep in mind two things. First, take care not to wield Scripture passages like commandments in which uncontrollable worry sounds like sin and thus increases feelings of guilt. Second, be careful not to convey the sense that merely accepting the simple truth of these passages should quickly make a hurting student feel better. Don't offer Scripture as a *simple* solution to any emotional problem. James 2:15-16 warns against offering a few quick words of comfort without addressing the real need. *Do* use Scripture to convey the truth that God loves the suffering person and cares about what bothers him or her (1 Peter 5:7). The love of Christ is made palpable when you allow it to be expressed through your own love for an anxious teenager (see Proverbs 12:25).

Additional Scripture passages that offer comfort for anxiety include Matthew 6:25-34 and Philippians 4:6-7.

---

[1]   Edmund J. Bourne, *The Anxiety and Phobia Workbook* (Oakland, CA: New Harbinger Publications, Inc., 1990), 70-74.

[2]   David D. Burns, *The Feeling Good Handbook,* Revised Edition (New York, NY: Plume, 1990, 1999).

STUDENT PAGE Use the photocopiable worksheet on page 50 to help a student develop skills in muscle relaxation. Encourage a teenager who is dealing with anxiety to use the worksheet at home to guide his or her muscle relaxation exercises. You may also want to practice this exercise with the student during a counseling session.

Instructions for Muscle Relaxation

This exercise calls for you to tense and relax various muscle groups one at a time. Doing this properly will leave you in a very relaxed state. After about three weeks of daily practice, you'll notice when you tense up, and you'll be able to quickly and easily let that tension go.

Find a quiet place, and sit or lie in a comfortable position. Tense each muscle group listed below. Hold the tension and concentrate on the feeling of tension in that area for about ten seconds. Then let go of the tension and concentrate on this sensation for about ten seconds. Notice the difference between tension and relaxation in each area as you do this. Repeat the tensing and relaxing so that each area is tightened and released twice before moving on to the next area. After you have gone through all of the areas, spend a few minutes remaining in this relaxed state. Enjoy this deep relaxation and allow your mind to relax as well.

Two notes of caution: First, while you can use this exercise to relax and help you fall asleep, don't count it as a practice session if you fall asleep in the middle of it. It's best not to practice late at night or when you are particularly tired. Second, take care of yourself by skipping any muscle group that would impact any medical problem or physical limitation you might have.

Face: Tighten the muscles of your face, scrunching up your face, and then relax.

Shoulders: Tighten your shoulders by raising them toward your ears, then relax.

Chest: Take a deep breath and hold it. Notice the tension in your chest, then let it out.

Arms: Bring your lower arms up toward your shoulders, tightening the biceps, then let your arms hang loosely.

Hands: Tighten your hands into fists, then relax.

Stomach: Tighten your stomach muscles, then relax.

Legs: Tighten the muscles in your upper legs by raising and holding your legs up, then relax.

Calves: Pivoting at the ankles, pull your toes up toward your shins, then relax.

Feet: Tighten your feet as if you were trying to make them into fists, then relax.

CHAPTER 6

Can't You Pay Attention?–
Working With ADD/ADHD Students

CYNTHIA LINDQUIST, M.S., AND LARRY LINDQUIST, Ed.D.

THE BASICS

You've probably heard about attention-deficit disorder or ADD. You may have seen magazine ads that celebrate the success stories of students who are on the latest treatment. Or you may have heard angry parents on TV talk shows arguing that it's all a conspiracy to put kids on medication. ADD is a controversial subject, and it's here to stay.

There are two main types of this disorder: attention-deficit disorder (ADD) and attention-deficit hyperactivity disorder (ADHD). (Throughout this chapter we'll generally refer to both disorders as ADD except in situations when the information applies specifically to ADHD.) There has been a great deal of research in the field, and we now know more than ever about ADD. Yet there still are many misconceptions, and there is still much to be learned about this disorder.

Attention-deficit disorder is the term that's been used for a number of years to identify children who are unable to focus, pay attention, and organize as well as other children their age. They have significant problems in the areas of attention, hyperactivity, and impulsivity. Issues related to ADD, such as identification of the disorder, medication, and management of behaviors, continue to raise new questions and cause controversy. By understanding the basics of the disorder, we can more effectively meet the needs of our students.

It's estimated that 3 to 5 percent of students have this disorder. We also know that "ADHD is diagnosed between three to nine times more frequently in boys than girls. It is believed that many more girls actually have ADHD and aren't diagnosed because often they exhibit fewer of the disruptive behaviors associated with hyperactivity and impulsivity. Many girls have the predominantly inattentive type of the disorder and are likely not being identified and diagnosed."[1] In people who are not hyperactive, their ADD can go undiagnosed for years or even for a lifetime.

ADD is a complex neurobiological disorder. Though much research is being done, it is still not clear what causes ADD. The disorder may be associated with a decreased production of certain neurotransmitters or with lower activity in certain areas of the brain. In people with ADD, the areas of the brain that control attention, organization, and related cognitive processes seem to function less efficiently.

A common misconception about ADD is that children outgrow it. In reality, ADD/ADHD is a lifelong disorder. Teenagers and adults don't outgrow ADD—they learn to manage it. Research also shows that ADD runs in families: "Forty to fifty percent of all children with attention deficits have at least one parent and thirty percent have a sibling with the condition."[2]

WHEN TO REFER

How can you know if a student has ADD? A diagnosis of ADD or ADHD is made through evaluations, parent-student interviews, classroom observations, and a medical examination to rule out vision and hearing problems and neurological disorders. There are no laboratory tests such as blood or urine screens that will identify ADD. Although many of us may look at a hyperactive adolescent and say, "That kid is as ADD as they come," it requires a thorough examination by a doctor to make a diagnosis. We can, however, make observations about a student's behavior and suggest an evaluation if it appears warranted.

There are several signs and symptoms of ADD. Not all people with ADD will display all of these characteristics; however, many students will exhibit most of them. Almost all people will show some of these characteristics at some point in their lives, but the degree and frequency to which they exhibit them is what sets ADD students apart from other students. If you have a student who exhibits many of these characteristics consistently, suggest to the parents that they have their child evaluated by a physician.

Signs and Symptoms

The following characteristics may indicate that a student has ADD or ADHD:

1. The student struggles with a limited attention span and the inability to concentrate, exhibited in the following behaviors.
   - The student has problems concentrating for long periods of time.
   - He or she quickly loses interest in tasks and activities.
   - The student daydreams and "spaces out."
   - The teenager does not pay attention to details and makes careless mistakes.
   - The student moves from one uncompleted task to another.

2. The teenager struggles with extreme impulsivity, which can be expressed in the following behaviors.
   - The teenager lacks the ability to stop and think before acting.
   - He or she rushes through work.
   - The student makes many careless errors.
   - The teenager talks excessively, blurts out ideas, and interrupts.
   - He or she doesn't wait for directions.
   - If the student is given a choice between a small, immediate reward or a larger one that he or she must wait for, the student chooses the more immediate reward.

3. The student displays excessive motor activity or hyperactivity and may exhibit the following behaviors.

- The teenager is restless and fidgety.
- He or she demonstrates a high degree of unnecessary movement (pacing, tapping feet, drumming fingers).
- The student makes inappropriate noises.
- The student invades other people's space.

4. The teenager displays emotional extremes or emotional overarousal.

- He or she has a short fuse (is easily angered).
- The student is moody and irritable.
- He or she gets frustrated frequently.
- The student loses control easily.
- The teenager becomes overstimulated and excited when he or she is in large groups.
- He or she experiences extreme emotions, such as anger, frustration, silliness, happiness, anxiety, or depression.

5. The student possesses poor social skills, which may be exhibited in the following behaviors.

- The student has difficulty getting along with others.
- He or she has difficulty making transitions.
- The teenager is socially immature and is unable to read social cues.
- The student has low self-esteem.
- He or she is bossy, aggressive, and competitive.
- The teenager often fights, yells, or offends others, leading to isolation and rejection.
- He or she is insensitive to others.

6. The teenager has poor organizational skills and may exhibit the following behaviors.

- He or she loses homework, books, or pencils.
- The student can't get started on tasks and doesn't know which step to take first.
- The student is unable to break tasks into manageable parts.
- He or she experiences difficulty in planning ahead for completion of long-term projects.

7. The student has an impaired sense of time as indicated by the following behaviors.

- The teenager can't manage time or judge the passage of time.
- He or she is often late.
- The teenager doesn't anticipate how long tasks will take.
- He or she procrastinates.

You have probably seen students with these characteristics in your youth ministry. If a teenager consistently has a limited attention span, is impulsive, displays excessive motor activity, gets easily excited, makes poor social choices, has poor organizational skills, and can't seem to manage his or her time, the student probably has ADD/ADHD. Talk with the student's parents about your observations, and encourage them to seek the help of a qualified physician.

COUNSELING IDEAS

Be a Coach

As a youth worker, you may be asked to play a special role in the life of an ADD student. Since these students have major problems with organization, time management, and memory, their needs extend beyond the school day. At school, their time is usually highly structured and tightly scheduled. ADD students often need models for time management and organization outside the classroom, and many ADD students seek a coach to guide them. A coach can help teenagers practice new, positive ways to deal with old, negative behaviors. A coach offers suggestions, advice, reminders, support, and encouragement. He or she may help the student become more organized, set and achieve goals, celebrate successes, and deal with failures.

The parents may not feel prepared to take on the role of coach because of the emotions involved, and they may seek help from an outside, neutral source. The parents may be overwhelmed dealing with the teenager in their home, and you can assist the parents with their spiritual needs as you help meet some very real physical needs. As a coach for an ADD student, you might meet the student face to face, or you may provide coaching by phone or e-mail on a weekly basis.

The task may seem enormous as you think, "How can I possibly pour that much energy into one of my students? I don't have time to mentor a student with significant needs." As difficult as the task appears, you have an opportunity to develop a leader in your youth ministry who has boundless energy!

Build on Strengths

What are some of the characteristics of an effective ADD coach? First, help the student discover his or her strengths and build on them. Does the student have great computer skills? He or she could be a part of the tech team in your youth group or church. Is the teenager talented in the arts? You may find a place for him or her in a drama production. Perhaps the student has an outgoing personality, but has crude social skills. As you model appropriate social behavior, you may help this student realize his or her ability to be a positive leader. You might also help the teenager work on social skills by pairing him or her with a reliable, more mature student in your youth ministry. Build on the teenager's positive traits. Give attention to his or her special qualities, and help the student maximize his or her strengths. Oftentimes this focus on the positive will help compensate for the teenager's weaknesses.

Recognize Weaknesses

Help the teenager deal with his or her weaknesses. If time management is a problem, help the student develop specific strategies to deal with that weakness. For example, you might suggest that the student wear a watch with an alarm or use a personal planner, or help the teenager set up a schedule with some extra time to get to important events. Helping him or her prioritize, as well as identifying busywork, will assist the teenager in managing time. Of course, setting an example in your own life is always important.

Focus on Learning Style

Assist the teenager in finding his or her dominant learning style, and teach to that style. Some students thrive when they see the information (visual learners); others learn best by listening (auditory learners); and still others learn by touching and by doing (kinesthetic learners). As you spend time with a student, you will probably begin to see his or her dominant learning style. Help the teenager build on that strength as well.

Ask Questions and Find Answers

Learn to ask good questions. Help the teenager find answers for himself or herself, and guide him or her in creating solutions. Encourage the teenager to be a good problem solver, and model this resourcefulness in your own life. In his book, *The Attention-Deficit Child*, Dr. Grant Martin uses a method for problem solving that he calls the SODA approach.[3]

Stop. Take a step back from the situation, and figure out what's causing the problem.

Options. Consider the many options that exist for dealing with the problem.

Decide. Weigh the options, and choose the solution that seems to be the best.

Action. Try out the solution, and evaluate the outcome.

Provide Structure

Provide some structure in the lives of your ADD students. As a youth worker, you may have to take into consideration the structure of your own youth ministry. Unfortunately, the environment of many youth ministries is just short of chaos. Does this mean that you'll need to restructure your youth ministry? It may. If nothing else, you may need to provide additional structure for your ADD students. For example, if you have an easily excitable student who quickly becomes out of control, consider having him or her run the PowerPoint presentation during your fast-paced crowdbreakers or upbeat musical numbers. This will include the student in the activity, while keeping him or her focused and preventing excessive moving around.

Encourage Taking Responsibility

Help the teenager take responsibility for his or her actions, and model this in your own life. Too often ADD is used as an excuse for poor behavior or inappropriate actions. The reality is that the student is still in control of his or her life, and the student's decisions and behaviors will affect his or her future.

Provide Support

Give the teenager unconditional acceptance. The student has to know that you really care before he or she will be willing to work with you. Share with the student your own struggles with weaknesses. It's helpful for a student to see that he or she is not alone in his or her problems. Explaining how you have coped with problems will give the student hope that he or she can succeed too.

Work With Parents

As you work with the parents of an ADD student, try to understand what the parents have been through. They probably have been criticized by family members, other parents, and professionals and have felt a certain amount of blame for their child's problems. They may have received repeated calls from others complaining about their child's behavior and have been told to fix it.

Don't assume the parents lack parenting skills or that they don't care about their child; instead, understand that it's possible that the parents may *also* have ADD. Gently express your concern for their child's difficulties.

- Don't blame or judge; be empathetic and supportive.
- Join with the parents; become a team.

Recommended Resources

Books

- *The ADD/ADHD Checklist: An Easy Reference for Parents and Teachers,* Sandra F. Rief. Paramus, NJ: Prentice Hall, 1998.

- *ADHD and Teens: A Parent's Guide to Making It Through the Tough Years,* Colleen Alexander-Roberts. Dallas, TX: Taylor Publishing Company, 1995.

- *The Attention-Deficit Child,* Grant Martin. Colorado Springs, CO: Chariot Victor Publishing, 1992, 1998.

- *The Parent's Guide to Attention-Deficit Disorders,* Angela Marie Bauer and Stephen B. McCarney. Columbia, MO: Hawthorne Educational Services, Inc., 1995.

- *Teaching Teens With ADD and ADHD: A Quick Reference Guide for Teachers and Parents,* Chris A. Zeigler Dendy. Bethesda, MD: Woodbine House, Inc., 2000.

- *Teenagers With ADD: A Parent's Guide,* Chris A. Zeigler Dendy. Bethesda, MD: Woodbine House, Inc., 1995.

- *You and Your ADD Child: How to Understand and Help Kids With Attention-Deficit Disorder,* Paul Warren and Jody Capehart. Nashville, TN: Thomas Nelson Publishers, 1995.

Web Resources

- www.add.org (Web site of the Attention-Deficit Disorder Association)

- www.ccpd.org (Web site of the Christian Council on Persons With Disabilities)

- www.cec.sped.org (Web site of the Council for Exceptional Children)

- www.chadd.org (Web site of CHADD—Children and Adults With Attention-Deficit/Hyperactivity Disorder)

- Ask the parents what has worked and what hasn't.
- Offer ideas you've found helpful in working with other ADD students.
- Keep the lines of communication open.
- Parents may need to learn to change their expectations for their child, and your neutral position outside of the family may help them do it.

---

[1] Sandra F. Rief, *The ADD/ADHD Checklist: An Easy Reference for Parents and Teachers* (Paramus, NJ: Prentice Hall, 1998), 5.

[2] Chris A. Zeigler Dendy, *Teaching Teens With ADD and ADHD: A Quick Reference Guide for Teachers and Parents* (Bethesda, MD: Woodbine House, Inc., 2000), 4.

[3] Grant Martin, *The Attention-Deficit Child* (Colorado Springs, CO: Chariot Victor Publishing, 1992, 1998), 114.

STUDENT PAGE Use the photocopiable worksheet on page 57 to help you determine if a student may need a referral and an evaluation by a professional for ADD/ADHD. Use this handout in a counseling session by having the student do the exercise and then using it as a discussion starter. Afterward total the ratings given by the student. A score of 66-80 strongly indicates that there is a need for a referral. Please keep in mind that *all* people will display some of these characteristics some of the time; but a pattern of extremes indicates the need for further investigation.

This Is Who I Am

Next to each statement, put the number (1-4) that best describes you. Answer the way that you really feel you *are*, not the way you think you *should be*.

1. Totally *not* me!
2. This is me, at least some of the time.
3. This is pretty much like me.
4. Wow! You're describing my life!

__ I can't study for long periods of time.

__ It is hard for me to stick to one thing for long periods of time.

__ I daydream a lot.

__ I interrupt other conversations.

__ I'm a risk taker!

__ I start a lot of things, but don't finish them.

__ I am often bored and impatient.

__ I bother people around me by tapping my feet, drumming my fingers, or moving.

__ I'm very talkative.

__ I have a very short fuse. I get frustrated easily.

__ I've been called moody.

__ I've been called bossy.

__ I have trouble getting along with others.

__ Sometimes I am too blunt or critical of others.

__ I tend to be messy.

__ I often turn in schoolwork late.

__ I'm always losing things.

__ I have trouble being on time.

__ I procrastinate (put things off until the last possible minute).

__ I can't tell how long a project will take me to do.

CHAPTER 7

I'm Ready for the World!–
Equipping Students to Make College and Career Choices

TREVOR SIMPSON, M.A.

THE BASICS

Perhaps there is no other time in a student's life that generates such a wide range of emotions as the second semester of a teenager's senior year in high school. Graduation is quickly approaching, and Timmy needs to decide how he is going to enter into the next phase of his life. He is clearly excited about his dreams of going to college and living on his own, under his own rules, and experiencing life from a new perspective. Not going to college was never an option for him. It was set in stone from the day he was born that he was expected to perform at a high level academically, go to college, get a good job, and be successful. Although he wants to be a teacher, he's not sure that it's really his dream. Both of his parents are teachers, but he finds himself wondering if he should pursue a degree in English and be a writer. At the same time, he's not really sure if he will be able to handle the stress of college life. He has to do well or his parents will not help him out financially.

Timmy's girlfriend of the last two years, Jessica, plans to stay in town and keep her job as a clerk in the hardware store. This was not a difficult decision for her because she's never had the desire to go to college. She'd rather make money and be independent right out of high school. Her parents did that, and they seemed happy in their jobs. Plus she wants a new car, and that just wouldn't happen if she had to take classes. She always figured that she would get married, and between her income and her husband's, she would be able to live comfortably.

The ideals of living out our dreams and being successful are both a blessing and a curse to all of us. These concepts also mean completely different things to different people depending on their upbringing, life experiences, cultural expectations, and resources. The idea of success motivates people to strive to reach their potential, which certainly can and does benefit the communities they live in. However, these ideals can also prompt people to look for their identity in what they *do*, rather than in their status as beloved children of God. This focus on what we do is apparent in every age group.

An adult might ask a young child what the child wants to be when he or she grows up. Almost invariably, the little one will spout out a romantic or adventure-filled vocation. The adult then smiles at the sincerity of the child's dream, knowing that it will probably not happen that way.

As early as junior high school, vocational classes become a part of the curriculum. In high school, vocational classes continue to be a part of the curriculum; however, the vocational focus is even more heavily emphasized as career assessment tests are administered and schools hold college and career days.

Even in adulthood, our vocation is quickly brought up as the primary identifying factor in our relationships. After introductions, the next question is always, "What do you do?" The person answering that question typically feels one of two things. The person is either proud of his or her job and says it with confidence; or the person is ashamed of his or her position and offers explanations as to why he or she is "stuck" in that job.

WHEN TO REFER

It's rare that a youth worker would find it necessary to refer a student with career questions to a professional counselor. At this point in their lives, most teenagers are uncertain about the future. We can probably assume, based on our own experiences, that a young person will change majors three times in college or change jobs several times in the next few years—but that's OK! It's a normal part of growing up.

Keep in mind that the student is still an adolescent! True, some teenagers have successfully chosen their paths or have sensed a calling from God during high school (or even earlier) and find vocational bliss for many years to come. Those aren't the students who are tormented and are knocking on your door asking you to help "find God's will for my life." In situations like those, remember that teenagers are not yet adults. Erik Erikson has identified the adolescent stage of life as "Identity vs. Identity Confusion."[1] Students are in the *process* of finding out who they are, how they fit in, and where they are going in life. This stage will last into a person's early twenties. As a result, trying to figure out what they want to do for the rest of their lives can feel frustrating and fruitless to teenagers.

The youth worker should refer a teenager to a professional career counselor if the student is experiencing unhealthy anxiety. (For more information about anxiety disorders, see Chapter 5). Anxiety about the future may cause feelings of hopelessness or depression or may negatively affect the student's relationships.

There are many excellent tools available from school counselors and career counselors that identify teenagers' strengths and weaknesses and provide vocational ideas. These tools are available from high schools and through the career placement offices at most community colleges. You might consider having a student make an appointment at a local community college to meet with a career counselor or use the database to do research.

COUNSELING IDEAS

Although career counseling with adolescents will rarely prompt a need for serious counseling, it's important for the youth worker to keep in mind several issues when discussing dreams, aspirations, and vocations with teenagers.

College and Career Decisions

Communicate an Appropriate Theology of "God's Will"

Perhaps one of the most abused clichés in Christian circles is the expression "God's will for my life." Although God does have a will for our lives, this expression is used so much that it loses meaning, and people often use it without thinking about the weight of what these words really mean. We know from Scripture that we were created to enter a relationship with God to bring honor and glory to him. We can say for certain that God's will for our lives is to honor and glorify him in all that we do.

During significant developmental changes or significant life changes, certain types of questions frequently arise: "Is this God's will for my life?" "Does God want me to go to this school or that school?" "Does God want me to work here or there?" These are sincere questions that deserve to be explored; however, we must also realize that we have been given a gift of freedom, and we are expected to use it. If a student is laboring over finding God's will for him or her after high school, the youth worker can direct the student toward a confident decision by asking the following questions:

- How would each of the choices give you opportunities to grow in your faith?
- Which of the choices would bring you to praise and worship God more easily and more fully?
- Which of the choices would allow you to be surrounded by people who would uplift you and encourage you in your faith?

No matter what a student's decision is, he or she has an opportunity to do God's will. Micah 6:8 says, "He has showed you, O man, what is good. And what does the Lord require of you? To act justly and to love mercy and to walk humbly with your God." That is God's will for his children. Pray with the student to experience a peace and joy in whatever decision he or she makes.

Know the Student

The best type of career counseling will come from the people who know the student the best. Ideally, youth workers should know their students well enough to be able to clearly articulate the characteristics that concern them and excite them about each student. Youth leaders can show love to students by being encouraging and by being honest about the students' strengths and weaknesses. Youth workers frequently fall into the trap of trying to be so uplifting and encouraging that they have a hard time giving any form of negative feedback. But for healthy relationships to develop, youth workers must be honest with their students.

If a student is laboring over decisions about his or her life after high school and is looking for some counsel, the youth worker should be honest and fair. For example, if Timmy is a complete goofball with little integrity, it may serve him well to hear that, as his friend and youth leader, you're concerned about his ability to meet the standards at the Christian college he'd like to attend.

Communicate Patience

This can be a sticky issue because much of the pressure is piled on by parents, schools, and society. There is a drive for students to get out and "do something" and to "begin the next phase." Most high school graduates have plans that involve going to college, entering the armed forces, traveling, getting a job, or some combination of these.

Some teenagers are totally clueless about what's next, though, and it really bothers them. Either *everything* sounds good to them or *nothing* sounds good to them. In this situation, it may be best for students to take their time in getting to where they think they need to go. It may be

College and Career Decisions

wise for a teenager to take a break and work for a year or take a wide variety of classes instead of immediately deciding on a course of study. This approach may alleviate stress and allow a student to grow through adolescence as the student figures out who he or she is.

Know Yourself

What were your own parents' expectations of you growing up? Do you feel that you've lived up to them? Were your parents' expectations too much or too little? Do you like where you are in your vocation? What mistakes have you made and what successes have you had in your career? How does this affect the way you view yourself and other people? How do you feel about college? Seminary? Blue-collar vs. white-collar careers?

Without exception, the way you answer those types of questions will affect the way you counsel teenagers. Projecting some of ourselves is a part of the counseling process—it is unavoidable and can create both good and bad counsel for those we are trying to help. As you counsel your students, it's very important to recognize that they are individuals who are very different from you. What worked for you may or may not be best for your students. Keep this in mind, and pray for the Holy Spirit to lead you in being objective and being aware of your students' needs.

Network for and With the Student

Perhaps one of the greatest things about being a part of the body of Christ is the fact that there are so many different people with different gifts. Keep in mind other people who could provide students with mentoring, counseling, or ideas about what to do next. If possible, have teenagers interview people and visit worksites to learn about different vocations. Remember that no matter where your students end up and whatever they do, they will have opportunities to honor and glorify God.

---

[1] John W. Santrock, *Adolescence,* Fourth Edition (Dubuque, IA: Wm. C. Brown Publishers, 1990), 53-55. See also Erik H. Erikson, *Childhood and Society* (New York, NY: W.W. Norton & Company, Inc., 1963).

Recommended Resources

Books
- *Occupational Outlook Handbook,* compiled by the United States Department of Labor, Bureau of Labor Statistics.

Web Resources
- http://online.onetcenter.org (Web site of O*NET, the Occupational Information Network)

- www.careermaze.com (Web site of Career Maze)

- www.octs.net (Web site of Orange County Testing Services)

- Search the Internet for the terms "career assessment" or "career counseling."

STUDENT PAGE Use the photocopiable worksheet on page 62 to help teenagers process their thoughts about future goals and choices. Allow the student to work on the handout independently, and then discuss the answers with the student during a subsequent meeting.

What's Next? First Steps in Figuring Out the Next Phase

You may feel stuck, scared, excited, anxious, or clueless (or all of these!) about life after high school. Join the club! It's probably going to be several more years before you really feel settled. Your job for now is to put yourself in situations where you can grow in your faith and your character. The rest will fall into place. Take some time and think seriously about the following questions. When you've finished answering the questions, discuss them with someone who will give you truthful advice and not just tell you what you want to hear. This isn't a test; you won't receive a grade. This is simply a way to gain insight into who you are and where you want to go in life.

What's your dream job? What's a fair wage to be paid for that job?

List five of your character traits that are strengths.

List five of your character traits that are weaknesses.

How do your strengths and weaknesses affect how you view yourself and your future?

What are three things you need in order to accomplish your wildest dreams, and how would these help you achieve your dreams?

What are three obstacles you face that may prevent you from accomplishing your wildest dreams?

How have the expectations of others (parents, friends, youth leaders, culture) affected the way you view your future?

If you could write a book about how you'd want your life to be, what would the next five years look like? What would the next ten years look like?

CHAPTER 8

I Can't Believe It Happened Here!—
Helping Students Face Community Tragedy

KYLE D. PONTIUS, Ph.D.

THE BASICS

Community tragedy, by definition, occurs on a large scale; for our purposes, on a scale that impacts an entire community, youth group, or school. Such tragedies include various types of natural disasters or accidents, as well as intentional acts such as the September 11 attacks, the Oklahoma City bombing, or the Columbine High School shootings. Psychological trauma may occur after experiencing an event that involves a threat of death or serious injury. But the event may also be one that is heard about secondhand, such as learning about the death of a family member. Even when a person is not directly involved, a wide range of psychological symptoms related to the tragedy can be present.

The human response to a traumatic event is fairly predictable. Following a tragedy, a person assigns meaning to the event, and from that meaning, emotions flow. Physiological responses to the emotions occur and can include hypervigilance, difficulty thinking, poor memory, increased heart rate, and other responses. Effectively working through this stress response results in a return to normal functioning—a person has been affected and changed by the event, but not crippled by it. Failure to effectively work through the stress response results in stress-related diseases or prolonged emotional problems such as post-traumatic stress disorder (PTSD).

In working with students who have been exposed to events that could evoke psychological trauma or other psychological effects, certain developmental characteristics should be considered. One of the main tasks of adolescence is for a teenager to separate from his or her parents and to move toward becoming a responsible adult. Youth ministry plays a vital role for many students as they begin to ask important life questions. In the youth group, students can separate from the direct influence of their parents, yet remain safe within a nurturing environment as they deal with the normal developmental tasks of adolescence.

The challenge for youth leaders is to develop an atmosphere of trust within the group and between themselves and individual students. The natural inclination for many students is to deal with life events on their own. While this is important, teenagers' lack of experience may result in their not asking for help or otherwise not being available to receive help from their parents or other adults. Even though the student may have the intellect of an adult, his or her lack of experience continues to make the teenager dependent upon adults much more than he or she would like to be.

When youth leaders work with students individually or in groups to process the psychological effects of a community tragedy, it's important to have already established trust and credibility so that the students can be as open with their experiences as possible. If a youth leader has already established a trusting relationship with the students prior to a traumatic event, it will help immeasurably in working with the students during the time of crisis.

Stress Disorders

In counseling students who have been directly affected by traumatic events, youth workers need to be aware of the symptoms of PTSD and the lesser-known syndrome acute stress disorder (ASD). These two conditions are basically the same with the exception of the time frame involved. In ASD, the symptoms last between two days and four weeks. PTSD requires the presence of symptoms for a minimum of four weeks.

Symptoms of PTSD and ASD include extreme feelings of shock and anxiety. Emotional numbing and detachment are also common. Other symptoms include a temporary reduction in cognitive abilities that results in a limited sense of awareness of oneself and the environment. There may be feelings of the event, the environment, or even of oneself as being "unreal." Forgetting important aspects of the traumatic event is common. Disrupted sleep, irritability, poor concentration, a heightened startle response, and restlessness are all symptoms of anxiety that may be present after experiencing a traumatic event.

To a large extent, these are normal processes that occur as individuals cope with tragedy, so it's important that people allow themselves to experience them. When individuals get "stuck" in the process, they may have symptoms of ASD and PTSD; this can result in recurrent and intrusive recollections (flashbacks) or dreams of the traumatic event.

Critical Incident Stress Debriefing

When traumatic events occur, there is generally some type of response initiated by emergency personnel to deal with the psychological trauma that may be experienced by those involved. Critical incident stress debriefing (CISD) is carried out by specially trained mental health professionals who are affiliated with the fire department, police department, school, or other institution. A facilitator works with small groups of individuals using a structured treatment protocol. It's important for youth workers to be aware of these services and to support the efforts of the professionals who provide them. If these services are not offered to the students, it may be appropriate to contact professionals to come in on behalf of the youth group. Local referrals may be obtained by contacting the schools in your area or the fire department.

Don't Forget About You!

Because of the nature of community tragedy, youth workers are also at risk for developing

Community Tragedy

the disorders described earlier. It's important for people who are concerned about providing help for others to take care of themselves. If you notice yourself experiencing any of the symptoms mentioned, seek support for yourself. Work to help your youth staff come together in support of each other. Consider bringing in a professional to work with the staff as a group, or encourage staff members to seek individual help. Unless you are able to cope well with the situation yourself, you will be limited in your ability to reach out and support your students.

WHEN TO REFER

Knowing when to make a professional referral is important in dealing with students who have been affected by a community tragedy. As a youth leader, you should let a professional make the diagnosis; but if any of the symptoms of ASD or PTSD become a problem for a particular teenager, be prepared to refer the student to a Christian counselor. Reacting with sadness and grief is natural when confronted with a community tragedy. Not everyone who is affected will need to work through the process with a professional—however, students who are stuck in the process; those who express recurrent, intrusive recollections or dreams of the event; or those who demonstrate other severe symptoms need help as soon as possible. PTSD may become a debilitating, lifelong condition if it is left untreated. Early intervention is the key to effective resolution of the symptoms. A student should be referred to a professional counselor in the following situations:

- when the student threatens to harm himself or herself
- when the student threatens to harm someone else (such as a perpetrator or a member of a group associated with the perpetrator)
- when alcohol or drug abuse is suspected
- when the student appears to have symptoms of ASD and PTSD
- when there are distinct changes in the student's functioning (such as changes in grades) or personality (such as appearing to be more depressed or manic than prior to the event)
- when the student asks for a referral
- when parents or friends express concern about the student

The treatment of choice for dealing with psychological trauma is psychotherapy. Medications are sometimes used as an adjunct; however, the initial referral should be for counseling, not for medical treatment. It is particularly important to refer Christian students to a Christian professional. For a Christian to effectively come to terms with a traumatic event, there must be a way to acknowledge God in the events that have occurred. A Christian counselor should be able to effectively integrate a Christian worldview into the counseling, using the Bible and prayer along with therapeutic techniques.

COUNSELING IDEAS

Counseling strategies for helping students deal with community tragedy should involve assisting individual students, small groups of students, and the youth group as a whole in coming to terms with the traumatic event. During these times, church youth leaders are in a unique and natural position to provide spiritual support and pastoral care to their students. Indeed, many students may feel that the youth group is the only place they can turn to for this type of help. Providing spiritual support should be the primary function for youth leaders as they counsel students during times of community tragedy.

Youth leaders need to keep in mind a number of things when they counsel students. First, effectively dealing with the psychological effects of a traumatic event doesn't necessarily mean that students will feel better about the situation right away. There are numerous ways of coping with a situation that provide initial relief; however, these coping methods are often unhealthy. Running away from the situation through drugs, alcohol, or other addictive substances or behaviors relieves pain for the moment, but it does nothing to bring resolution to the problem. Watch for students who use unhealthy ways of coping, and make referrals when appropriate.

Talking about the traumatic event—how a person felt when it happened, his or her current feelings, and thoughts the student has regarding the tragedy—can be painful. Expressing oneself verbally, however, facilitates the natural healing process.

In addition to verbal expression, healing can also take place through symbolic expression. When a person expresses his or her feelings through art, music, poetry, or another medium, it seems to bring about healing at a different level. Use care, however, when you're directing symbolic expression in a counseling context. Students may object because of a perceived lack of talent, or they may become suspicious, believing that their artwork may tell more about themselves than they are willing to share or perhaps know themselves. Reassure hesitant students that the activity is not a contest, you are not an art critic, and the activity is not about discovering hidden meanings. No matter what techniques are used, healing will take place as a natural process, helped along by the trusting relationship between the students and the youth worker.

As you counsel individuals or small groups concerning a traumatic event, focus on present experiences. It's OK to talk about history—and, in fact, remembering the past is a present activity and helps students continue to develop a perspective on past events. Take care, however, not to cause a student to remain stuck in the past.

Asking Questions

In general, ask descriptive questions that begin with "what," "where," and "how." These questions will encourage students to observe themselves, noticing their own processes of coping with the event. Asking "why" questions tends to put people on the defensive and increase their anxiety. The following are examples of questions that encourage self-exploration:

- What did you see when [the event] happened?
- Where were you when you first heard about it?
- What did you do next?
- How did you feel when that happened?
- What do you think about [the event/situation]?

People experience life on four levels: cognitively, emotionally, behaviorally, and physically. Keeping these areas in mind as you ask descriptive questions will help you guide the students into greater self-awareness.

What Not to Say

Affirm the students' experience by letting them know that what they say is accepted. Avoid telling the students that you know "exactly how they feel." *No one* knows exactly how another person feels, and a teenager who hears this message will most likely feel misunderstood and may shut down. It's important to convey understanding and empathy while encouraging continued verbal sharing. Some students may feel as if they're going crazy. Communicating to students that they are understood and accepted gives them permission to accept themselves and the painful experience they're going through.

Avoid making attributions of causality concerning the event unless you are absolutely sure. The healing process involves a person's being able to make as much sense of a traumatic event as possible. Attributions that are later shown to be in error will challenge the way a person has come to deal with the event and may inflict further harm.

Using Scripture to Understand Tragedy

For Christians to come to terms with a traumatic event, they must be able to reconcile the event with their view of God. Youth leaders should be prepared to deal with students' questions of how evil and suffering fit into God's plan and how their view of a loving God can remain intact in light of tragic events. There are numerous Scripture passages that can be used, and many of them speak specifically to situations associated with traumatic events. Consider using the following passages as you help students deal with tragedy:

- Job (the entire book but especially 42:1-6)
- 2 Corinthians 1:3-5; 12:9
- Psalms 27; 40; 71; 86; 121; and 139
- James 1:12

Creative Activities

A number of activities can be used to facilitate healing in medium-sized or large groups. An obvious way to promote healing is to hold a memorial service. Involving the students in planning and leading the service will help them work through the stress response. It might also be helpful for teenagers to make murals, quilts, or other memorials. Set up a Web site or Internet bulletin board where students can write out their feelings and post their submissions for others to see. Start a memorial fund or scholarship. Teenagers could also raise funds for groups such as the Red Cross or The Salvation Army. Activities such as these can do a lot to pull the students together and give them a sense that they are contributing to the healing of the community.

Recommended Resources

Books

- *Critical Incident Stress Debriefing: An Operations Manual for CISD, Defusing and Other Group Crisis Intervention Services,* Third Edition, Jeffrey T. Mitchell and George S. Everly, Jr. Ellicott City, MD: Chevron Publishing Corporation, 2001.

- *The Skilled Helper: A Problem-Management and Opportunity-Development Approach to Helping,* Seventh Edition, Gerard Egan. Pacific Grove, CA: Brooks/Cole Publishing, 2002.

Web Resources

- www.cmionline.org (Web site of the Crisis Management Institute)

STUDENT PAGE Use the photocopiable worksheet on page 68 to help teenagers understand their feelings about a tragic event. Allow a teenager to work on the page at home, then invite the student to discuss his or her thoughts about the exercise with you during a subsequent meeting.

Dealing With Tragedy

Dealing with the emotional impact of a crisis involves developing a view of what happened. In order to move on after the event, somehow we need to fit the crisis into the way we view the world. Writing about your thoughts, emotions, and other experiences helps. Going through the following journal exercise will help you explore your thoughts and feelings more deeply, allowing you to know yourself better and become stronger as you cope with the crisis. If you aren't keeping a journal now, you can start one and use this exercise as the first entry; or simply use a couple of sheets of paper.

Start by *describing the tragedy* in as factual a manner as you can—describe what happened to you and what you did at the time. When you've finished, begin to write about your *thoughts* about the event. Include any evaluations you made or opinions you formed at the time. Don't include any ideas you've had or conclusions you've drawn since then; just concentrate on what you thought about when it happened. Next write about the *emotions* you had at the time. Try not to include your current emotions (we'll get to that in a moment). Finally, write about how you felt in your body. What *physical experiences* did you have when the crisis happened?

After you've finished writing about these four areas, read through what you wrote. Spend a minute or so reflecting on what you are aware of in each of these areas now. But instead of concentrating on the current facts, observe your current thoughts, feelings, behavior, and physical experience.

This exercise may be difficult to do and may take several days to complete. If you begin to feel overwhelmed as you go through this activity, find someone to talk with, or take a break for a while and complete the activity later.

CHAPTER 9

I'm Pregnant!–
Loving Students Through Unplanned Pregnancy or Post-Abortion Stress

COLLEEN J. ALDEN, M.A.

THE BASICS

I'm sitting downstairs in the home of a family I have known for years, listening to the sounds generated by twenty-five or so teenagers who unexpectedly showed up for a night of playing Ping-Pong, eating chocolate chip cookie dough, and watching DVDs. I hear the sounds that anyone who has been around teenagers knows well: sounds such as intermittent peals of laughter, sarcastic tones, and thumping on the ceiling from impromptu wrestling matches. This particular family is characterized by health—Allison, Amy, and Evan have grown up with the security that allows them to know themselves and know what they want out of their interactions with others. As any youth worker knows, many teenagers are not so fortunate. Some people never learn how to choose healthy relationships.

Teenagers are working on figuring out how they fit into the world around them. They are asking questions such as, "Who am I?" "Who do I want to be?" "Do I have what it takes to become that kind of person?" Students are making their own decisions, such as what friends to spend time with or what activities to be involved in. Some are beginning to be involved in intimate relationships, which is an area confusing even to adults. It's a major challenge for young people, these not-quite-adults, to navigate the turbulent waters of dating relationships. The sting of rejection and the ache of being unwanted are felt deeply in a teenager's fragile heart.

Society does not help us as we work to guide teenagers toward sexual purity. Abstinence is viewed as an archaic idea. (For more information about abstinence and sexual choices, see Chapter 22). At Alternatives Pregnancy Center in the Denver area, young girls look at me as if I have two heads when I bring up the topic of abstinence. In other settings, students are handed free condoms and told that they are incapable of controlling their urges. Young people today are catapulted into an adult world for which they are emotionally unprepared.

This chapter discusses the all-too-common problems of teenage pregnancy and abortion. An unexpected pregnancy will change the course of a teenager's life forever, regardless of how she responds to her situation. Another challenge many teenagers face is post-abortion stress. I speak with many young women each month who say they are against abortion, but who are considering abortion as they find themselves having to decide what to do about the baby growing inside. They often make choices out of fear—choices they come to regret. The issues of unexpected pregnancy and abortion have significant impacts on the heart of a teenager. Those closest to the young woman—including you as her youth leader—need to know how to address these issues effectively and compassionately.

WHEN TO REFER

As a youth leader, there are many situations for which you will want to enlist the help of others for your hurting students. Ask God to help you know when you are in over your head. For some teenagers, pregnancy may be the result of sexual abuse, rape, or incest. In these cases, referral to a professional counselor is imperative.

Watch for these signs in teenagers, whether or not they are pregnant, and remember that these behaviors can occur in teenagers struggling to come to terms with a past abortion.

1. The student displays signs of depression, including the following:
   - ongoing loss of energy; she can't seem to "get going" anymore
   - isolation, withdrawal, or loss of interest in people or activities
   - loss of hope about the present or future
   - unusual restlessness, irritability, or lack of concentration
2. The student displays signs of suicidal tendencies, such as the following behaviors:
   - talking about ending her life (saying things such as "why bother living?")
   - giving away treasured possessions
   - showing an unusual obsession with death and dying, which may be apparent in her writing, drawings, conversation, or choice of music or movies
3. The student displays destructive behavior such as the following:
   - eating disorders
   - self-injurious behaviors such as cutting, scratching, or burning herself
   - excessive drug and alcohol use, partying, or having indiscriminate sex

From the time a young woman learns of her pregnancy, she will probably be bombarded with opinions. She may have to face several forces in her life that are pushing her to have an abortion. Abortion is *never* the best option, no matter what the circumstances are. She may feel immediate relief, but her choice will hurt her in the long run. Her parents or boyfriend may not understand this, and it is a secret that society does not readily share.

Working With a Local Crisis Pregnancy Center

If one of your teenagers is facing an unplanned pregnancy, contact a local crisis pregnancy center. Keep in mind that it's easy to confuse these centers with family planning clinics; they are not one and the same. (Included in the Recommended Resources at the end of this chapter is the

Web site for Care Net, an organization that will connect you with a crisis pregnancy center in your area.) At a crisis pregnancy center, the student will be encouraged to explore her options and hear the truth about abortion. She will not be judged, but empowered, and will be less likely to make a decision out of fear. The young woman and her baby will be prayed for by countless men and women who support the center. If appropriate, she might consider having her parents or boyfriend come with her.

When you refer a teenager for further counseling, your role in her life does not change. She needs you now more than ever. Do not be tempted to think of a Christian counselor or treatment program as a cure. A young woman's soul was fashioned for relationship, and her healing will come as she is shown constant, abiding love. Jesus spent time with his disciples, and his presence changed their lives! His presence in you can change your student's life, too.

COUNSELING IDEAS

The following are some ideas about where to focus as you counsel a teenager who is struggling with a current pregnancy or a past abortion. Given the sensitivity of these issues, I suggest that only women work with female students. Likewise, if there is a young man involved, he should be counseled by a male youth leader.

For the Pregnant Teenager

A teenager has just taken a home pregnancy test. It was positive. She tells you she doesn't know what to do; she feels paralyzed. Everybody else seems to have an opinion. Her "fear factor" is sky-high—she may cover it up, but inside she is scared to death. She may feel that her life is over. An unexpected pregnancy and the thought of unplanned motherhood "represents a threat so great to modern women that it is perceived as equivalent to a 'death of self.'"[1] Without a voice of truth, comfort, and reason, there's a good chance that she will do what she thinks will solve her problem— she will have an abortion. Pressure from others and a natural impulsivity often put teenagers at an even greater risk than adults for having an abortion. You have the opportunity to speak truth to the teenager and help calm her fears so that she can make a clear decision. But how do you do this?

- Before you do anything else, *listen*. When I first began working at the pregnancy center, I was amazed at how few people my clients had in their lives who simply listened. Women in particular need to talk about their lives and relationships. They need someone who will hear them. So bite your tongue, and simply listen. You'll have a chance to speak later, and waiting will give you the opportunity to be prayerful about what you say. Once a young woman knows that she has been heard, your words will have greater impact.
- Find out what her pressures are (such as her parents, boyfriend, finances, reputation). Being able to identify why she feels like Gumby—stretched in all different directions— will help her make clearer decisions. Talk about the impact that each of these people or circumstances has in her life.
- Find out what the student's fears are. Naming her fears takes away some of their power, and it will help her to know what she's up against. Talking about fears with a compassionate listener often helps to lessen them.
- Help her identify her feelings. God gave us feelings, but we often bury our feelings when they

become threatening to us. The young woman may need help recognizing what she feels and why she feels that way. The student page (p. 74) includes an inventory of emotions—let her see how many of her feelings she can identify. If she likes to write, buy a journal together and share it, writing back and forth to each other. Or cut up some old magazines and make collages together—the end result can be a window into her emotions.

- If she has supportive female friends, start a small group. Open your home, cook dinner for them, and talk about whatever they need to talk about. Young women thrive in relationships, and you can help them learn to support each other in crisis.

For the Post-Abortive Teenager

God did not design the female heart to have to make a decision about whether or not to end the life of her child. Yet today's teenagers live in a society where abortion has been legal since before they were born. A teenager who makes the decision to have an abortion can be left with a train wreck of emotions. A list of common signs of post-abortion stress is included at the end of the chapter (p. 75). Here are some ways you can help:

- Help her get into group or individual Christian counseling. Crisis pregnancy centers are great resources for this. I recommend group counseling whenever possible because it's healing for a young woman to talk with others who know what she has been through.
- If her abortion is a secret, help her find safe people to tell. Talk with her about her relationship with her parents, and help her decide if, when, and how they should be told. Every teenager's situation is different, and there are no easy answers.
- The young woman is probably working her way through a cycle of grief. Memorializing her child's life somehow will help her find closure and grieve in a healthy way. This needs to be done in her own time, however. I encourage a teenager to give her child a name, make something for the child, or take a trip to a local memorial for unborn babies. The teenager might wish to order a plaque with an inscription from The National Memorial for the Unborn.[2]
- Pray for the teenager. She needs your prayers more than anything else.
- One last suggestion: examine yourself, and do not judge. The most important challenge as you counsel the teenager is to withhold the judgment that can flow from your own attitudes. Keep in mind the grace that Jesus communicated to a woman who had been caught committing adultery and who was brought before him (John 8:1-11). He alone has the right to judge—you and I do not. He loved the woman, even as he spoke truth to her. Seek to speak the same kind of truth to the teenager you're working with, with the same kind of love.

For Guys Only

As mentioned earlier, it's often best if a young man talks with a male counselor. So what should you do to counsel a guy whose girlfriend becomes pregnant or has an abortion? He may be experiencing a profound sense of helplessness because this is an area that's unfamiliar to him. He doesn't get to make the most important decisions; those decisions belong to the young woman, whether he agrees with her or not. His influence on her can be enormous, however, and he needs someone to help him respond in an honorable way.

You can help by listening and by making sure he knows that he has been heard. Let him know that you will stick by him. Encourage his involvement during this time of crisis, but help him sort out his responsibilities and establish boundaries. For example, how can he support the young woman without making impossible promises? What can he do, and what should he not do? This is a teachable moment in which you can help a young man learn a great deal about integrity and responsibility in relationships.

God's Redeeming Love

Students who are facing an unplanned pregnancy or dealing with an abortion need to know that there is *hope*. Their difficult situation isn't the end of the story! The circumstances that a teenager believes may signify the end of her life may instead positively affect her future choices and ministry opportunities. Pregnancy and even abortion can be used by a redemptive God to save and impact lives in the future. A student who has made it through the challenge of teenage pregnancy or abortion can help others make the right choices in the future. You can't know all that God is doing in a student's life, but you have the chance to build a relationship with a young woman and offer the support, connection, and hope she so desperately needs.

---

[1] Paul Swope, "Abortion: A Failure to Communicate," First Things (April 1998), 31-35.

[2] For more information about the National Memorial for the Unborn, call 1-800-505-5565.

Recommended Resources

Books

- *Equipped to Serve: Caring for Women in Crisis Pregnancies,* Fourth Edition, Cynthia R. Phikill and Suzanne Walsh. Sparta, MI: Frontlines Publishing, 1999.

- *The Missing Piece Meets the Big O,* Shel Silverstein. New York, NY: HarperCollins Publishers, 1981.

- *A Season to Heal,* Luci Freed and Penny Yvonne Salazar. Nashville, TN: Cumberland House Publishing, 1993.

Web Resources

- www.care-net.org (Web site of Care Net)

STUDENT PAGE Use the photocopiable worksheet "How Are You Feeling?" (p. 74) to help teenage girls and guys who are facing crisis pregnancy or abortion situations understand and verbalize their thoughts and feelings. Use this student page in a counseling setting by talking through the exercise with the teenager. Use the worksheet on page 75 as your own resource to help you recognize possible symptoms of post-abortion stress in students.

How Are You Feeling?

If you feel it, circle it. Then talk about it with your youth leader.

Abandoned	Comforted	Fierce	Murderous	Silly
Able	Confident	Forgiving	Nasty	Small
Adequate	Confused	Fragile	Neglected	Spirited
Admired	Considerate	Furious	Nervous	Stable
Adored	Content	Genuine	Obstinate	Stranded
Affectionate	Cool	Glad	Optimistic	Strong
Afraid	Courageous	Gloomy	Outraged	Sure
Aggravated	Cranky	Grieving	Overlooked	Suspicious
Aggressive	Cruel	Happy	Overwhelmed	Sweet
Alarmed	Crushed	Hateful	Panicked	Tearful
Alienated	Daring	Helpless	Pathetic	Tender
Alone	Deadly	Honest	Poisonous	Terrified
Amused	Defeated	Hopeless	Powerful	Thoughtful
Angry	Defective	Humiliated	Proud	Thrilled
Annoyed	Deficient	Hurt	Pulled apart	Timid
Anxious	Delighted	Ignored	Reckless	Tormented
Awful	Demolished	Impatient	Resentful	Touchy
Awkward	Desolate	Imprisoned	Restless	Tough
Battered	Despairing	Inadequate	Revengeful	Tremendous
Belligerent	Desperate	Incapable	Ridiculed	Trustworthy
Bewildered	Despised	Incompetent	Right	Unable
Biting	Determined	Inferior	Righteous	Understanding
Blamed	Devoted	Insecure	Rotten	Unloved
Blissful	Disabled	Jealous	Rude	Unlucky
Bloodthirsty	Discarded	Justified	Ruined	Unmerciful
Bold	Disgusting	Kind	Ruthless	Useless
Brave	Durable	Lame	Sad	Weak
Bright	Embarrassed	Laughed at	Satisfied	Well-equipped
Broken	Empathetic	Lonely	Savage	Wise
Bullied	Energetic	Lost	Scared	Wishful
Burned	Enraged	Lovely	Secure	Witty
Callous	Envious	Mad	Self-confident	Worried
Calm	Exalted	Mean	Selfish	Worthless
Capable	Exhausted	Mighty	Sensitive	Wrathful
Caring	Exposed	Mishandled	Shaky	Wrecked
Castoff	Fearful	Mocked	Shamed	
Cheap	Fearless	Moody	Shy	

How Can I Know What's Wrong?

POST-ABORTION STRESS SYMPTOMS

Are you concerned that a teenager you're working with may be suffering from post-abortion stress? The following behaviors and emotions are signals that a student may need help for PAS:

- ❑ She avoids any person or situation that could trigger painful emotions related to pregnancy or abortion, such as pregnant friends, infants, or routine appointments with a gynecologist.
- ❑ She appears to be preoccupied with becoming pregnant again in an attempt to replace the child who was lost.
- ❑ She expresses a fear of being infertile.
- ❑ She suffers from "anniversary syndrome"—an increase in symptoms around the time of the abortion or due date of the baby.
- ❑ She significantly alters her sexual behavior (she may exhibit promiscuity or a heightened interest in sex).
- ❑ She develops unhealthy eating habits or an eating disorder as an expression of self-contempt.
- ❑ She has sudden or unexplainable bouts of crying.

POST-ABORTION STRESS TRIGGERS

The following events may trigger the symptoms of post-abortion stress:

- ❑ Interaction with infants or other young children
- ❑ Significant dates, such as the anniversary date of the abortion or the baby's conception or due date
- ❑ Media attention to the abortion issue
- ❑ Death of a loved one or other losses in life
- ❑ Holidays or other significant family times

GENERAL SIGNS OF POST-TRAUMATIC STRESS

The following are signs of post-traumatic stress that can result from traumas such as abortion, sexual abuse or rape, crisis pregnancy, or miscarriage. These signs may also indicate another issue requiring counseling that is unrelated to pregnancy or abortion.

- ❑ Addictions or substance abuse to dull emotional pain
- ❑ Feelings of intense grief or symptoms of depression
- ❑ Unexplainable or ongoing anger
- ❑ Nightmares or flashbacks to the traumatic event or situation
- ❑ Feelings of panic and anxiety, or more severe anxiety disorders such as panic attacks
- ❑ Denial or repression of painful emotions
- ❑ Suicidal or self-injurious thoughts or actual attempts to kill or injure oneself
- ❑ Extremely negative self-image
- ❑ Intentional social isolation
- ❑ Feelings or expressions of regret

Depression

CHAPTER 10

More Than Just a Bad Day—
Understanding Depression

SALLY SCHWER CANNING, Ph.D.

THE BASICS

Everybody feels down sometimes. Life can be difficult, and growing up brings all kinds of challenges and transitions along the way. There probably isn't a person in the world who hasn't felt sad or depressed at one time or another. Sadness is simply a part of life. But how do you know when normal sadness crosses the line into depression? Depression is more than just feeling low for a few days after a negative event like failing a test. It's also different from the sorrow that comes in the normal process of grieving the loss of a loved one. Depression is an illness that disrupts the thinking, feelings, and behavior of an individual. The National Mental Health Association lists the following symptoms of depression:[1]

- persistent sadness and hopelessness
- withdrawal from family, friends, and activities that were once enjoyed
- increased irritability or agitation
- missed school or poor school performance
- changes in eating and sleeping habits
- indecision, lack of concentration, or forgetfulness
- poor self-esteem, guilt, overreaction to criticism
- anger, problems with authority
- frequent physical complaints, such as headaches or stomachaches
- lack of enthusiasm or motivation
- drug or alcohol abuse
- recurring thoughts of death or suicide

Depression can come in many forms and at different levels of severity. Some individuals are persistently depressed, others experience cycles of depression alternating with periods of health or mania (excessively elevated mood). In some rare cases, depression is accompanied by psychotic symptoms such as hallucinations. Depression is sometimes linked to a particular season or can appear after the birth of a baby. It might occur after a significant life event or appear to have no identifiable precipitating factors. The risk for depression and other mood disorders seems to run in families.

Depression can be accompanied by anxieties. The teenager may be anxious in social situations, worried about bad things happening to him or her or to people he or she loves, or have fears that go beyond what would be expected for normal adolescents. Teenagers with mood problems such as depression and anxiety may exhibit disruptive behaviors, including severe and persistent opposition to parents, school personnel, or other authority figures. They may exhibit conduct problems such as truancy, substance use, or aggression. These behaviors easily command the attention of adults and can elicit strong responses. Sometimes, however, these troublesome behaviors mask accompanying mood problems that require skillful and compassionate attention.

WHEN TO REFER

Clinical depression is a debilitating illness that can be life-threatening. It is one of the most common mental health problems, affecting many children, teenagers, and adults each year. Despite this fact, depression often goes unrecognized and can be particularly easy to miss in adolescents. If a student's life is being disrupted and he or she is exhibiting some of the signs of depression listed earlier, it's important to make a referral to a professional Christian counselor, psychologist, or psychiatrist. If the adolescent appears to be at risk for hurting himself or herself, you will need to refer the student to a physician or mental health care provider immediately (or make a trip to an emergency room). (See Chapter 25 for additional information on recognizing and responding to the risk of suicide in young people.)

Because the risk of depression appears to run in families, be sensitive to how parents and siblings of the student are doing. There may be other family members who also should be referred for help. Treatment of depression may be in the form of individual or group therapy, be cognitive or interpersonal in nature, and may include medication.

COUNSELING IDEAS

A student who is seriously depressed needs to be in the care of a trained mental health professional; the primary responsibility for treatment of the depression will rest with that person. The youth worker can play an important role as a source of support for the student. Being in relationship with a depressed teenager can be challenging, however. The thinking of a depressed individual can be distorted in several ways. Concentration, attention, and problem-solving abilities can be negatively affected. The flat or irritated demeanor of a depressed teenager can make it hard to feel connected to that person. You may experience feelings such as frustration, boredom, or a depressed mood yourself after spending time with a depressed student. Remaining aware of your feelings is important so that you can avoid acting on them and instead stay focused on being an attentive, warm, supportive presence.

Working With Depressed Students

Here are some tips for working with a depressed teenager:
*   Take the person seriously—do not minimize the situation.
*   Show respect for the thoughts and feelings that the student has shared with you. A student

who is depressed may view things in a distorted way, but it's important to understand that it's his or her present reality.

- Practice active/reflective listening—make good eye contact, be attentive, reflect back to the person what you've heard him or her say.
- Be alert to "all or nothing" thinking ("Everyone was laughing at me"); catastrophizing ("Getting a C on this test will ruin my life"); and misplaced responsibility (for example, a teenager who is convinced that his father's inconsistent visits are all his fault).
- Explore the possibility that there are alternatives to these depressive ways of thinking. The point is not to shame the person, but to gently open up the possibility of thinking more objectively about the situation, which may help to reduce the distress the student feels and help him or her to constructively move forward.

Overcoming Isolation—Setting Achievable Goals

Another way you can help is by joining with the student in planning and carrying out positive, achievable goals that will move the student along the road toward wellness. This important role must be approached with caution, however, because it's very easy for a person who is not depressed to underestimate how debilitating the illness really is. It may be very difficult for the depressed individual to even imagine finding the energy or optimism to carry out an action that seems simple to you. Even making a phone call to a friend or taking a walk around the block can seem like almost impossible tasks.

There are a number of things you could encourage a young person to do that may help him or her feel better. The first concerns the social isolation that often accompanies depression. Unfortunately, this isolation can become a downward spiral. The more lonely or depressed the student feels, the more difficult it can be to connect with others in positive ways; the less a teenager connects with others in positive ways, the more lonely and depressed he or she can become. A youth leader can go a long way toward supporting a depressed student by encouraging him or her to increase the amount of time spent in positive social interactions. This is not always easy to do, as the student may lack energy, be fearful of negative responses from others, or lack the skills necessary to meet people and form friendships. Here are some ways that you can help:

- Explain to the student that there is a link between being isolated and feeling lonely or depressed. Let the teenager know you will support him or her in decreasing the isolation.
- Identify someone the student already interacts with or something the student already does successfully that will help the teenager connect with others. (For example, the student may have a friend that he or she already feels comfortable calling on the telephone to ask about a school assignment.)
- Make a plan for the teenager to carry out that particular activity this week. Be specific about what the student will do and when he or she will do it. Write down the plan, and consider having the student rehearse it in a role-play—try to keep it light and fun.
- Follow up with the student the next week.
- Come up with another activity that's a bit more of a stretch. Go slowly, though, because a depressed individual can easily become discouraged. The idea is to help the student grow in his or her abilities and have as much success as possible along the way. For a student who

is comfortable calling a classmate with a question regarding schoolwork, the next step might be to encourage the student to comment about another topic and broaden the conversation.

- Consider role-playing the new assignment. Discuss what obstacles might prevent the teenager from completing the assignment and how he or she might tackle those obstacles. Talk about how the student might feel and what he or she could do if things don't go as planned.
- Meet each week to review how things went and to set a new goal.
- Make it clear that growth takes time and sometimes includes twists, turns, and setbacks along the way.
- Point out the reality that not all of our social interactions result in close friendships. Talk about the positive aspects of having acquaintances, such as discovering what sorts of people we feel comfortable with and enjoy spending time with.
- Make a deal with the teenager to celebrate effort and perseverance, not just success.
- Try to identify skills the student may need help with, such as starting conversations with peers that the student doesn't know very well. Work with the student to improve his or her skills in these areas.

The Physical Effects of Depression

Depression affects not only the thinking and social behavior of a person, but also the body. Depression often disrupts the activity level as well as the eating and sleeping habits of the affected person. Regular aerobic exercise along with a healthy diet can, over time, contribute significantly to a young person's mental well-being.

If the student experiences premature awakening in the middle or late part of the night, has difficulty falling asleep, or sleeps an inordinate amount of time at night, the student should discuss sleep strategies with his or her family physician or mental health practitioner. Teenagers with sleeping difficulties will probably be advised to remove caffeine and other stimulants from their diets and avoid highly stimulating activities for several hours before bedtime. It's also important for a student to keep to a regular sleep routine (same time to bed, same time to rise) that allows for at least eight or nine hours of sleep a night. In some cases, medication prescribed by a physician or psychiatrist may be recommended. As a youth minister, you can talk with the teenager and plan how to accomplish realistic, manageable steps toward caring for his or her physical health. To do this, follow steps similar to those outlined earlier regarding social isolation.

Problem Solving With Depressed Students

Students who are depressed may have difficulty with problem solving. They may feel overwhelmed by problems that seem small to others and have difficulty concentrating well enough to generate solutions. You can help the teenager break problem solving down into a more manageable process.

- Help the student identify a problem that he or she is currently facing. Choose something relatively small to begin with, such as finding the energy to study for a test, instead of resolving a student's anger about his or her parents' divorce. Define the problem together as clearly and objectively as you can.
- Identify as many solutions to the problem as you can. In the brainstorming process, you

- are not allowed to edit; all ideas are welcome at this stage.
- Talk through the pros and cons of those solutions.
- Help the teenager decide which solution to pursue. Choose a Scripture passage that delineates the nature of Christian life, such as Galatians 5:22-26 or Philippians 4:4-8, and use the passage to help you evaluate the solutions.
- Role-play the solution if appropriate.
- Help the student plan how and when to carry out the solution.

Using the Bible With Depressed Students

The psalms have offered great comfort to many people through the ages. Teenagers can identify with the portrayal of the realities of life—the pain, the joy, and the struggles. There are many chapters and verses that are appropriate for a depressed person. One suggestion is to give the student an assignment to read a specific passage several times a day; other students may benefit from reading a few chapters each day.

Psalm 139 assures us that God is with us, no matter what state we find ourselves in. It also reminds us that we are precious in God's sight, even as we were being formed in the womb. Other appropriate Scriptures include Psalms 20; 30; 42; and 100; along with passages in the New Testament such as Matthew 11:28-30; 2 Corinthians 1:3-5; and Ephesians 1:3-21.

Supporting the Adolescent in Treatment

As a youth minister, you can play an important role in supporting the student in treatment by providing encouragement and accountability. Check in with the student to see that he or she is attending doctor's appointments or therapy sessions as well as completing "homework." Encourage openness and honesty in the student's relationship with his or her healthcare providers. Affirm the student for his or her courage and for taking care of himself or herself by getting treatment. Show optimism about the teenager's ability to get better.

Recommended Resources

Books

- *Feeling Good: The New Mood Therapy,* David D. Burns. New York, NY: Avon Books, 1980, 1999.

Training

- *Adolescent Coping With Depression Course*, Gregory Clarke, Peter Lewinsohn, and Hyman Hops (1990). Available at the Kaiser Permanente Center for Health Research Web site, www.kpchr.org/info/newACWD.html.

---

[1]   This list of symptoms, as well as other information about depression, is available from the National Mental Health Association at www.nmha.org.

STUDENT PAGE Use the photocopiable worksheet on page 81 to help teenagers find encouragement in the midst of depression. Let the student work on the page at home. At your next meeting, invite the student to share what he or she drew or wrote.

You Are Important!

1. Read aloud Psalm 139 (or another psalm chosen by your youth leader). Ask God in prayer to speak to you personally through the words of the Scripture. Write a poem or draw a picture on the back of this sheet about something in the psalm that touched you in a special way. For example, if you read Psalm 139, you might feel touched knowing that God knew you and cared about you even before you were born (verses 13-16). You might draw a picture of God wrapping his arms around a baby or write your feelings in a poem. After you've finished, show your youth leader what you wrote or drew, and talk about it.

2. God gives each of his children gifts to use to serve him. Some people are good listeners, hard workers, or loyal friends. Others can sing or draw or appreciate other people's talents. Some have a great sense of humor or can play sports. The important thing to realize is that everyone has a gift to share—everyone!

Ask two or three people (parents, friends, a youth leader, or others) to tell you at least one gift they see in you. Write down what they say, even if it's hard for you to believe right now.

_____

_____

_____

Write about at least one gift you see in yourself that you can offer back to God and to others.

_____

_____

_____

Come up with five ways you could share the gift with God or with others, and write those ideas below. Put a check by one idea that you can do this week, and write the date that you plan to do it. Your youth leader will ask you how it went the next time you meet. Then sign your name to the bottom and get started on a good week!

Ideas		Dates
	❑	
	❑	
	❑	
	❑	
	❑	
	Signature	

CHAPTER 11

Changing Families—
Helping Students From Divorced, Single-Parent, or Blended Families

TERRI S. WATSON, Psy.D.

THE BASICS

Ministering to families in the twenty-first century necessitates an understanding of the experiences of teenagers and families as they move through the transitions related to divorce, single parenthood, and remarriage. Nearly half of all children in the United States will live in one of these types of families at some point during their lives.[1] Our definition of what constitutes a family in the twenty-first century needs to be broadened to include adoptive parents, grandparents, aunts and uncles, stepparents, stepsiblings, and half siblings.

A critical challenge facing the church today is the need for Christian communities to be hospitable, healing, and supportive havens for teenagers and parents in transition. Many families are isolated, overwhelmed, and lacking in support as they face the challenges of divorce. Without help, teenagers who are experiencing stressors brought on by divorce can develop significant emotional, relational, and behavioral problems that interfere with the healthy transition through adolescence to adulthood. The church can take an active role in helping teenagers and families find stability in Christ and in Christian community. What are the common challenges that families face, and how can youth leaders help provide for families' needs? In this chapter, we will examine the experience of divorce in the family, the effects on teenagers, and specific counseling strategies that youth leaders can use in ministering to divorcing, single-parent, and remarried families.

The Experience of Divorce: Transitions and Challenges

Families and teenagers face numerous challenges as they transition from a two-parent household through the initial separation, adjustment to two households, and often remarriage. While there are important cultural and religious differences in the meaning and experience of divorce, most teenagers and families experience the following common challenges.

The Initial Impact of Divorce

When he was asked to draw a picture of his family, Charlie drew Mom, Dad, Dad's new girlfriend, himself, and his sister all on a Ferris wheel. Chaotic, confusing lines were drawn between family members, who were each alone in separate cars, hanging terrifyingly over empty space, spinning endlessly. Charlie's picture captures the essence of this transition through divorce for children and families. Tremendous feelings of grief, confusion, anxiety, and loss of confidence in the stability of the world often result. Families at this stage often face a range of challenges including the following:

- dealing with feelings of grief and loss. For parents, it can be grief over the loss of the marriage; and for teenagers, grief over what feels like the loss of both parents (one parent moves out, and the other parent is often less available due to his or her own emotional turmoil).
- feeling that "it's my fault." Children and teenagers often feel responsible for the breakup or feel a sense of failure that they couldn't prevent it.
- facing changes which may include relocation, adjustment to two households, and a change in the standard of living.
- establishing a cooperative parenting relationship between parents who may be estranged.
- negotiating legal decisions including custody, child support, and visitation, without placing the children in the middle of an adult conflict.

Single Parenthood

Jamie is proud to be her mom's best friend. "She tells me everything," Jamie says. She likes the new apartment, and she doesn't even mind having to give up after-school activities to babysit her younger siblings. She can't seem to get past her anger at her dad, though, and fights with him about why he doesn't pay more for child support. Jamie is struggling with adjusting to living in a single-parent family. Single-parent families are becoming more prevalent in the United States, with one out of every four children living in a single-parent home, mostly headed by mothers.[2] Families at this stage often face challenges, including

- increasing responsibility for the teenager, including taking care of younger siblings and sometimes even the parent.
- dealing with a decreased standard of living and loss of financial resources. This situation, too, often results in increased responsibility for the teenager. (For example, a student may have to get a part-time job.)
- balancing the parents' emotional need for support with the establishment of healthy parent-child boundaries.
- establishing and maintaining relationships with both parents.

Blended Families

Cecilia, a sci-fi fan, described her frustrations with living in two families in this way: "It's like going back and forth between two warring planets—each with its own set of rules, customs, and even language. And I don't really fit in either place." Some family researchers suggest that the remarried family will constitute the most common family type in the twenty-first century.[3] Families at this stage face numerous adjustments, including the following:

- allowing new family members into their lives, including stepparents, stepsiblings, and

other members of the stepfamily
- dealing with divided loyalties between two families
- establishing parental authority and determining the role of stepparents in parenting and discipline
- figuring out cooperative parenting for the long haul
- balancing the teenager's need for "a life" with parental visitation rights

The Effects of Divorce on Children and Adolescents

Judith Wallerstein, one of the foremost experts on the impact of divorce on children, describes four major effects of divorce on children as they grow into adulthood.[4] First, children of divorce experience anxiety and self-doubt about their ability to establish successful love relationships. Wallerstein suggests that these children lack an "inner template" of what a successful marriage is like. Second, children of divorce experience more feelings of uncertainty and insecurity about the future, which is likely related to the losses that the child experienced growing up. Third, children of divorce experience some loss of stability and parental protectiveness, and parents are less attentive to the needs of their children. Wallerstein suggests that as parents work to rebuild their lives economically and emotionally, it often interferes with their availability to meet their children's needs. Finally, Wallerstein notes that children of divorce are often stronger and more independent, and they view themselves as survivors because they have become more independent at a young age. This can be a positive trait that facilitates adjustment to the responsibilities of adulthood.

WHEN TO REFER

The experience of divorce places a tremendous amount of stress on all family members. Most families attempt to negotiate the crisis without support. While the church can provide a supportive environment for healing, most families can benefit from counseling as well. Parents should not assume an easy adjustment and acceptance of the divorce by their children, even when no emotional or behavioral problems are evident. Checking in with a mental health professional for assistance can ensure that adjustment problems do not go unnoticed.

It is imperative to refer teenagers for professional help if their responses to family changes begin to interfere with school, social relationships, or behavior. Statistics on children of divorce suggest that increased behavioral and emotional problems are common. The importance of counseling increases proportionately to the degree of ongoing conflict between divorcing parents, since conflict will interfere with cooperative parenting and with parental support of children through the divorce process.

COUNSELING IDEAS

The support of the church as a "third family" for teenagers whose families are experiencing divorce can provide much-needed physical, emotional, and spiritual resources. This section will give general guidelines for working with teenagers and families and suggest specific counseling strategies for each stage of the family's transition through the divorce.

General Guidelines

Counseling teenagers and families during the divorce requires tact, sensitivity, and good communication skills on the part of the youth leader. Consider the following guidelines:

- Establish the church as a neutral, hospitable, safe place for healing and support. Avoid making judgments, taking sides, and placing blame.
- Make contact with both parents as soon as possible. Offer to keep them informed about church or youth ministry activities. This will enhance the involvement of the student— even when the teenager is visiting the other parent.
- Use a family approach to counseling the teenager. Frequent contact with the parents, visits to the home, and counseling assistance to the family are all important tasks.
- Support the teenager's relationships with both parents, except in cases of documented abuse of the child by a parent.
- Present yourself as a neutral party as you look out for the teenager's best interests.
- Establish a confidential, supportive place where you can discuss your own feelings and reactions to working with the family. This is a key factor in preventing burnout.
- Did I mention the importance of maintaining neutrality?

Counseling Divorcing Families

Few experiences are more painful for a child than seeing the stability and security of his or her parents' marriage and family come to an end. Teenagers have many questions about why their parents are divorcing, whether they had anything to do with it, and what's going to happen in their lives. They are also concerned about practical issues such as financial needs. Some students are required to take on increased responsibility for their siblings and also, unfortunately, for their parents' emotional needs.

Youth leaders can play an important role in helping the teenager at this point. Listening to a student's concerns and fears and providing a supportive environment during the time of transition are crucial counseling responses. Other suggestions for helping teenagers and families at this stage include the following:

- Help parents talk to teenagers about divorce in an age-appropriate way—for example, reassuring teenagers that the divorce is not their fault, explaining why the parents are divorcing, and telling teenagers what will happen next. It may help the family for you to be present as a neutral third party during these discussions.
- Encourage the parents to parent cooperatively despite their personal differences. Help them come up with ways to enhance communication between them. For example, parents could pass a notebook back and forth between visits to keep informed about things such as medical needs, school assignments, or functions that the teenager needs to attend. As much as possible, help parents negotiate conflicts without placing the teenager in the middle.
- Help the teenager set appropriate boundaries with his or her parents. Often the student will need to take on more responsibilities at home, but this should not unduly interfere with normal developmental needs. A teenager may also need help in discouraging parents from sharing too much personal information with him or her, overutilizing the teenager for emotional support, or putting down the other parent.

Counseling Single-Parent Families

Once the initial crisis of the news of the divorce has passed, families are faced with establishing two households. Single-parent families often face great demands on financial and emotional resources. The church can play a critical role in the assistance and support of these families. Specific counseling suggestions include the following:

- Explore the family's needs, which may include child care, shelter, food, financial assistance, or vocational training. Many single parents have never faced the challenges of daily living alone, and they may need practical assistance during the time of transition. Youth leaders can help single parents find the necessary resources.

- Help single parents establish a support network, including extended family, church fellowship, and other single parents.

- Reinforce the single parent's authority. This can be an especially challenging task for single parents with teenagers, particularly mothers with sons. Youth leaders can support the parent's authority in the presence of the teenager, encouraging the teenager to respect and obey the parent.

- Help the teenager cope with changes as new people enter and exit the family, particularly as parents begin dating. Most teenagers have conflicting feelings about this. Helping parents balance their own social and relational needs with the emotional needs of the teenager can be an important task for the youth leader.

Counseling Blended Families

Most single-parent homes will at some point transition to blended families as parents remarry. Establishing relationships with new family members can be a challenging task for teenagers, particularly at a time when they are striving for independence and moving away from the family. Consider the following counseling suggestions to assist families with this transition:

- Counsel the biological parent in the blended family to maintain the primary responsibility for disciplining the teenager. This will give the new spouse time to develop a friendship with the teenager before trying to move into the role of parent.

- Help the teenager adjust to new household rules and expectations by empathizing with his or her frustrations. Have the student make a list of the differences between the households, with specific "survival" strategies for each location.

- Encourage parents to be flexible with visitation and family expectations to allow the teenager to engage in activities at school and home with minimal disruptions.

- Provide hope for blended families, and make sure they realize that adjustments will take a long time. Remind parents that it's counterproductive to try to *force* teenagers to attach to new family members.

Counseling the Teenager

Reminding adolescents of the unchanging nature of Christ's love can provide a necessary anchor during stressful family transitions. In the midst of the teenager's rapidly changing and unstable world, encourage the student to meditate on Christ's constancy and reliability. Consider memorizing together and discussing Hebrews 13:5-8. Talk about the implications of this passage for the teenager's life. Remind the student often of the reality that Christ will *never* leave or forsake him or her.

Divorce

Youth leaders can also help teenagers develop skill and confidence in forming healthy relationships. Modeling and mentoring in the area of relationships can help teenagers rebuild trust and hope, and it can help prevent premature involvement in romantic and sexual relationships. An adolescent girl who has experienced family separation or divorce may be at greater risk for premature romantic relationships and sexual behavior—particularly if she has not maintained a close relationship with her father. An adolescent boy needs a good model of a committed husband and father—and may especially need a male adult to identify with if he is living in a single-parent home headed by his mother and has limited contact with the father. By teaching on God's intentions for relationships, and providing accountability, the youth leader can provide an important source of support to teenagers who are dealing with their parents' divorce.

What role can the church and the youth leader play in helping to ease the effects of divorce on children as they grow to adulthood? A number of studies on the effects of trauma on children indicate that the presence of one caring, supportive adult in the life of a traumatized child can make a huge difference in decreasing the impact of the trauma. While you may despair over your inability to "fix" the teenager's challenging family situation, you should not underestimate the importance of being a caring companion and a representative of Christ's love and protection for the student through these difficult years of transition.

---

[1] Anne C. Bernstein, "Reconstructing the Brothers Grimm: New Tales for Stepfamily Life," Family Process (vol. 38, no. 4, Winter 1999), 417. See also Judith Wallerstein, Julia Lewis, and Sandra Blakeslee, *The Unexpected Legacy of Divorce* (New York, NY: Hyperion, 2000), xxviii.

[2] Terry A. Lugaila, "Marital Status and Living Arrangements: March 1998 (Update)." Report P20-514 from the U.S. Census Bureau, issued December 1998.

[3] Anne C. Bernstein, "Reconstructing the Brothers Grimm: New Tales for Stepfamily Life," 417.

[4] Judith Wallerstein, Julia Lewis, and Sandra Blakeslee, *The Unexpected Legacy of Divorce*, xxviii-xxx.

Recommended Resources

Books

- *Blended Families: Creating Harmony As You Build a New Home Life,* Maxine Marsolini. Chicago, IL: Moody Press, 2000.

- *The Blended Family: Achieving Peace and Harmony in the Christian Home,* Edward Douglas and Sharon Douglas. Franklin, TN: Providence House Publishers, 2000.

- *Ministering to Twenty-First Century Families: Eight Big Ideas for Church Leaders,* Dennis Rainey. Nashville, TN: W Publishing Group, 2001.

Web Resources

- www.crown.org/SingleParents (Web site for the Single Parent Ministry of Crown Financial Ministries)

- www.parentswithoutpartners.org (Web site of Parents Without Partners)

- www.saafamilies.org (Web site of the Stepfamily Association of America)

STUDENT PAGE Use the photocopiable worksheet on page 88 to help teenagers understand their feelings related to their parents' divorce. Use the student page during a counseling session, allowing the teenager to draw his or her picture, and then discussing the questions together.

Who Is My Family?

Draw a picture of your family in the space below. Write family members' names near their pictures.

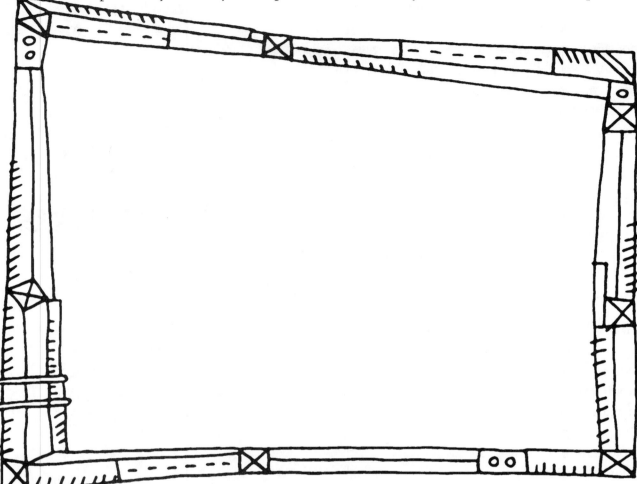

Questions for Discussion

Share your drawing with your youth worker, and use the following questions for discussion.

1. Tell a little about each family member. Does that person live with you? If not, how often do you see him or her?

2. Who do you feel the closest to in your family? Why?

3. Who do you feel the most distant from? Why?

4. Is there anyone you consider "family" who is not related to you? What makes that person so important to you?

Thoughts to Consider

Read Matthew 12:46-50 together with your youth worker. Who does Jesus consider to be his family? What does this say about Christian community as family?

CHAPTER 12

Beyond "Just Say No"–
Counseling Students With Drug and Alcohol Problems

JAMES D. FROST, M.A.

THE BASICS

Alcohol and drug use can be understood as a continuum, beginning with abstinence and moving through experimentation, abuse, and finally dependency. A teenager at the experimentation level is exposed to a substance and decides to try it. The student's normal curiosity may increase because of his or her exposure to the effects of the substance on a peer or a familiar adult. Or a young person may drink at parties not so much out of a desire to try alcohol, but rather to avoid standing out in the crowd by abstaining. Students often try popular and easily obtained drugs, such as marijuana, because of peer pressure, and treat the experience as "no big deal."

While any adolescent who uses alcohol or drugs can develop a problem, our current understanding suggests that many young people experiment at least once with one or more mind-altering substances without experiencing any significant harmful effects.[1] They don't all become addicts; some of them learn their lesson the first time. While any experimentation with drugs and alcohol can be dangerous, it is critical to identify students who are at risk of developing serious problems (such as habitual use or addiction) and to be ready to intervene as soon as is possible. The risk of substance abuse and addiction increases when any of the following factors are present:

- Genetic—there is a history of substance abuse or dependence in a biological relative.
- Environmental—a student was raised in a home where substance abuse was modeled, whether by biological parents, siblings, or a stepparent.
- Social—a student has friends who use drugs or alcohol or the student attends social gatherings where peers have come together primarily to use alcohol or drugs.
- Psychological—the student uses alcohol or drugs in an effort to cope with problems or block out painful emotions.

Use vs. Abuse

Substance *use* and substance *abuse* are both problematic, and both require intervention. Teenagers who experiment with drugs or use alcohol infrequently, but who are not substance abusers, still face the possibility of legal, physical, and relational consequences. The distinction between use and abuse is not necessarily tied to the amount or frequency of substance use. Instead, it is based primarily on the consequences of drug or alcohol use in the student's life and his or her willingness to curtail use to prevent further consequences. Abuse of alcohol or drugs may be indicated when a pattern of use is associated with one of more of the following signs:[2]

- The student fails to fulfill obligations or responsibilities at work, home, or school.
- There is recurrent use in dangerous situations (such as driving while under the influence).
- The teenager has repeated legal troubles associated with use of the substance.
- The student continues to use drugs or alcohol despite problems the substances have caused, including problems in relationships with family or friends.

Symptoms of Dependence

Dependence on a substance may be manifested through physical or psychological symptoms. The hallmarks of physical dependence are tolerance and withdrawal. Tolerance is indicated when a person's sensitivity to a substance decreases with repeated use of the substance over time; a certain amount of the drug no longer produces the same effect that it once did, and the student must use greater amounts of the substance to get the desired effect. For example, a teenager who became inebriated after several beers when he or she first started drinking may, with continued heavy drinking over time, require three or four times that amount to feel the same effect. Withdrawal refers to uncomfortable and sometimes dangerous physical symptoms that are experienced by a person who stops or decreases the use of a substance that he or she had used regularly.

Various abused substances can differ greatly in their potential for tolerance and withdrawal. Continued use of alcohol, sedatives, and barbiturates (or "downers") leads to tolerance and dangerous, potentially lethal withdrawal. Tolerance to cocaine and other stimulants (or "uppers") as well as narcotics (often available as prescription painkillers) can develop rapidly and is associated with withdrawal that is painful but not particularly life-threatening. Marijuana's potential for physical dependence has been debated, but psychological dependence on this drug is a significant risk.

Signs of dependence include the following:

- loss of control over use (using more over a longer period than intended or repeated unsuccessful efforts to stop or curtail use)
- going to great lengths or taking risks to obtain the substance
- spending a great deal of time using the substance or coming down from the effects of using the substance
- giving up important social, occupational, or recreational activities in order to use the substance
- experiencing alcohol-induced blackouts
- continuing to use the substance in the face of adverse consequences, especially when those consequences will be made worse by continued use

With dependence comes the sense that one cannot function "normally" without the substance, even in the absence of physical withdrawal. The dependent teenager can become preoccupied with obtaining the drug or planning the next time he or she will be able to use it. As use of the substance becomes increasingly necessary, it can take precedence over activities, and even relationships, that were previously important. A student may sell prized possessions in order to fund his or her drug use.

"Blackout" is a term used to describe a person's inability to recall what he or she did while drinking. It is not the same as passing out because it refers to periods in which the person was conscious. A common example of this alcohol-induced memory loss is when a student remembers drinking at a party but cannot remember how he or she got home. Blackouts are associated with moderate to heavy drinking and may indicate the early stages of brain damage.[3]

Any use of inhalants, often referred to as "huffing," is particularly dangerous. The most commonly used inhalants include glue, gasoline, paint thinners, other solvents, spray paints and other aerosols, or other petroleum-based products. Addiction to inhalants can occur very rapidly, and death can occur anytime an inhalant is used.

WHEN TO REFER

Refer the student to a Christian counselor, psychologist, or substance abuse specialist if any of the following conditions apply:
- withdrawal symptoms are observed or are acknowledged by the student
- the student admits to having blackouts
- tolerance to alcohol or any drug is admitted
- alcohol or drugs are being used at school
- the student has used inhalants

COUNSELING IDEAS

Assessing the Issues
- It's a good idea to know which drugs are currently popular and which are used in your particular area. The drugs of choice within a geographical area change from time to time based on factors such as the availability of particular substances or the introduction of novel "designer" drugs to the area. Youth leaders should stay abreast of what young people are exposed to and may be offered. The students themselves can be a great source of such information.
- When you're working with a student, carefully examine the teenager's life for problems that may create a need to use alcohol or drugs. Under the best of circumstances, adolescence is a tough phase of life marked by rapid physical and psychological changes. Teenagers often face significant social pressures or family problems. At the same time, though, they do not have fully developed problem-solving skills, nor are they afforded the social standing to initiate solutions to many of the problems that they face. All of this can create a desire to escape and increase a student's vulnerability to the mind-altering effects of alcohol and drugs. It is important to look for problems in a student's life that may drive a need to flee from reality; focus on helping the student develop more effective ways of problem solving.
- Assess the extent of a student's alcohol and drug use. Find out about current and past substance use patterns. Determine when drugs or alcohol were first used and under what

circumstances. Discover when the last use of any substances occurred, as well as how much and how often they are being used. Look at how the frequency and amounts of substances used have changed since the student first used alcohol and drugs. Explore the reasons for any change in the teenager's drug of choice, especially if the change is to a more rapidly intoxicating form of the substance (such as a transition from beer to hard liquor) or a change in how a drug is administered (such as moving from inhaling cocaine to injecting it or smoking it). When a student moves toward more rapid or more frequent intoxication, it's a bad sign.

- Look at the context of drug use. Is it limited to situations in which peers are also using, such as drinking beer at a party? Or is the person using in unusual situations or at unusual times (such as before school)? Has the teenager tried unsuccessfully to control or stop using the substance? If so, this is a significant sign of trouble.

- Together with the student, carefully examine how drug or alcohol use has impacted the major areas of the student's life. A teenager may not show the physical signs of addiction (such as withdrawal) that are seen in adults who have abused a substance for decades. However, there are other ways in which drugs or alcohol affect a student's life. Look at the lengths to which he or she will go (and risks he or she will take) to obtain and use substances and the extent to which he or she persists in use despite negative consequences. Use the student page (p. 96) to help a teenager identify the adverse effects of substance use in some major life areas. Also help the student see how additional consequences might occur if he or she continues to use alcohol or drugs, such as the risk of legal trouble because of underage drinking or from the use of illegal drugs.

- Assess the student's motivation to change. Some positive signs are a student's awareness that his or her alcohol or drug use is causing problems, an awareness that he or she is not able to control the drug or alcohol use, and a willingness to listen to or seek help from others in making a change. These indicators roughly correspond to the first three of the Twelve Steps of Alcoholics Anonymous (see page 94).

Dealing With Denial

Individuals who have an alcohol or drug abuse problem but who are unmotivated to change are often referred to as being in denial. One form of denial involves the failure to recognize problems related to substance abuse or the tendency to attribute the problems to some other cause. For example, a teenager may say, "I didn't make the team this year because the coach doesn't like me," without admitting that his drinking affected his performance. Even when the consequences of alcohol or drug abuse are acknowledged, denial may appear in the mistaken belief that "I don't need any help. I can cut down (or stop) by myself."

When working with a teenager who is in denial, it's important to follow these guidelines.

- Use confrontation gently and respectfully. When denial is present, regardless of the form it takes, it will likely stop the addicted person from fully committing to the changes needed to halt his or her substance abuse. This is why is it often said that a person must "hit bottom" (experience consequences that are so prolonged or so severe that the individual can no longer stay in denial) in order to stop substance use or abuse. While there is some truth to this, you can play a role by gently leading a person to see the consequences of his or her drinking or drug use and weakening the student's denial through tactful but persistent confrontation.

The word "confrontation" often carries with it a connotation of forcefulness, which runs counter to the respect that should be maintained. By confrontation I simply mean pointing out inconsistencies or realities that the student would rather not face. I try to demonstrate a link between the consequences the student is experiencing and the substance abuse. I rarely argue a point if the person disagrees with the connection, other than to maintain that my observation, while perhaps not right, is reasonable. The best approach is one of persistence (showing one connection after another), rather than power.

When my work becomes confrontational in this way, I often use the analogy of a lighthouse keeper to illustrate how I view my role. I explain that my job is to shine the light to signal the presence of dangerous rocks. I point out that the student is the "captain" of his or her own life and can "steer the ship" as close to the rocks as he or she chooses. What I will not do, however, is allow the student to pretend the rocks are not there. In other words, I respect a student's right to make his or her own decisions, but I want the choices to be honest and made with no pretense regarding the possible consequences.

- Don't label the teenager or his or her use of alcohol or drugs. Labeling the student as an alcoholic or addict is likely to increase resistance and denial. Instead, accept whatever terms or language the teenager uses. For example, a student may say, "I may go a little overboard every now and then, but I'm not an alcoholic." What the student calls his or her substance use matters less than helping the student come to see the situation and its consequences accurately.

Evaluating Their "Rules"

Work with teenagers to build insight into out-of-control use of drugs or alcohol. Once students have an awareness that drinking or drug abuse is a problem, they will usually respond with efforts to convince themselves that they are in control. This is sometimes done through setting limits on what substances will be used (such as "only beer and not liquor"), amounts ("only two joints"), or under what situations ("only at parties"). My approach is to allow teenagers to try to stick to their own rules for use, but I encourage them to evaluate those rules using the following two tests:

- Do your rules work? ("If the rule of drinking only beer is designed to keep you out of trouble, can you successfully drink only beer and still stay out of trouble?")
- Can you follow your own rules? ("If you intend to limit yourself to two beers and end up having more, then you're unable to follow that rule.")

I impress upon teenagers that rules which don't work or can't be followed are useless and need to be revised. In other words, rather than push a specific goal on a resistant student, I allow him or her to make and revise personal rules until he or she comes up with something that works. I tell students that if they are honest about this process of testing the rules, they will either teach themselves how to control the substance abuse or else they will come to understand that they can't control the dependence. If, however, a teenager's drug or alcohol abuse escalates and the student exhibits the symptoms on page 91, it's time to refer the student to a professional counselor.

Teach Surrender

My goal in working with a resistant but substance-dependent teenager is to bring him or her to an awareness that he or she cannot control the substance use and thus needs to abstain. This often takes some time of trial-and-error learning, but once this awareness develops, I recommend using the Twelve Steps of Alcoholics Anonymous (A.A.) to provide a framework for the student's recovery. The first three of the Twelve Steps are as follows:[4]

1. We admitted we were powerless over alcohol—that our lives had become unmanageable.

2. Came to believe that a Power greater than ourselves could restore us to sanity.

3. Made a decision to turn our will and our lives over to the care of God *as we understood Him.*

In determining a person's readiness for the Twelve Steps, it's important to note that the first step has two parts—the awareness that "I cannot control my use" and the awareness that "my use is wrecking my life." I have had students tell me that they were unable to control their drinking, and yet they denied that this was causing them any problems. I have also had students who recognized that drinking was wrecking their lives but still believed that they could control it themselves. A teenager with a substance abuse problem must come to the point of recognizing *both* aspects of Step 1.

Once a student has admitted his or her powerlessness over drugs or alcohol, it is crucial for the person to develop a sense of hope, which is what Step 2 is about. The biggest step of all, however, may be Step 3—that of surrendering to a higher power. The importance of this step spiritually is the person's plea to God for deliverance from addiction; this reliance upon God for help signals a readiness to accept direction from others with regard to decisions that have a bearing on recovery.

The Twelve Steps of Alcoholics Anonymous

1. We admitted we were powerless over alcohol—that our lives had become unmanageable.

2. Came to believe that a Power greater than ourselves could restore us to sanity.

3. Made a decision to turn our will and our lives over to the care of God *as we understood Him.*

4. Made a searching and fearless moral inventory of ourselves.

5. Admitted to God, to ourselves, and to another human being the exact nature of our wrongs.

6. Were entirely ready to have God remove all these defects of character.

7. Humbly asked Him to remove our shortcomings.

8. Made a list of all persons we had harmed, and became willing to make amends to them all.

9. Made direct amends to such people wherever possible, except when to do so would injure them or others.

10. Continued to take personal inventory and when we were wrong promptly admitted it.

11. Sought through prayer and meditation to improve our conscious contact with God, *as we understood Him,* praying only for knowledge of His will for us and the power to carry that out.

12. Having had a spiritual awakening as the result of these steps, we tried to carry this message to alcoholics, and to practice these principles in all our affairs.

New Patterns

Encourage the teenager to break patterns associated with the substance abuse. As hard as it is for some teenagers to give up alcohol or drugs, they may find some other things just as hard to live without. There is a saying that substance abusers must change "playmates, playgrounds, and playthings." What does this mean for teenagers? It means that a student who is trying to recover from drug or alcohol dependence should not continue to hang around with the same people, go to the same places, or engage in the same activities that were associated with his or her substance abuse.

This need to change friends (at least those who were partners in substance abuse) is often an especially sore point with newly recovering teenagers. Although their attachment to their friends may be rooted in their mutual interest in drugs, they are reluctant to walk away from friends who have come to be their primary associates. Peer acceptance is very important to teenagers, and they do not want to be disloyal to these friends or face the uncertainty of being accepted by a different peer group. It has been my experience that adolescents often have to learn the lesson of "playmates, playgrounds, and playthings" the hard way. Nonetheless, it's important to encourage the newly recovering teenager to break patterns that were part of his or her life as an alcohol or drug abuser.

You'll also want to teach teenagers skills for refusing drugs. Find out from the student under what circumstances he or she might anticipate being offered drugs or alcohol. Help the student plan how to avoid such circumstances, as well as what he or she can say and do to get out of those situations should they occur. Consider using role-plays to help the student practice refusing drugs.

Finally, encourage "one day at a time" thinking. Once a teenager becomes dependent on a substance, he or she may have a hard time imagining life without it. Impress upon the student the importance of making changes in manageable bits. Encourage the young person not to think about never having a drink again, but rather to focus on not having a drink *today*.

---

[1] Vincent B. Van Hasselt and Michel Hersen, *Handbook of Adolescent Psychopathology* (New York, NY: Lexington Books, 1995), 390.

[2] *Diagnostic and Statistical Manual of Mental Disorders*, Fourth Edition (Washington, DC: American Psychiatric Assocation, 1994), 182-183.

[3] Robert Jean Campbell, *Psychiatric Dictionary*, Seventh Edition (New York, NY: Oxford University Press, 1996), 99.

[4] *Alcoholics Anonymous*, Third Edition (New York, NY: Alcoholics Anonymous World Services, Inc., 1976), 59.

Recommended Resources

Books

- *Alcoholics Anonymous,* Third Edition. New York, NY: Alcoholics Anonymous World Services, Inc., 1976.

- *Counseling for Relapse Prevention,* Terence T. Gorski and Merlene Miller. Independence, MO: Independence Press, 1982.

- *Drugs, Society, and Human Behavior,* Ninth Edition. Oakley Ray and Charles Ksir. New York, NY: McGraw-Hill Higher Education, 2001.

- *Staying Sober: A Guide for Relapse Prevention,* Terence T. Gorski and Merlene Miller. Independence, MO: Independence Press, 1986.

STUDENT PAGE Use the photocopiable worksheet on page 96 to help teenagers understand the effects of their alcohol or drug use. Use this student page in a counseling situation by talking through the questions with the teenager and actively listening to his or her responses.

Drugs and Alcohol

Examining the Impact of Your Alcohol or Drug Use

Carefully and honestly answer the following questions about how your alcohol or drug use may have affected these areas of your life.

Physical: Have you experienced physical or medical problems (such as stomach pain or liver damage)? Have you been injured in an accident or fight while under the influence? Have you had memory lapses?

Family/Social: Have you had arguments with family or friends because of your drug or alcohol use? Have you stopped spending time with former friends, or have you increased time with friends who like to use drugs and alcohol? Have you lost friends because of your drug or alcohol use?

Educational: Have you skipped class or missed classes (for example, because of a hangover)? Have you gone to school while under the influence? Have your grades gone down or has the quality of your schoolwork suffered? Have you been unable to concentrate or had memory lapses? Have you dropped out of school?

Employment: Have you missed work to use drugs or alcohol or because you were under the influence? Have you gone to work high or with a hangover? Have you been fired because of drug or alcohol use?

Financial: How much money have you spent on alcohol or drugs? How much have you had to pay in fines or legal fees related to abuse?

Legal: Have you been arrested for substance abuse? Have you been placed on probation? Have you lost your driving privileges because of substance abuse? Do you face the possibility of being arrested?

Psychological: Have you experienced a worsening of mood problems or other previous problems because of your alcohol or drug use?

Spiritual: Have you had a change in values or a change in what's important to you? Have you experienced a decline in the practice of your faith? Have you changed your religious beliefs? Have you felt distant or separated from God? Have you felt that your drug or alcohol use controlled you instead of that you controlled your use?

CHAPTER 13

Starved Self-Esteem—
Helping Students With Eating Disorders

KYLE D. PONTIUS, Ph.D.

THE BASICS

Mention "eating disorder" and a variety of images and ideas come to mind. Of the many emotional and behavioral problems, eating disorders get a lot of press. Anorexia nervosa (or simply anorexia) became a familiar term following the well-publicized death of singer Karen Carpenter in 1983. Other celebrities have suffered from and confessed to having eating disorders—anorexia nervosa, bulimia nervosa (or simply bulimia), or binge eating—capturing headlines along the way.

In general, the age of onset for eating disorders is during adolescence. It's important for youth workers to be aware of the symptoms, as most of the students who develop eating disorders will develop them during the years when their youth leaders have the most impact on their lives.

For a formal diagnosis of anorexia nervosa, a person must be refusing to maintain a body weight that is considered normal for that height. As a rule of thumb, this would be an individual whose weight drops below 85 percent of what is considered normal. There is usually also an intense fear of gaining weight or becoming fat, even when a student is underweight. People affected by anorexia are driven by their obsessions over body image and are usually difficult to talk to about their weight because of the distortions in thinking. Even after an individual has acknowledged the disorder and become intent on recovery, compulsive behavior may continue to be a problem.

Anorexia can be short-lived or a lifelong struggle. Generally, the disorder is more difficult to treat when there are other mental or emotional problems involved or when the onset is prior to adolescence. Even though bingeing and purging is typically associated with bulimia, this behavior also occurs in people who have been diagnosed with anorexia. Sufferers of anorexia may binge and purge to maintain their underweight condition or even to lose additional weight.

People with bulimia generally don't actively refuse to maintain their normal weight. However, they will binge eat and then either purge the food from their bodies by vomiting or by misusing laxatives, diuretics, or enemas; or they will compensate for the food intake through fasting or excessive exercise. This behavior is recurrent, happening a couple of times a week over at least a three-month period. Generally, individuals who suffer from bulimia do so for a longer period of time before receiving treatment than those who have anorexia. People with bulimia may also have more chronic problems with their eating than those with anorexia.

Interestingly, anorexia and bulimia seem to be primarily a product of industrialized societies. That would explain why there are few passages in Scripture having to do with problem eating; such references involve only gluttony, such as Proverbs 23:20-21, which associates gluttony with drunkenness and laziness. Gluttony is not the same as what we are addressing here, and it is outside the scope of this chapter to build a theology of eating disorders. I would suggest, however, that misuse or abuse of food—whether it is gluttony, severe restriction, bingeing, or purging—is against God's will for his people.

Body Image

With both anorexia and bulimia, body image plays a critical role. This is reflected in the prevalence of these disorders in societies that place a high value on appearance and weight, particularly in women. For both of these disorders, over 90 percent of those affected are female. Anorexia and bulimia both appear to have a genetic component and can co-occur with other disorders such as depression or substance abuse.[1]

Binge-eating disorder is similar to bulimia, except there is no attempt at purging the consumed food. Interestingly, only about 30 percent of those involved in weight-control programs could be considered to have this disorder; and of those, women are about 1.5 times more likely to have this disorder than men.[2]

In addition to those with full-blown eating disorders, there are people who experience many of the symptoms but fail to meet the full diagnostic criteria. Consequently, the number of students who abuse food could be much higher than what one would expect simply by looking at the statistics. Food-abusing students who do not meet the diagnostic criteria could easily slip through the cracks and never get the help they need.

Serious health problems can result from eating disorders, and treatment is best when it's approached by a team of professionals consisting of at least a physician, a psychotherapist, and a dietician. Hospitalization may be a necessary first step to ensure the physical health of the eating-disordered person. Other treatment options include residential, day treatment, and outpatient treatment programs, as well as self-help groups. The most effective treatment program will be the one that best fits the affected individual.

Theories concerning eating disorders are hard to prove; however, the most helpful ones view an individual's relationship with food as a substitute for healthy interpersonal relationships or as an attempt to deal with the damage done from troubled early relationships. For example, anorexia might be seen as an expression of a power struggle between a student who wants desperately to grow up and become more independent and his or her overcontrolling parents. Binge eating may be viewed as an act of reaching out to food for comfort and acceptance instead of receiving this support from healthy relationships.

Assuming that these theories have merit, teaching about healthy relationships and self-esteem within the youth group can be very beneficial. The church should actively address the unhealthy messages that students receive concerning their bodies and their value before God. Offering parenting classes or organizing social activities that involve the student's parents and siblings can help to reach families on a larger scale.

WHEN TO REFER

An eating disorder can be a life-threatening condition. Fortunately, the social nature of a youth group can provide a context in which many of the symptoms of eating disorders can be observed. Act carefully when you notice any of the symptoms. An overreaction can alienate a leader from the student; however, not taking symptoms seriously can be worse if the student's health is at risk. A referral may be appropriate in any of the following situations:

- when a student, family member, or friend requests a referral
- when you notice food-abusing behavior. (Many youth group activities involve food and provide an opportunity to observe the student's eating behaviors, including avoiding food and indications of purging.)
- when you notice dramatic weight loss in a teenager or see the student dress in such a way as to hide changes in appearance
- when you hear a teenager talk about losing weight or when the student seems to have an abnormal focus on his or her weight
- when friendships are disrupted as a result of a food abuse. (Watch for conflicts that occur within the group or unusual isolating behavior.)
- when a student is obese or exhibits significant weight gain. (Obesity is a problem with binge eaters. Lovingly pay attention to overweight students, and offer your help if symptoms are observed.)

The above situations can be even more serious when other problems, such as depression or substance abuse, are present. Carefully assess each situation. Don't betray the trust of a student, but remember that an eating disorder can be life-threatening. It's important to make a referral to a professional who specializes in eating disorders or to refer the student to an eating-disorder program. A professional counselor or psychologist is generally a good first referral. This professional can act as a case manager, recruiting and coordinating services with others on the treatment team.

COUNSELING IDEAS

Counseling is certainly a major activity of youth leaders, and one that needs special attention when other counseling professionals are involved in helping a student. When several people are involved in the care of an individual, it is vital to delineate roles so as not to compromise treatment. This is particularly important in dealing with a student who has an eating disorder because the student should also be receiving medical, nutritional, and psychotherapeutic help.

Because the youth leader is on the front lines, he or she is more likely to be aware of how a student is abusing food and is therefore one of the first people who could identify a problem and offer a referral. The youth leader can present biblically based material about eating disorders, body image, self-esteem, and healthy relationships as part of the overall youth ministry programming on the large-group as well as small-group and interpersonal levels. The youth leader can also address healthy family relationships, both educationally and spiritually, on each of the above levels.

Eating Disorders

It's important for the youth leader to know his or her limitations, as well as have an understanding about how he or she can best be involved in the lives of students and their families. The role of the youth leader is unique because he or she has not been brought in specifically to address the eating disorder and may remain in the student's life long after treatment by a professional counselor has ended.

Partnering With a Therapist

When a student has been referred to a professional counselor, the youth leader should consult with the therapist to discuss appropriate ways to be involved in working through the eating disorder with the student. The difference in roles between the youth leader and the therapist can be used powerfully in addressing the needs of the student, but it can also be destructive if not managed well. The counseling provided by the youth leader is generally best when it is episodic rather than ongoing. An ongoing counseling relationship may interfere with the therapy as well as with a healthy relationship between the student and the youth leader. The youth leader can help in the following ways:

- Initially the youth leader can provide the student with a safe relationship in which the student can vent his or her feelings and know that the youth leader has heard and understood. When you accurately reflect and paraphrase what a teenager has said, it allows the student to feel a human connection. Reflecting is simply restating what the student has said as a means of both checking the communication and letting the student know his or her message has been received and understood. Paraphrasing condenses the message and may make reference to earlier messages. Lifting your voice a bit at the end of a statement, or even phrasing the statement as a question, allows the student to comment on your understanding of what he or she has said. Avoid giving advice when reflecting and paraphrasing—simply focus on giving the student the experience of being understood and accepted.

- The youth leader should discuss spiritual issues with the student. Praying with the student and addressing the application of Scripture provides the teenager with much needed pastoral care. Here again, it's important to coordinate with the student's treatment team. For example, trying to incorporate fasting into a student's prayer life would *not* be a good idea for the student who is struggling with anorexia. There may be more subtle areas that need to be clarified with the therapist as well. This type of dialogue is helpful in that the therapist could guide the youth leader in ways to best support the student's treatment, and the youth leader could inform the therapist of how the student is participating in the youth program and in relationship with the leader.

  Scripture passages dealing with self-esteem, body image, self-discipline, and spiritual maturity can be appropriately addressed with the student depending on his or her needs and the specific eating disorder. The following are a few helpful passages that might be used for individual or group study:

  Proverbs 14:30
  Proverbs 31:30
  Matthew 22:37-40
  1 Corinthians 6:19-20
  Galatians 5:22-26
  2 Timothy 1:7

Eating Disorders

- The youth leader can act as a coach or accountability partner for the student. The leader can help the teenager follow through on the treatment program, check in with the student about his or her eating behaviors, offer the student encouragement, and be available when the student needs support. Many of the same reflecting and paraphrasing skills described earlier can be used by a youth leader in this role.

- The youth leader can work to boost a student's self-esteem and can be an example for the student. Treating the student with respect, showing the teenager that his or her opinions are important, and letting the student know that he or she is valued for his or her thoughts and abilities—and not just for his or her outward appearance—will go a long way toward boosting the student's self-esteem. Strive to model healthy living (including eating) and healthy relationships. Allowing the student to see a healthy marriage at work and giving the student a chance to observe the application of appropriate parenting techniques can challenge the teenager's perceptions of what is normal if he or she comes from a dysfunctional family.

Self-Help Programs

Many churches offer self-help groups based on an adapted Twelve-Step model for people who are affected by eating disorders. Popularized by Alcoholics Anonymous, the Twelve Steps are essentially the gospel without Jesus Christ. Christian programs adapt the Twelve Steps by replacing A.A.'s generic "higher power" with who we know God to be, and providing support from Scripture for each of the steps. Twelve-Step meetings provide teaching, support, and accountability to the participants. Self-help groups are not meant to be used in place of treatment, but they *can* be a powerful adjunct to treatment.

---

1 *Diagnostic and Statistical Manual of Mental Disorders,* Fourth Edition, Text Revision (Washington, DC: American Psychiatric Association, 2000), 587-588, 592-593.

2 *Diagnostic and Statistical Manual of Mental Disorders,* Fourth Edition, 786.

Recommended Resources

Books

- *Diagnostic and Statistical Manual of Mental Disorders,* Fourth Edition, Text Revision. Washington, DC: American Psychiatric Association, 2000.

- *Fat Is a Family Affair,* Judi Hollis. Center City, MN: Hazelden, 1985.

- *The Lies We Believe,* Chris Thurman. Nashville, TN: Thomas Nelson Publishers, 1989.

- *Love Hunger: Recovery From Food Addiction,* Frank Minirth, Paul Meier, Robert Hemfelt, Sharon Sneed, and Don Hawkins. Nashville, TN: Thomas Nelson Publishers, 1991.

- *The Outpatient Treatment of Eating Disorders: A Guide for Therapists, Dietitians, and Physicians,* James E. Mitchell, editor. Minneapolis, MN: University of Minnesota Press, 2001.

- *The Twelve Steps and Twelve Traditions of Overeaters Anonymous.* Torrance, CA: Overeaters Anonymous, 1990, 1993.

Web Resources

- www.celebraterecovery.com (Web site of Celebrate Recovery)

STUDENT PAGE Use the photocopiable worksheet on page 102 to help teenagers understand their feelings related to their eating habits. Let the student complete the page at home, then discuss it with the student during a subsequent meeting.

Seeing Yourself

Our self-concept plays an important part in our approach to food. This exercise is designed to heighten your self-awareness and to let you decide if the way you view yourself is helpful or not.

Begin with a blank piece of paper and some colored pencils. First draw a self-portrait. Approach the drawing from the perspective of how you see yourself. You may include other people or objects in your picture; however, the main figure in the drawing should be you.

Now draw two more self-portraits. Approach one of these drawings from the perspective of another person. This other person may be a friend, parent, sibling or other important person in your life. Approach the third drawing from God's perspective. Ask yourself how God sees you, and draw yourself through his eyes. Again, you may include other people or objects in your pictures—just make sure that you are the most prominent figure.

Place the three drawings next to each other and write about the pictures in your journal. If you don't keep a journal, use the blank space at the bottom of this page, a spiral notebook, or even a computer file that you can keep safe. Compare the drawings. How do you like each of your drawings? What would you change? What would you keep the same? When you're ready, share your drawings and journal entry with your counselor, youth worker, or someone else you trust, and get that person's feedback.

CHAPTER 14

Faith Development—
Understanding Stages of Growth

LARRY LINDQUIST, Ed.D.

THE BASICS

Men of faith, women of faith—how do people become defined that way? What are the criteria used to assess someone's level of faith? Beyond that, how does a person's faith develop? Can we assist students in the development of their faith? If so, how? It is certainly our goal to send out men and women of great faith from our ministries. But how do we define or plan for that development?

While researching this chapter, I found an overabundance of literature focusing on the development of character. Traits such as honesty, respect, and courage are frequently addressed in youth ministry resources to help leaders develop those traits in students. However, in all of this literature, little is dedicated to the issue of faith development. And there's even less curriculum specifically designed to develop faith in students.

There is a growing field of literature on the topic of faith development. Most of it is based on the concept of stages and is supported by well-known theorists including Jean Piaget, Lawrence Kohlberg, and James Fowler. These stages are sequential but not guaranteed. A person's faith can continue to grow, or a person can reach a particular stage and stagnate. Each stage is defined, allowing a person to identify the level of faith exhibited by a student. Of the stages proposed by the theorists mentioned above, Fowler's stages are the most recognized. Using the stages Fowler identified[1] as a basic outline, here's my own summary of the stages of faith development.

Stage One: Intuitive-Projective Faith

This is the level of faith normally exhibited by preschoolers. They know nothing of faith except what is based on intuition and projected upon them by their parents or significant caregivers. Children derive their image of God from the people who are closest to them. The family's perspectives on death, taboos, and values become part of the child's values.

Stage Two: Mythic-Literal Faith

As children enter the early grades of elementary school, their understanding of faith is essentially a reflection of the concepts and beliefs of others. I call this level of faith the "umbilical cord" faith, in which children simply feed on the predigested faith and beliefs of others. However, it is at this level that children are exposed to people who have faiths that are different from theirs. A Christian second-grader may sit next to a Muslim student in school. Their conflicting faiths may begin to cause tension. Often students at this level of faith are intolerant of people who have different faiths. They view everything as black and white.

Stage Three: Synthetic-Conventional Faith

This stage typically begins in early adolescence. Since agreement and conformity are paramount to young people, compartmentalizing their faith accommodates the tension that was experienced in the previous stage. Students at this stage still do not "own" their faith. They are masters of camouflage! Their faith is synthetic in the sense that it is not authentic—they simply exhibit a faith that is conventional to the particular environment in which they find themselves. Know any students who are like this?

Stage Four: Individuative-Reflective Faith

This stage normally begins to appear in late adolescence. A student's faith begins to become his or her own. Teenagers at this stage begin living and expressing their faith, though this usually causes relationship tension, and friendships may begin to change. The teenager's faith is individuative in the sense that the student can articulate it, and reflective in the sense that he or she has the ability to defend it. There is no better way for a teenager to own his or her faith than having the ability to know why he or she is not of another faith. That requires reflection. The burden of responsibility to establish personal values, beliefs, and attitudes rests on the individual alone. At this stage the student's life is usually filled with tension and questions, but the teenager *owns* his or her faith.

Stage Five: Conjunctive Faith

This level of faith is a synthesis of previous stages. At this stage, an individual is able to see and understand perspectives other than his or her own. This level of faith is rarely achieved without direct, extended immersion into a culture and ideology other than one's own.

Stage Six: Universalizing Faith

Individuals at this level are called "saints." Very few people ever arrive at this level of faith. It's a total commitment to the guiding presence of God or whatever the person recognizes as the ultimate authority. Gandhi, Martin Luther King, Jr., Mother Teresa, and Dietrich Bonhoeffer are examples of individuals who attained this level of faith. Their faith was not a part of their life— their faith *was* their life.

WHEN TO REFER

Referral is not often an issue in this area of ministry. However, there are a few situations in which you would refer a student to someone else. For example, if a student describes a spiritual

Faith Development

encounter (such as exorcism, expressing manifestations of the Holy Spirit, or epiphany) that's beyond your knowledge or comfort level, seek someone who has good biblical knowledge about the particular experience and make a referral. Even though you have referred the student, go with the teenager to the appointment if you can, and learn more about the issue.

As the spiritual mentor of a student, it's important that you understand where *you* are in your personal faith development! There is a great deal of truth to the saying "you can't lead students to places you haven't been." If a student is moving beyond your own level of faith development, place him or her in the hands of someone who is at the next stage. That's a humbling thing to do, but failing to do it will impede the faith development of the student.

COUNSELING IDEAS

Use the handout "How Deep Is Your Faith?" (p. 109) to help a student identify the level of his or her faith. (The stages are modified slightly on the handout.) When the teenager better understands the level that he or she is at, you'll be better able to facilitate the growth of the student's faith. However, make sure to allow *the student* to identify himself or herself among the levels of faith. Don't argue with his or her self-assessment; guide the teenager by making sure that he or she understands the particular level of faith. Once a student has identified where he or she is at, begin meeting together to encourage the teenager to grow in his or her faith. Remember that identification is only part of the process. To pigeonhole students at a particular level of faith will excuse and stagnate them. It is our mission as those who love students and seek the deepening of their faith to challenge and encourage them to reach higher levels of faith.

Helping Students Transition From One Stage to the Next

The transition from the first stage of faith to the second stage is prompted by the development of concrete operational thinking. Students begin to understand distinctions between what is real and what only seems to be real. As students grow in their ability to think abstractly, they will also begin to understand the need for faith in things they cannot test or see. Scripture defines faith as "being sure of what we hope for and certain of what we do not see" (Hebrews 11:1). Talk with the student who is at this level of faith about the necessity of placing faith in things we cannot see—things beyond ourselves.

When someone asks them about their faith, students at this level commonly respond with, "Well, that's what my church believes," or "That's what my parents believe." When they are asked to participate in a questionable activity, their response will likely be, "My church won't let me." The security of this "umbilical cord" faith is very comfortable. However, the only way to help a student move to higher levels of faith is to provide opportunities in which the student can't rely on the umbilical cord. If someone at this level asks a sincere question about his or her faith, don't provide the appropriate denominational response! Cut the umbilical cord by forcing the student to look at Scripture himself or herself. Give hints, but encourage the student to find answers on his or her own.

In his book *Fire Up Your Life!* Ken Davis speaks to this critical point as he talks about teenagers who have gone off to college: "Within months, many of these young people leave the 'faith of their fathers' behind. This is sad but not surprising...Only the convictions that are *personal*—that come from the inside out, that are *their* convictions rather than their *parents'* convictions or their *church's* convictions—will stand."[2]

The transition to the third stage follows a conflict or contradiction in one's faith, causing the student to reflect on those ideas; formal operational thinking allows this reflection to occur. A common conflict of faith for students comes when they are faced with the issue of abortion or the topic of creation vs. evolution in school. These and other points of tension in the faith of a student are not bad things! In fact, one of the best ways to strengthen a student's faith is to have him or her defend the opposing view. The best way for a person to understand why he or she does not follow another faith is to have a better understanding of that faith. While I was in high school, I was assigned such a task. I had to defend the evolutionary explanation of our existence. It was a faith-developing exercise for me. I have never forgotten it, and I am better able to defend my faith as a result.

Doubts are often a huge part of this transition. Assure the student that doubts are not a bad thing. There are many characters in Scripture (such as Moses, Abraham, Gideon, and Thomas) who came to this level of faith development through their doubts. Doubts push us to further questioning and investigation. Investigation has never threatened God or his Word; encourage it in your students. Talk to students about their doubts. Unpack some of your own.

Transition to stage four follows more intense conflict or contradictions between valued authorities. The natural tendency of students is to steer clear of conflict to avoid being perceived as odd. They desperately seek to blend in with others and maintain separation of their "worlds." Their faith can be fragile at this level. It is protected and submerged whenever they are with people who would exclude or ridicule them for it. Their behavior is often inconsistent with their faith. However, when students are free to exhibit their faith, it can appear very strong!

The most powerful way to bring a student to the next level of faith is to create an environment where the teenager's "worlds" collide. Have a student's friend from school attend a youth group event or have a student run into the youth leader at the mall—suddenly the student's worlds collide. All at once, the student's faith is threatened. This is a dangerous point in the teenager's faith development. It's important that you do not *force* this collision—it can break a student's trust, and the teenager may eliminate you from his world entirely! Find creative ways to cross these borders. Go to high school sporting events (with the teenager's permission). Or invite the student and his or her friends from school to your home for a barbecue.

The transition to this fourth level of faith is usually marked by emotion. Paradoxes from a student's own traditions may break up the neatness of the previous levels of compartmentalized faith. When the conflict of colliding worlds becomes too disturbing for the student, he or she will often make a major decision of personal faith. Guidance is critical at this point in the student's faith development. Encourage the student. Pray with him or her. One of the dangers of this emotional commitment to personal faith is the development of a "crusader type" fervor in which those of a different faith are seen as the enemy. Zeal without knowledge and truth without grace are dangerous combinations.

The transition to stage five requires a tempering of the student's faith—not the lessening of passion, but an ability to embrace those who differ with him or her. In an effort to move the high school students in my ministry to this next level of faith, I invited people of various faiths to share their beliefs with my students. It was a wonderful challenge to my students, and it began the process of tempering them in their relationships with people whose faith differed from their own. They began to interact with people of other faiths, grew in their apologetic skills, and even saw an individual from another faith return to our group on a regular basis. That person eventually committed her life to Christ, and she married one of the members of our group! When students reach the fifth level, they need opportunities to interact with others in a constructive, loving format. Ecumenical retreats and cooperative interfaith missions endeavors are both wonderful ways to develop faith at this level.

The transition to the sixth stage comes when an individual sees the world through the eyes of his or her faith. The student has moved from owning and defending his or her faith to the point at which *faith owns the student*. Feeling the call to missions or ministry is common during this stage. Sacrifice is the definition of faith at this level. Self is gone; living the life of Christ before others is all that is important. Galatians 2:20 describes faith at this level: "I have been crucified with Christ and I no longer live, but Christ lives in me. The life I live in the body, I live by faith in the Son of God, who loved me and gave himself for me."

Cognitive Dissonance

In the process of counseling a student through the various stages of faith, a key element is something called cognitive dissonance or disequilibrium. A major part of our responsibility as people who love students and seek the development of their faith is to create environments of dissonance and disequilibrium. That may sound odd, but let me explain. Can a fish know what it is to be wet? Think about that for a minute. If a fish has never experienced "dry," how could it know "wet"?[3] The experience is defined by its opposite! In faith development, we must bring experiences and dilemmas into the teenager's life that serve as catalysts to help the student define his or her faith. These experiences may cause tension in the teenager's mind (cognitive dissonance), but that's exactly what brings about growth in the student's faith.

I think of it as a controlled crisis. I never want to place a student in a dangerous, uncontrolled situation. However, I will do everything I can to bring a student to the end of his or her cognitive rope if it will help strengthen that teenager's faith. I often say that there are two places where God loves to hang out. (Please, I know about omnipresence—I'm just making a point!) One place is Starbucks (love my java!); the other place God loves to be is at the "end of our rope." The problem is, not many of us make it there (to the second place, not the first) because of an independent spirit and our constant effort to keep our lives at peace. God waits for us at the place we struggle to avoid!

How can you create cognitive dissonance in

Recommended Resources

Books

- *Fire Up Your Life!* Ken Davis. Grand Rapids, MI: Zondervan Publishing House, 1995.

- *Stages of Faith: The Psychology of Human Development and the Quest for Meaning,* James W. Fowler. New York, NY: HarperCollins Publishers, 1995.

- *Will Our Children Have Faith?* Revised Edition, John H. Westerhoff, III. Harrisburg: PA: Morehouse Publishing, 2000.

Periodicals

- "Adolescent Spirituality: What Can We Expect?" Les Parrott III. Youthworker (Spring 1995). www.youthspecialties.com/ywj/articles/results/adolescent.html

Web Resources

- www.youth.co.za/model/faith2.htm#2 ("Faith Development Theories" at the Web site of The Edge Consulting) the minds of your students? One way is to have your students talk about the situations on the student page at the end of this chapter ("Dissonance!" p. 110). After a student has read each scenario, ask him or her to share his or her thoughts. Your students will express their level of faith, and the exercise will help them grow.

---

[1]   See James W. Fowler, *Stages of Faith: The Psychology of Human Development and the Quest for Meaning* (New York, NY: HarperCollins Publishers, 1995).

[2]   Ken Davis, *Fire Up Your Life!* (Grand Rapids, MI: Zondervan Publishing House, 1995), 146-147.

[3]   Also see Fowler, *Stages of Faith*, 161-162.

STUDENT PAGES Use the photocopiable worksheets on pages 109 and 110 to help teenagers identify their level of faith and be challenged to grow. Use "How Deep Is Your Faith?" (p. 109) with a student to guide a discussion in a counseling session. Use "Dissonance!" (p. 110) as a discussion starter as well, encouraging the student to read and think through the scenarios and then explain what he or she would do and why.

How Deep Is Your Faith?

"Examine yourselves to see whether you are in the faith; test yourselves" (2 Corinthians 13:5).

Everyone fits somewhere among the levels of faith listed below. Where are you? Where do you want to be? Where do others think you are?

Level 1—Umbilical Cord Faith

People at this level have a faith that is not really their own; they simply reflect the faith of significant individuals in their lives. If someone asks them about their faith, people at this level respond with the things they've been taught or have seen in their parents or pastor. They depend on the faith of others.

Level 2—Confused Faith

People at this level of faith have been confronted by individuals whose faith is different from their own. For example, a Christian and a Muslim might sit next to each other and discover their differences. They learn that their faith may be "wrong" and others may be "right"! That can lead to confusion, frustration, and doubt.

Level 3—Chameleon Faith

A chameleon can change its color to blend into the environment. In the same way, individuals at this level adjust their faith to blend with those around them. They seek to avoid conflict and arguments.

Level 4—Unashamed Faith

People at this level of faith are committed to their beliefs and do not budge. They realize that conflict may come as a result, but they will defend their faith to people who have different beliefs. Their parents may disown them or their friends may leave them, but they will not give up their faith.

Level 5—Loving Faith

This level includes people who are unashamed of their faith and are loving toward people whose beliefs differ from theirs. They understand that those of other faiths are not the enemy, but rather are victims of the enemy.

Level 6—Sacrificial Faith

This is the highest level of faith development. At this level, a person has moved from "I own my faith" to "My faith owns me!" A person's life totally reflects sacrifice for his or her faith. At this stage, an individual's life revolves around the teachings of his or her faith. Death is no threat if it is the result of a person's living out his or her faith before others.

Dissonance!

Dissonance is the awkward feeling you get when something doesn't feel quite right to you. Most of the time we want to get rid of the tension in a particular situation. To do that, we try to figure out a way to resolve the situation—to make the tension go away.

Read the paragraphs below, and think about what you would do in each situation. Be ready to talk about your answers. There is no right answer—it all depends on your own perspective.

Thief or Savior?

Your best friend has been diagnosed with a rare disease. He will die in just a few weeks if he doesn't get treatment with a very expensive drug. His family could never afford the medication, and their insurance will not cover it. Your friend's older brother decides to break into the hospital and steal the drugs. But he can't do it alone and asks for your help. What do you do?

Punishment or Praise?

You've just gotten your permit to drive! However, you've been firmly told by your dad that you cannot drive unless there's a licensed adult in the car *and* you have your dad's permission. On Saturday, you're relaxing at the park when a woman nearby breaks her leg! She desperately needs medical attention and begs you to drive her to the hospital a mile away. You drive her to the hospital in her car. When you get home and tell your father what happened, he takes away your driving privileges for a month. How do you react?

Enemy or Friend?

You sit next to a student in history class who has become a great friend. However, he has just told you that he is a Muslim. When you explain that you're a Christian, he begins to explain why your faith is flawed. How do you respond? Do you sit somewhere else? Argue with him? Has your friend become your enemy?

Beating Your Pastor

You're at a prayer meeting in a foreign country. Suddenly police enter the room and begin to beat the pastor who is leading your meeting. When the police have finished, they demand that you and the others in the group beat your pastor! If you don't, they will beat *you*—possibly to death! The others in the group begin to beat the pastor. What's your decision?

CHAPTER 15

Family Conflict—
Overcoming Communication Challenges Between Teenagers and Their Families

TERRI S. WATSON, Psy.D.

THE BASICS

"All my parents do is nag—they don't want to listen!"

"I can handle it on my own."

"My mom is too nosy—she won't leave me alone. Why should I talk to her?"

"When we talk, we always end up fighting and somebody leaves mad."

For many families, common complaints such as these are the "background music" of everyday life with a teenager. One of the greatest challenges for families with teenagers involves the increase in family arguments, power struggles, and value clashes combined with a sense of being closed out of their teenagers' lives. Adolescents are at the age where they increasingly value the opinions of peers over parents, want independence instead of depending on parents' views, and tend to value freedom of expression over conformity. Escalating family conflict is often the natural result of the push for independence.

Research informs us that it's particularly important for families to have good communication during their children's teenage years. Active parent-adolescent communication can have a preventive effect on a number of serious teenage problems, including drug and alcohol abuse and teenage pregnancy. Adolescents who can "talk out" their problems and concerns with their parents are much less likely to "act out." Adolescents who are able to assertively express their needs to others are less likely to be aggressive. And most important, healthy family communication can enhance a teenager's spiritual development. The importance of good family communication during the teenage years cannot be overstated. How can a family practice good communication and collaborative problem solving in a way that maintains healthy parental authority, while taking into account the emerging need for independence of the teenager?

Youth ministers have an opportunity to play a key role in helping students and families keep the channels of communication open. This chapter will attempt to equip youth ministers to support students and families in open communication and conflict resolution.

Healthy Communication

Successful family communication allows for a clear authority structure in the family and keeps parents in charge while allowing for increasing respect and attention to the concerns, needs, and views of the teenager as he or she grows toward young adulthood. The goal of family communication should be to create an atmosphere of mutual caring, respect for differences, and tolerance for both positive and negative emotions where all parties are free to state needs and concerns. Good communication involves much more than simply winning arguments or getting the kids to obey. Parents can help teenagers understand the reasons behind family rules or guidelines, with the goal of helping their children internalize these values and make them their own.

Froma Walsh is a family therapist who has studied the characteristics that make families resilient and strong. She identifies three critical components of good family communication that allow families to maintain strong relationships and yet still attend to the needs of family members.[1] First, Walsh suggests that clear, consistent, "truth speaking" is an essential element of good communication. Family members can be challenged to be direct about their needs and expectations, rather than hoping unrealistically that others will be able to read their minds.

Second, Walsh identifies open emotional sharing as a characteristic of healthy communication. Parents and teenagers can foster an atmosphere of trust and openness by respecting and listening to one another. Honest sharing of a full range of emotions, both positive and negative, is important.

Third, Walsh suggests that collaborative problem solving through shared decision making is essential for healthy family communication. As families encounter normal, day-to-day stresses and make everyday decisions (use of the family car, curfew, or choice of friends), as well as face more severe family stressors (divorce, health problems, or financial difficulties), the ability to work together to generate solutions is critical for family functioning.

Common Barriers to Communication

A number of factors can interfere with a family's ability to have caring, open, and clear communication and can lead to conflict and misunderstanding.

- Some parents fear that allowing open communication and negotiation will undermine their authority. Not so! Two-way communication increases teenagers' respect for their parents and increases compliance.
- Other parents, after listening to their teenager's feelings and concerns, feel that they cannot say no, and they don't take enough of a position of authority. This may be a challenge particularly in single-parent families.
- Many families are unable to deal with the expression of negative feelings such as hurt, anger, or disappointment; family members "tiptoe" around each other, and honest communication is lost. Families can be encouraged to honestly express concerns in a respectful manner, and parents must model this for the children.
- During discussions, some families quickly escalate to hurtful expressions of anger, blame, and criticism that destroy trust.

- Parents or teenagers may have unrealistic, perfectionist expectations for themselves and others or harbor excessive shame and guilt that interferes with their ability to admit their mistakes and seek reconciliation.
- Indirect communication, vague threats, or passive-aggressive communication are also barriers to identifying and addressing the cause of the family conflict.

WHEN TO REFER

While some degree of conflict is normal and even healthy in families with teenagers, it's important that a youth minister knows when family conflict places a student at risk for more serious emotional and behavioral problems and warrants a professional referral. Families should be referred to a licensed marriage and family therapist or mental health professional in the following situations:

- when the family conflict is interfering with the normal adjustment of the teenager (such as affecting the student's schoolwork, relationships, or job)
- when the student makes subtle or obvious references to behaviors such as running away, substance abuse, or physical violence, or when the teenager has suicidal thoughts
- when a teenager has a long history of defiance of authority or acting-out behaviors
- when the student exhibits symptoms of excessive sadness, mood swings, anxiety, or excessive shame that may indicate the presence of a depressive disorder or anxiety disorder
- when the church's attempts to decrease family conflict have not been successful
- when conflict in the family leads to emotionally or physically abusive behavior by the parents or teenager

In this last situation, most states require by law that youth ministers report the abuse to their state's child protective services. Families are particularly at risk if one of the family members has a substance abuse problem.

COUNSELING IDEAS

Prevention

The old adage "an ounce of prevention is worth a pound of cure" is certainly the case when it comes to family communication. Families start building a strong foundation for trust and open communication early on in the lives of their children. Consider providing parent education and support classes in your church where characteristics of good parent-child communication are explored. Helping parents identify potential communication blocks early on can prevent the development of more serious conflicts in parent-child relationships as the children grow older. The biblical principles of mutual respect, anger management, and Christlike behavior are the foundation for fostering an emotionally and spiritually healthy family atmosphere in which openness and sharing can occur.

Ground Rules for Counseling Teenagers and Families in Conflict

The following guidelines can help a youth minister navigate the rough waters of family conflict and maximize the potential that counseling will be helpful:

- Adopt a family perspective in your counseling. Involving both parents and teenagers in counseling is critical.

- Look for the family's strengths. All families bring unique abilities to the art of communication, including humor, tact, or strong mutual caring. Find these strengths, and help the family use them in times of conflict.
- Maintain neutrality. A neutral third party can offer much assistance to parents and teenagers who are stuck in conflict. Avoid placing blame, and focus on the communication style as the problem, rather than a particular person.
- While often youth ministers feel an especially strong alliance with the students, it is important not to undermine parental authority.
- Help the family redefine the problem. For example, the pronouncement "Jonny has just become so rebellious" can be reframed in a more positive light as "Jonny is trying to be more independent." "Mom and Dad are such nags" can be redefined as "Your mom and dad care enough to want to really be involved in your life."
- Slow down family discussions, making sure that all family members get to present their views. Sometimes it can be helpful to ask the family to practice reflective listening. For example, you might say to a teenager, "Jonny, would you repeat back to your parents what you just heard them say about why curfew is so important to them—just to make sure you heard them right." Be sure that only one family member speaks at a time.

Helping Families Negotiate: The Art of "Contracting"

One technique for helping students and families work through specific issues involves the collaborative development of parent-teenager contracts related to specific issues. Behavioral contracting allows the family to clearly communicate values, expectations, and implications in a way that promotes collaborative problem solving. Youth leaders can facilitate family meetings where contracts are negotiated and agreed upon. The handout at the end of this chapter (pp. 117-118) can be used with parents and teenagers to help them negotiate conflict around a specific issue.

Guidelines for Negotiating Values Conflicts

One challenge for teenagers and parents involves differences in values. Often adolescents will test their developing values on their parents as a way of establishing a separate identity. Parents can clearly communicate their values while still remaining open to gaining a better understanding of their teenager's point of view. Encourage parents to be respectful of the values and beliefs of their teenager, even if they disagree. Encourage parents to make it their goal to truly understand their teenager's point of view, rather than convincing the teenager of their own. Other suggestions for parents include the following:

- Encourage parents to present their position on issues in a calm manner without lecturing. Teenagers do not respond well to absolutes or ultimatums—they will be much more interested in why the parents think the way they do.
- Help parents resist the temptation to use power (such as force, punishment, or threats) in conflict situations about values. Power tactics almost never work. The motivation to change values must be internal—that is, the teenager must want to change his or her views. Parents can help the most by giving the teenager an opportunity to think through and analyze his or her developing attitudes and values.

- Help parents think creatively about the many ways they can communicate important values to their children—through initiating family discussions of current issues, through allowing parental actions and behaviors to speak for themselves, and through making themselves available and open to questions from their children. Older teenagers can benefit from hearing about their parents' own journeys in the development of important values.

Parents and teenagers will not always agree on values. What is most important is that the channels of communication remain open. Focusing on the topic at hand, rather than focusing on the disagreement, can foster lively discussions where all family members feel free to share their opinions and views.

Handling Angry Teenagers and Parents

Few behaviors shut down communication and collaborative problem solving more quickly than angry words, gestures, or actions. Both parents and teenagers must commit to finding that balance between honest expressions of feelings and destructive expressions of anger. As a barrier to communication, anger can be employed in an attempt to have power or control over another; it is at times an expression of frustration or even desperation. Inappropriate expressions of anger can be prevented by helping teenagers and parents learn assertive communication to avoid aggressive confrontation. Helping each person communicate his or her position in a clear, calm, direct manner can allow productive discussions to occur.

First, the youth minister should assess the severity of the anger. Does the parents' anger place the student at risk for being verbally or physically abused? Might the student assault the parents? Asking families to describe in detail the times when conflict has escalated may help the youth minister assess this. Look for common anger triggers, and identify ways to avoid them. As always, when there is concern that the degree of anger places a family member at risk, a referral should be made to a licensed mental health professional or to a marriage and family therapist.

What about families who struggle with escalating anger that does not cross this line? These families should be encouraged to make safety their first priority in communication. When a family member feels that tempers are getting out of control, the family should be encouraged to take a "time out" from attempts to resolve the conflict (possibly with family members in separate rooms), and then agree on a time to continue the conversation. If the youth minister is present when this conflict occurs, he or she can meet briefly with the parents and the teenager separately and help them find more assertive and less provocative ways to express themselves. The family meeting can then continue.

When Families Are "Stuck"

When parents and teenagers are stuck in conflict, the following ideas may help to open the channels of communication and help the family move forward:

- Have the student express himself or herself through writing a letter to his or her parents. The teenager can work on the letter with the youth minister in a counseling session, and then read the letter to his or her parents. This allows the student to gather his or her thoughts and consider the most productive way to state his or her needs and feelings.
- For a family that's gridlocked in conflict, consider assigning a mentor family in the church. Ask the parents of the family in conflict to meet with the teenager of the mentor family, and ask the

parents of the mentor family to meet with the teenager of the conflicted family. This can help the family in conflict gain perspective and pick up practical ideas from the mentor family.

- Assign a gridlocked family the homework of planning and taking a fun family outing together where no problems or concerns can be discussed. This will help them begin to learn collaborative problem solving around a less emotionally charged issue while at the same time help build a foundation of positive emotional experiences together.

- Family rituals that allow family members to air conflicts and concerns as a part of every-day life can be helpful—such rituals might include family meetings, dinnertime conversations, or weekly check-ins with each child in the family. This can have the added benefit of preventing the buildup of conflict and resentments. For example, asking family members to talk during dinner about the best and worst parts of their day helps families build a tolerance for both positive and negative emotional experiences and conversations.

Adopting Christlike Attitudes in Family Communication

Scripture provides us with important principles for family communication. Parents and teenagers can be counseled to take on Christlike attitudes in their interactions with one another. In Philippians 2:1-11, Paul encourages believers to be of the same mind, united in spirit, intent on one purpose, not looking out solely for one's own interest, but for the interests of others. Most important, Paul reminds us of Christ's attitude of humility and service to us—and tells us that we should adopt this attitude in our interactions with others. Parents and teenagers can be encouraged to identify ways they fall short in their behavior and confess to one another. For example, this might mean that, at times, parents lay aside their authority in the family and truly listen to their teenager without defending themselves, allowing the teenager to have a say in family decisions. For teenagers, a Christlike attitude of humility may mean accepting their parents' decisions even when the decisions feel unfair or unreasonable. Families who strive to follow Philippians 2 in their interactions with each other may find their conflicts redeemed as opportunities to love and serve each other in the name of Christ.

Recommended Resources

Books

- *Angry Kids: Understanding and Managing the Emotions That Control Them,* Richard L. Berry. Grand Rapids, MI: Fleming H. Revell Co., 2001.

- *The Family: A Christian Perspective on the Contemporary Home,* Second Edition, Jack O. Balswick and Judith K. Balswick. Grand Rapids, MI: Baker Books, 1999.

- *Resolving Conflict,* Josh McDowell and Ed Stewart. Nashville, TN: W Publishing Group, 2000.

Web Resources

- www.family.org/pplace/youandteens (Web site of Focus on the Family)

---

[1]   See summary table in Froma Walsh, *Strengthening Family Resilience* (New York, NY: The Guilford Press, 1998), 107.

STUDENT PAGE Use the photocopiable handout on pages 117-118 to help families negotiate serious conflicts. Make a copy of the worksheet for each family member. Instruct families to work through the contract together at home or with your help during a counseling session.

Making a Family Contract

Families frequently face challenging decisions that require conversation, collaboration, and compromise. A family contract is a helpful tool for involving all family members in the decision-making process. This worksheet will walk your family through the steps needed to reach a solution together. All you'll need is a Bible, a copy of this worksheet for each family member, and a pen or pencil for each person. Find a quiet place with few distractions, and agree as a family to set aside an hour for this exercise. You might find it helpful to have a family friend or a youth minister help you go through this the first time.

Step 1: Read Philippians 2:1-11 as a family. Write down the Christlike attitudes identified in the verses. Make a commitment to each other to practice these attitudes during your discussion. Open your family meeting in prayer.

I will practice these Christlike attitudes:

Step 2: What do you think are the biggest areas of disagreement in your family (such as curfew, homework, or use of the family car)? List the areas of conflict, go over your lists together, then decide together which issue will be the focus of the family contract for this meeting.

Today we'll focus on this area:

Step 3: Take a minute to think about your feelings and concerns about this issue. What is it that you want? Why is this important to you? Write down your thoughts, and then take turns reading them to each other. Make sure that you understand everyone else's position on the subject, and that you have been able to clearly state your position.

My expectations are...

This is important to me because...

Step 4: If there are differences between family members on this issue, take a minute to brainstorm possible solutions and compromises that you personally are willing to make. Come up with at least three ideas. Read these solutions to each other. Just listen—don't comment on each other's ideas yet.

1.
2.
3.

Step 5: Talk together about the pros and cons of everyone's suggestions. As a family, decide which idea is the best compromise for everyone, and write down the expectations related this issue (for example, curfew times or homework expectations).

Step 6: What do you think are fair consequences for not following through on these responsibilities? Each person should list at least three ideas.
1.
2.
3.

Step 7: What do you think are fair rewards for following through on these responsibilities? Each person should list at least three ideas.
1.
2.
3.

Step 8: Take turns readings your lists. Decide together on one reward and one consequence. Write down your specific contract here.
Expectation:

Reward for following through:

Consequence for not following through:

Step 9: Set up a time to re-evaluate this contract. Two to four weeks is usually sufficient to see if the contract is working well. Agree to renegotiate the contract if necessary.
We will re-evaluate this contract on _____.

Step 10: All family members should sign the contracts. Keep one copy of it in a visible place such as on a family bulletin board or refrigerator door.

_____   _____
SIGNATURE   **SIGNATURE**

_____   _____
SIGNATURE   **DATE**

CHAPTER 16

Gender Questions—
Recognizing Sexual-Identity and Gender-Role Issues

JULIE A. ODELL, M.A.

THE BASICS

Tammy is an attractive high school freshman. Unfortunately, when she attends youth group functions, she wears provocative, revealing clothes and surrounds herself with male attention. Tammy appears to seek out and cling to males who are sexually suggestive in their behavior toward her. Both male and female youth leaders have noticed her inappropriate behavior, but they aren't sure how to bring up the subject with her.

It's possible that Tammy was sexually abused as a child and is now acting out her perceived role as a sex object. Or perhaps Tammy believes that her value as a female is directly related to her sexual appeal to members of the opposite sex; her self-esteem may be largely based on her physical appearance. Or maybe Tammy is simply starved for attention and has found an effective way of getting noticed. A concerned youth leader could approach Tammy and begin with a nonjudgmental statement, such as, "I've noticed that you spend a lot of time with the guys—are they good friends?" or "It seems like you're getting a lot of attention from the guys. What do you think about that?" If the door for discussion is open, the leader could try to develop a better understanding of the reasons behind Tammy's seductive behavior, and thus would be equipped to minister to her more effectively.

Steve is eighteen years old and has never been on a date with a girl. His mannerisms and behavior are perceived by many as effeminate, and he is often teased by the other teenagers in the youth group. Steve approaches a trusted male youth leader and confesses that he has had sexual dreams involving other males, and he is concerned that he may be homosexual. If the youth leader is uninformed about gender-identity issues, he or she may assume that Steve is definitely struggling with homosexuality. On the other hand, a knowledgeable leader could assure Steve that those types of dreams are normal and that it doesn't mean that Steve is destined to be homosexual. Hopefully, the leader could then begin a discussion with Steve, validating his unique masculine qualities and characteristics.

Peer and Media Influence

Tammy, Steve, and other teenagers all are attempting to discover who they are, what their role is in society, and what it means to be female or male. According to the stages of psychosocial development proposed by Erik Erikson, the major task of developing a stable identity takes place during adolescence, when teenagers struggle to overcome confusion concerning their social roles. In Erickson's words, "To keep themselves together, they temporarily overidentify, to the point of apparent complete loss of identity, with the heroes of cliques and crowds."[1]

As teenagers develop their social identity, they are often confronted with questions concerning their gender identity (which can be defined as their sense of being male or female) and their gender role (the behaviors, attitudes, and characteristics associated with each gender).[2] Masculine and feminine roles are largely defined by popular culture; sometimes they are consistent with Scripture, and sometimes not. The fact that most teenagers are bombarded with inappropriate and unrealistic media images of "ideal" teenage appearance and behavior further adds to the confusion. The role models that many teenagers identify with as they are searching for identity are often overly sexualized and illustrate extreme sex-role stereotypes: males are macho and muscular; and females are a paradox, both seductive and sexually submissive.

Adult Models

In addition to learning about gender roles through peer influence and the media, children also learn about these roles through adult modeling; they observe the significant men and women in their lives and develop ideas about appropriate ways for each gender to behave. Families tend to have rules surrounding gender roles—some are spoken, and others are unspoken but understood. For instance, many families have gender roles dealing with work and responsibilities: Dad may be responsible for the yardwork while Mom maintains the home; Dad may watch TV after work while Mom fixes dinner and cleans the kitchen. Families also have gender roles related to appearance: Dad may make negative comments about women who are overweight or men who are not tough; Mom may place an emphasis on looking presentable, which means having perfect hair and makeup every day. Children integrate all of these rules and stereotypes about men and women into their own developing concepts of gender roles and gender identity.

Changing Bodies

During the adolescent years, teenagers must attempt to incorporate all of these ideas into their rapidly changing identity as they figure out who they are as young men and women. Adolescence is a period of major growth and change, physically, emotionally, and cognitively. Some preteens seem to blossom overnight, and may become overwhelmed, confused, and self-conscious about the sudden and obvious changes in their appearance. Students who mature early in terms of physical development are often treated by peers and adults as if they were older, which further adds to their confusion. Many teenagers may still *feel* like children, yet they are expected to behave like adults because they have adult bodies. Youth leaders have the tasks of serving as a positive model for healthy gender-identity and gender-role development and providing a safe sounding board for students who are struggling with these issues.

WHEN TO REFER

If the student exhibits the following behaviors, a referral to a professional Christian counselor or psychologist is highly recommended:

- The student reports previous sexual abuse or sexual assault.
- The student is engaged in sexually promiscuous behavior and is putting himself or herself in high-risk situations.
- The student reports repeated sexual fantasies with members of the same sex, or is involved sexually with a same-sex partner.
- The student reports feelings of being trapped in the body of the wrong gender or expresses a desire to look like and dress like members of the opposite sex.
- The student is significantly distressed about his or her gender identity or appropriate gender role, and the situation is beyond the leader's comfort level.

COUNSELING IDEAS

Be Understanding

The most beneficial thing that youth leaders can do to help teenagers who are struggling with issues of gender identity or gender roles is to express understanding. Often students feel isolated because they don't realize that their experiences are normal. Males may be concerned about common experiences such as nocturnal ejaculations, a desire to masturbate, or sexual dreams involving other males. Females may be concerned about their rate of physical development, desires to appeal to the opposite sex, or sexual dreams involving other females. Therefore, a major task of youth leaders is to normalize the student's troublesome thoughts and feelings. This can be done by using simple statements such as, "I've heard that your experiences [thoughts, feelings] are fairly common" or "I remember feeling like that when I was your age."

Control Your Reactions

Another way to help students feel normal is to subdue your own emotional responses during the conversation, particularly concealing any reactions of shock or disapproval. For example, if Dave confesses to his youth leader that he is sexually attracted to another male, it's essential that the leader respond with a nonjudgmental statement. A response such as, "Well, why don't we talk about it," is likely to invite the student to continue the conversation. On the other hand, if the leader expresses disapproval or is judgmental and says, "Well, obviously that's not God's will. We had better pray for you," the student will probably clam up before a productive discussion can take place. Along the same lines, if Sandy shares that she was sexually molested as a child, a response of empathy and concern, rather than shock, will facilitate the discussion so that a referral to a Christian counselor or psychologist will be well-received. Anytime a student brings up a gender-identity issue that is beyond the youth leader's knowledge or comfort level, a referral to a mental health professional is recommended.

Body-Image Issues

The majority of teenagers struggle with body-image issues to some extent, which may be tied to their gender identity. Leaders can address this by emphasizing the importance of character and personality over appearance. As 1 Samuel 16:7b tells us, "The Lord does not look at the things man looks at. Man looks at the outward appearance, but the Lord looks at the heart." While this Scripture may not necessarily comfort a student in terms of his or her relationship with peers who are focused on the external, hopefully it will at least introduce a different perspective on body image. Students may be able to retrain their thought processes and stop negative or troublesome thoughts about body image.

Youth workers can teach students to recognize when they begin thinking negative thoughts such as "I wish I looked like her" or "My face is ugly." Once teenagers become more aware of their negative self-talk, they can stop the thoughts and replace them with positive thoughts such as, "I'm thankful that I'm able to use my strong legs" or "Thank you, Lord, for the body you've given me." This simple exercise will encourage students to focus on their body in terms of function rather than appearance.

Gender Identity

Teenagers may have general concerns about gender identity and wonder, "Am I masculine (or feminine) enough?" Of course, the answer to this question will depend to some extent on each student's concept and understanding of appropriate gender roles. It may be helpful for leaders to affirm the student's *value as a child of God*, perhaps reading Psalm 139:13-16 with the student. Youth leaders can also facilitate a study on men or women in the Bible or on the characteristics of Jesus himself. The goal is to help the student focus on God's perspective of masculinity and femininity, rather than on society's perspective. In doing this, some of the teenager's stereotypes may be challenged as he or she discovers that men and women often possess characteristics in common, such as strength, courage, sensitivity, leadership, submissiveness, boldness, and humility.

Students will benefit from having their own (and society's) stereotypes about masculinity and femininity lovingly challenged. All humans, both male and female, are created in God's image, and all possess similar characteristics. Regardless of their gender, their appearance, or their masculine and feminine characteristics, all teenagers need and deserve to have their individual value affirmed and celebrated.

Recommended Resources

Books

- *Someone Like Me: A Youth Devotional on Identity*, Annette LaPlaca. New York, NY: Random House, 2001.

- *So What Does God Have to Do With Who I Am?* Joey O'Connor. Grand Rapids, MI: Fleming H. Revell Co., 2001.

Web Resources

- www.freetobeme.com (Youth Web site of New Direction for Life Ministries)

---

[1]   Erik H. Erikson, *Childhood and Society* (New York, NY: W.W. Norton & Company, Inc., 1963), 262.

[2]   Carol Lynn Martin, "Gender Identity," in *Encyclopedia of Psychology*, Volume 3, edited by Alan E. Kazdin (Washington, DC: American Psychological Association; New York, NY: Oxford University Press, 2000), 444.

STUDENT PAGES Use the photocopiable worksheets on pages 123 and 124 to help teenagers process gender-identity issues. Use the "For Guys" student page with young men and the "For Girls" student page with young women. During a counseling session, invite the teenager to work through the questions on the appropriate student page, then discuss the responses together.

Gender-Identity Development

For Guys

Answer the following questions, and then discuss your responses with your youth leader.

Think of someone you look up to—it might be a male friend, an older sibling, or a male character in a TV show or movie. Make a list of the qualities that you admire in that person.

Think of your dad, or another adult male, and list the qualities that you admire in him. What makes him a "good" man—the kind of man you would like to be?

Which of these qualities do you already have? What other favorable qualities do you possess?

Identify one or two qualities or character traits that you would most like to develop in yourself, and ask your youth leader to hold you accountable in these areas.

Gender-Identity Development

For Girls

Answer the following questions, and then discuss your responses with your youth leader.

Think of someone you look up to—it might be a female friend, an older sibling, or a female character in a TV show or movie. Make a list of the qualities that you admire in that person.

Think of your mom, or another adult female, and list the qualities that you admire in her. What makes her a "good" woman—the kind of woman you would like to be?

Which of these qualities do you already have? What other favorable qualities do you possess?

Identify one or two qualities or character traits that you would most like to develop in yourself, and ask your youth leader to hold you accountable in these areas.

CHAPTER 17

Help for the Hurting—
Dealing With Grief and Loss

JULIE A. ODELL, M.A.

THE BASICS

Amanda is a social seventeen-year-old. Four weeks ago, her closest friend, Emily, committed suicide. Since Emily's death, Amanda's behavior has been inconsistent and unpredictable. At times, she vocalizes anger toward her deceased friend ("How could she do this to me? She's so selfish!") as well as confusion and anger toward God ("Why would God let this happen? He's supposed to be loving!"). At other times, Amanda appears to blame herself for her friend's suicide. She says that she should have been there—that she should have done something to help. During these latter conversations, Amanda appears sad and discouraged.

Greg, a junior high student, is Emily's younger brother. Since his sister's suicide he has withdrawn from his friends and has rejected offers to hang out with the youth leaders. When others visit him at home, Greg is quiet or tearful. He cries and says, "I can't believe Emily is gone." He recalls memories of their last day together, telling and retelling the story to anyone who will listen.

Although Amanda and Greg are both grieving the loss of a loved one, they are grieving differently. Amanda's reaction fluctuates between the various, somewhat predictable, stages of grief. Greg, on the other hand, appears to be stuck in the depression and sadness of grief, and therefore may need individual counseling to progress through the stages. The grief process consists of typical and predictable components; however, it is still unique to each situation and each individual.

Stages of Grief

The many stages of grief include shock or denial, anger, guilt, bargaining, anxiety, sadness or depression, and acceptance. Denial is a normal coping mechanism that protects the individual from experiencing a flood of intense emotions too quickly. If a student instantly realized and accepted the full reality of a loved one's death, with all of the ramifications, he or she would be overwhelmed. However, by accepting the loss in bits and pieces, the individual can deal with it slowly.

Once a student begins to *feel* his or her emotions, he or she will not progress through the stages of grief in a linear fashion, by completing one stage and moving to the next. Instead, a grieving person typically cycles through the stages, thus making it possible to experience anger one day (or even one hour) and sadness the next. It may be easier for family and friends to deal with the individual's sadness because it is the most acceptable and expected emotional reaction to loss. However, it is crucial that a person be allowed to experience and work through *each* of the stages and emotions.

Although anger is a normal and important part of the grief process, that emotion is sometimes discouraged by family and friends in an attempt to be positive or optimistic. A grieving teenager may feel anger toward the deceased, toward himself or herself (which often leads to feelings of guilt), toward medical staff, or even toward God. It may be helpful to interpret the person's anger as a feeling of helplessness over the situation.

The intensity and duration of grief will vary depending on factors such as the type of loss, an individual's coping skills, previous experiences, and the availability of resources and support people. Typically, teenagers may experience loss in the form of the death of a loved one, death of a pet, divorce of their parents (see Chapter 11), breakup of a romance, injury or illness (see Chapter 20), or even the loss of a goal or dream. However, the death of a family member or other loved one often invokes the most intense grief reaction.

Sudden or violent deaths tend to be the most difficult for survivors to deal with because they lack the opportunity to prepare for the death. Survivors often experience nightmares and flashbacks and may require professional counseling to successfully negotiate the grief process. Hearing the voice of the deceased loved one or seeing the person's image or face in a crowd is not unusual.

Survivor guilt is common, as survivors question whether *they* should have been the one to die. Like anger, guilt is another normal emotion that is often misunderstood and is therefore discouraged by friends and family of the bereaved. Students may feel guilty about things they did or didn't say, behaviors they did or failed to do, and even negative thoughts they may have had about the deceased loved one. When the survivor and the deceased person are close in age, it's also common for an individual to have fear or anxiety about personal safety and death in general.

Regardless of the circumstances surrounding the death, grief is a necessary and normal reaction to a loss. It may take up to two years to fully accept the death and to recall memories without feeling the intense pain of loss. Thankfully, the Bible shows us that Jesus also experienced loss, as he grieved the death of Lazarus and his betrayal by Judas. Bereaved students can find strength and comfort in Jesus. The most important thing that youth leaders can do is to pray for grieving students and pray for wisdom in ministering to them.

WHEN TO REFER

If a student exhibits the following behaviors, a referral to a professional Christian counselor or psychologist is recommended:

- The student is unwilling or unable to talk to anyone about his or her feelings about the death.
- The student's eating or sleeping patterns have significantly changed since the loss and are disrupting daily functioning.
- The student is using drugs, alcohol, food, or sex to cope with the loss.
- The student has withdrawn to the point of completely isolating himself or herself from friends and family.

- The student appears to be stuck in one of the grief stages, and the youth worker has exhausted his or her time and emotional resources in trying to help.

COUNSELING IDEAS

Building a Support System

Ministering to someone who has recently lost a loved one can be physically, emotionally, and spiritually draining. Developing a support system is critical. A youth leader can assist the student in identifying friends and family who are available for support. It may be possible to find a support group for the teenager to attend. If the student is unable to tap into other resources, the youth leader may need to actively include others in the ministry process by asking them to call or otherwise check in with the student. It is also helpful to talk with the parents to identify specific needs of the family or the student and to determine convenient times for phone calls or visits so that the family can maintain structure during the time of crisis.

Educating Students About Grief

During periods of acute grief, it's common for people to feel out of control because emotions fluctuate drastically. Youth leaders can normalize students' experiences and feelings by educating students about the grief process, typical reactions, and emotions. Hopefully teenagers will find relief in knowing that they are not crazy and that their feelings and experiences are part of the normal process of grieving. In addition, leaders can share their personal experiences of bereavement and their feelings about the present situation.

Grieving students will probably be forgetful and disorganized. Again, leaders can inform students that this behavior is both normal and expected. Youth workers can offer practical assistance by helping students write "to do" lists or encouraging them to keep track of assignments and obligations in a notebook.

Listening

The most beneficial thing that a youth leader can do for a grieving teenager is to be a good listener. The bereaved student will need, and therefore will seek out, a safe place to share feelings and thoughts. Being a good listener requires time and energy. Grieving individuals may want to talk about the deceased incessantly, often repeating stories and memories. Effective listening also requires that helpful advice remains unspoken until the student wants input and is ready for advice. Preaching about God's sovereignty or reminding teenagers that "things happen for the best" is *not* recommended and may be perceived as insensitive.

As a student shares difficult emotions such as anger, guilt, or sadness, it may cause the youth leader to feel awkward or uncomfortable. In addition, it may bring up previous feelings of loss in the youth worker. Either of these situations can lead the listener to discount the feelings of the student. For example, if a student comments that she is angry at a loved one for dying, and the leader responds with "Oh, you don't really mean that," or "But you know that she isn't really to blame," it doesn't give the grieving person permission to express his or her true feelings. If, on the other hand, the leader responds with a general statement that indicates he or she has heard and understood, such as "It sounds like you're really feeling angry right now, and that's OK," the student is more likely to feel free to talk openly.

Providing an environment in which a student can share true feelings requires trust that the information will be kept confidential. The grieving teenager will be more likely to open up if he or she is confident that the leader will not share with others the details of a conversation. However, if the student expresses a desire to hurt himself or herself, confidentiality must be broken. In this case, the student's parents should be notified, and steps should be taken, with the assistance of a mental health professional, to ensure the safety of the student. (For more information about dealing with students who have suicidal thoughts or feelings, see Chapter 25.)

Encouraging the Expression of Feelings

Leaders can facilitate the expression of students' feelings by asking open-ended questions about the deceased person, such as

- What's your favorite memory with [the deceased loved one]?
- Which object or activity most reminds you of him [her], and why?
- Which quality did you most appreciate about him [her], and why?
- What would you most like to tell him or her?

Writing in a journal is an effective way for a teenager to express and work through feelings individually. The youth leader can encourage the student to write in the journal before bed each night, to recap the events of the day and to identify the various emotions that the student experienced. A teenager can read his or her journal entries with a friend or support person, or he or she may decide to keep the journal private.

Similarly, the student can be encouraged to write a letter to the deceased person to share his or her thoughts and feelings. A letter of apology to address unresolved disagreements or feelings of guilt can be a powerful tool in the healing process. The bereaved individual can apologize for any hurtful words or actions or for missed opportunities to express love in the relationship. The student can write about feelings of guilt, then the youth leader can pray with the student for forgiveness and freedom from guilt. It may be therapeutic for the leader to actually write the word "Forgiven" across the letter in red ink, symbolizing forgiveness though the blood of Jesus.

Therapeutic Activities

The youth worker can also participate in therapeutic activities with the student. Asking the student to show and discuss pictures of the deceased is an easy and enjoyable way to facilitate the process of grieving. Other activities symbolize letting go, such as sending a toy boat down a river together or releasing balloons into the air. It may be helpful for the bereaved person to write a good-bye letter first and then attach the letter to the boat or balloons. The youth leader may wish to pray aloud or read a Scripture passage, such as Psalm 121, prior to releasing the symbolic item.

Students can express anger through safe physical activities such as punching a punching bag, screaming into a pillow, ripping up pieces of paper, or throwing small rocks into a lake. These and similar activities are helpful because they allow students to release physical energy and express frustration and anger in ways that do not cause harm to themselves, others, or valuable property. The youth leader can initiate these activities and even participate in them with the student.

In addition to activities that are specifically therapeutic, any physical activity is recommended because it can ease feelings of depression or help with insomnia. A grieving student would benefit greatly from an invitation to go on a hike or play sports. Regular exercise should be strongly encouraged.

Monitoring Progress

A weekly check-in is an easy way to connect with the grieving student. The youth leader can ask the student which emotion, or which stage of grief, the teenager primarily experienced during the week, and which emotions the student is dealing with that day. The youth leader should keep in mind, though, that the student may not want to talk about his or her feelings at the moment. Rather than forcing the issue, the leader can simply remind the teenager that he or she will be available to talk later if the student wishes.

If the youth leader does not see the student on a weekly basis, phone calls or visits will be necessary. However, simply telling a person to "call if you need something" is not effective because oftentimes a student will not take the initiative to do so. Remember that regular phone calls or visits are appreciated even weeks or months after the funeral, after most friends and acquaintances have stopped mentioning the loss.

Recommended Resources

Books

- *Don't Ask for the Dead Man's Golf Clubs: Advice for Friends When Someone Dies,* Lynn Kelly. Littleton, CO: Kelly Communications, 2000.

- *The Grieving Teen: A Guide for Teenagers and Their Friends,* Helen Fitzgerald. New York, NY: Simon & Schuster, 2000.

- *Part of Me Died, Too: Stories of Creative Survival Among Bereaved Children and Teenagers,* Virginia Lynn Fry. New York, NY: Dutton Children's Books, 1995.

- *When a Friend Dies: A Book for Teens About Grieving and Healing,* Marilyn E. Gootman. Minneapolis, MN: Free Spirit Publishing, 1994.

STUDENT PAGE Use the photocopiable worksheet on page 130 to help teenagers understand their feelings of grief after the death of a loved one. Use the student page in a counseling session by talking through each emotion with the teenager and perhaps watching one of the suggested movies together. You could also have a teenager work through the student page at home during the week, and then discuss it during a subsequent meeting.

Dealing With Grief

What You May Be Feeling...

Read through the following list of emotions, and think about how you've been experiencing them.

- **shock or disbelief**—I can't believe this happened.
- **anger**—I'm mad at [person's name] for dying; at God for allowing it to happen; at the doctors for not stopping it; or at myself.
- **guilt**—I wish I would have...; I wish I wouldn't have...; I should have been the one to die.
- **anxiety**—I'm afraid I might die; I'm concerned about my future.
- **confusion**—I feel overwhelmed; I just can't figure things out.
- **sadness**—I feel sad; I can't stop crying.
- **acceptance**—I think that things will be OK.

List any other feelings and emotions you are experiencing.

Suggested Activity

With a family member, friend, or your youth leader, watch a movie that talks about grief and loss, such as

- *Beaches*
- *Forrest Gump*
- *My Girl*
- *Patch Adams*

Identify which emotions the characters in the movie are experiencing, and discuss how the characters are dealing with their grief.

CHAPTER 18

Identity Development—
Answering the Question "Who Am I?"

SCOTT GIBSON, M.S.W., L.C.S.W.

THE BASICS

I remember the moment like it was yesterday. It was the morning after my high school graduation. I was lying awake in my bed and doing some serious thinking about my life. I looked back at the previous four years and started a list in my mind. On one side of this list were all the things that I liked about myself. On the other side were all the things that I wished were different. There were some good points in the first column, but they were outweighed in number and impact by the things in the second column. At that point, I made a decision that would influence the next few years of my life. I decided to become someone who wasn't those not-so-great things.

For the next several years, I put tremendous amounts of energy into creating a mask that I thought I would like better. During high school I had been on only a few dates. The mask I created was a person who had many dates each weekend. I had also been very quiet and uninvolved during high school. The mask I created ran for class treasurer as a freshman in college and won. Anytime I felt some of the things on the "don't like" column peeking through, I intentionally tried to be the opposite. For a while this seemed to work...or at least I thought so. But there came another moment when I looked closely at my life and realized something else: I didn't like this mask either. It felt as if no one knew the real me. It felt like my real self was very alone. At this point, I made another important decision. I decided that I needed help to work on understanding who I *really* was.

Creating a Sense of Self

One of the fundamental developmental tasks of adolescence is forming a personal identity—a sense of self. Our personal identity answers the question, "Who am I?" There are many aspects of a person's identity that change during the teenage years. During adolescence, a student's body is changing. Teenagers no longer see themselves as children, but as young men or women. During these years, teenagers' mental abilities are expanding. Prior to adolescence, children's thinking is dominated by a need to have concrete examples; their thinking is constrained to what is real and physical. During adolescence, however, individuals begin to recognize and understand abstractions. They are increasingly aware of their own selves and the standards and expectations of society.

At my youngest son's ninth birthday party, the other boys were all laughing and enjoying noticing their differences. One boy said, "I wear glasses and have a notch in my ear." Another boy commented, "My two fingers are shorter than anyone else's." A third child said, "I have freckles all over my body." These nine-year-olds enjoyed the reality of being themselves. It was my junior high-age son's reaction that interested me. He said, "Just wait until you get to junior high—you might not be laughing so much." My older son knew only too well that the rules about how people treat each other and how people think about themselves change as kids develop.

My sense of self gives me the ability to see me for who I am—it's an awareness that we are all very similar and yet very unique in our own ways. It allows me to appreciate you for being you and me for being me. John describes Jesus in John 1:14 as "full of grace and truth." Having both grace and truth about who I am allows me to accept myself as I am and also to understand that there are things within me that need work to continue to grow and develop.

The mistake I made as an older teenager was one that many students make. As teenagers evaluate who they are, they decide to allow others to squeeze them into a mold of how they should fit into this world. This is a tragedy for both the individual and our world. If God the creator uniquely created each one of us for a divine purpose, then we all benefit when we each are who we were meant to be.

In this chapter, we'll look at some ways for youth workers to help students in the process of discovering who they are. But as we focus on students, don't forget about yourself either! The greater sense of self that *you* have, the better able you will be to guide others in their journey.

WHEN TO REFER

Students exhibit many behaviors that scream out, "I don't know or like who I am!" It's important, however, to discern the difference between normal adolescent struggles and struggles that need professional intervention; different types of situations will require different levels of response. First are those situations in which you "hop on it ASAP." These situations require intervention *now*, and you will take action while the student is with you or immediately after he or she leaves. Second are situations in which you will encourage a student to go for professional help. Third are situations in which you will listen, encourage, and pray with the student; the teenager is probably just going through normal struggles and needs someone to talk to about it.

The following types of symptoms would require you to take action immediately:
- when a student talks about ending his or her life
- when a student is involved in regular drug or alcohol use
- when a student is involved in self-injurious behaviors (such as cutting)
- when a student is involved in abnormal eating behaviors such as bingeing and purging or starving himself or herself
- when a student is sexually promiscuous

In the following situations, you will want to strongly encourage a student to seek counseling:
- when a student struggles at school, with grades, or with friends

- when a student struggles with controlling his or her anger or with conflict at home
- when a student has intermittent drug or alcohol use
- when a student is sexually acting out

COUNSELING IDEAS

Recognizing the Lifelong Process

Struggling with personal identity is not something that's unique to adolescence. As you work with students, remember that all of us are in a continual growth process. Paul says it best in Philippians 1:6: "...he who began a good work in you will carry it on to completion until the day of Christ Jesus." Christians often take the Bible and the ideal of who we are becoming in Christ and try to fake being that *now*. But what Paul is saying is that each one of us is a *work in progress*. This truth helps me in understanding my role in helping others—it's ultimately God's job to bring about a person's growth, not mine. I don't have to figure out anybody except myself. This truth also gives me great hope in telling students that they can figure out who God made them to be.

When a person has a greater sense of self, that person can be more of who he or she is and, in turn, bring honor and glory to God. I know a man who once worked at a bank. He was good at the job, but after a while he realized that his job didn't fully express who he was. So after a lot of thought and prayer, he ventured out to pursue something he loved—he opened up a toy store. He encountered people who judged and criticized his bold move, but what motivated him to make the change was to express how God had wired him. Recently I visited the man's toy store. It was an amazing place where kids were playing and having fun. But the person who was having the *most* fun was this man who had followed his dream of being who he was. In the end, my friend felt more joy and pleasure in his walk with God, and others were blessed because he was free to live out his true identity. What an awesome privilege you have in helping students become who God made them to be!

The "Bus" Approach

When it comes to helping a teenager in his or her journey, I find that having a mental picture of what's going on inside is helpful. The picture I often use with a student (and with myself for that matter) is a bus with passengers in the seats. I tell the teenager to imagine himself or herself as a bus. The teenager is the driver, and all of the parts of himself or herself (personality traits, fears, interests, desires, and so on) are seated on the bus. The goal of this visualization is to help a student drive his or her bus, with Jesus' help, and recognize and value all of the parts. Teenagers with a strong sense of self are able to drive their buses and understand what all of the parts of themselves want and need.

Avoiding Burnout

The role you play in counseling is that of a fellow bus driver. You can't drive the student's bus—you have your own bus to drive. But your experience in dealing with some of your own "passengers" will help students in dealing with theirs. It's a common tendency for people in the helping professions to play a bigger role than they need to. Many of us have a part that wants to help out and rescue the world. I have seen many youth workers become burned out by allowing this part of themselves to drive their buses. Remind yourself often of Philippians

Identity Development

1:6, and remember that God will do this work with the students—you don't have to. You're just a fellow bus driver who has your own passengers to care for, but you can offer support to your students by helping them manage the passengers on their buses.

Who's Driving?

In helping a student manage his or her bus, the first parts of the student's personality that I try to address are the parts that have been doing the driving. These dominant traits learn to read the cues of society and the family and help the teenager fit in. One student I worked with had an outstanding reputation at his school and church. He was involved in many healthy activities and had a good sense of what he wanted to do in life. But the way this student lived out his "plan" was to shame any of the parts of his personality that he feared would not be accepted by others. He put these parts of himself in the back of the bus and hoped they would go away. But remember what usually happens in the back of a school bus? The parts that he shamed ended up acting out. After his girlfriend got pregnant and his grades went down, he got the wake-up call and decided to deal with what was going on inside of him.

The first thing to acknowledge was that the part that was currently driving was trying to help him. That part wanted to go in some positive directions, but it was doing so by trying to get rid of some of the other parts of who he was. At one point, I asked the student to imagine what would happen if Jesus was riding on his bus. Together we decided that Jesus wouldn't come on the bus and start throwing passengers off, but would instead be with each one of them and help them with what they might be going through.

We don't develop a strong sense of self by getting rid of parts of who we are. This is a common tendency in our culture, but Paul challenges us in Romans 12:2 and says, "Do not conform any longer to the pattern of this world." The driving parts that try to rid us of "unacceptable" parts are doing so in hopes of making us loved and accepted by others in this world. One young woman I worked with pleaded with her mother to let her get plastic surgery to change some of the aspects of her face that she didn't like. Adolescents are still in the transition from thinking concretely to thinking abstractly, so an abstract idea such as being loved can attach itself to a concrete idea such as getting plastic surgery. My work with this student focused on helping her work with the "bus driver" in her personality that wanted to get rid of some of her physical attributes and helping her understand different ways to feel loved.

Other students have personality traits that are unwelcome and unloved by them. One teenager I worked with didn't like how shy he felt around people. He constantly received negative messages from family and friends about how quiet he was. What he heard from these interactions (though no one ever *said* it) was that others didn't like who he was. So he worked really hard at being more outgoing, but he would panic, feeling that people might see the quiet part of him and wouldn't like it. I worked with the teenager and with his family at learning to affirm him for the times he chose to be quiet. He was a great listener, and people loved to tell him all types of stories. This young man began to understand what the quiet part could do for him; that part helped him be a great friend and be there for people. Once he started liking the quiet part of himself, he brought it up from the back of the bus and started to feel more comfortable around people.

Involving Students in Service

One powerful tool that works in helping adolescents find out who they are is involvement in service projects. A key element in discovering one's identity is going out in the world and trying new experiences. I've led numerous service adventures with students, and I always conduct a group debriefing afterward. Asking students these three questions usually generates a lot of discussion:

- What part of the project *didn't* you like?
- What part of the project do you feel like you did a good job at? Why do you think that particular job gave you joy and confidence compared to the part that you didn't like?
- What did you observe in each other throughout the day? What roles did each person play? How did you see others serve?

Using Scripture With Students

Finally, you can help students understand what the Bible says about who they are and how God sees them. In Psalm 139, David says that God knit us together in our mothers' wombs and knows our inmost being. God's response to us is not one of shame or repulsion, so why should ours be? Share this and other Scripture passages with students to help them see themselves through God's eyes.

Recommended Resources

Books

- *Helping the Struggling Adolescent: A Guide to Thirty-Six Common Problems for Counselors, Pastors, and Youth Workers,* Les Parrott III. Grand Rapids, MI: Zondervan Publishing House, 1993, 2000.

- *Internal Family Systems Therapy,* Richard C. Schwartz. New York, NY: The Guilford Press, 1995.

- *Reviving Ophelia: Saving the Selves of Adolescent Girls,* Mary Pipher. New York, NY: Ballantine Books, 1995.

- *The Search for Significance,* Robert S. McGee. Nashville, TN: W Publishing Group, 1998.

- *See Yourself As God Sees You,* Josh McDowell. Wheaton, IL: Tyndale House Publishers, 1999.

STUDENT PAGE Use the photocopiable worksheet on page 136 to help teenagers work through their identity development. Use this student page during a counseling session by inviting the teenager to work on it independently, then discussing it with him or her. Or have the teenager work on it at home, and then, at your next meeting, invite the student to share what he or she drew and wrote.

Identity Development

Who Is on My Bus?

Take your Bible, a pen, and this sheet to a quiet spot.

Read Psalm 139:13-16.

What are some of the parts of your "inmost being" that you like?

Imagine yourself as a school bus. You are the driver, and the passengers in the seats on your bus are the many different aspects of who you are. There might be parts that excel at certain things and other parts that struggle to get by. There may be physical traits, mental talents, fears, or feelings of inadequacy. In the bus below, put in some of the parts you know about. Think about where the parts would sit—do they sit in the front of the bus near the driver, or are they pushed to the back of the bus? What parts sit close to other parts, and what parts sit far away from other parts?

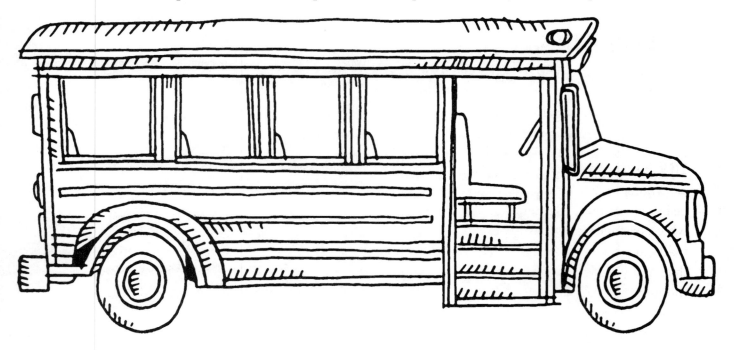

Put a heart by the parts you like and an X by the ones you're not so fond of. Then pick one of the parts with an X by it.

What do you dislike about having that part on your bus?

What might be good about having that part on the bus?

When you've finished, discuss your drawing with your youth worker or a close friend.

CHAPTER 19

Interpersonal Communication—
More Than Just Enunciation

TREVOR SIMPSON, M.A.

THE BASICS

Watching preteens and teenagers try to communicate what they're thinking and feeling can be both hilarious and tragic. The ability to communicate is one of the many important areas in which teenagers are weirdly developing. Many teenagers are emotionally, physically, intellectually, and socially disabled due to hormones, growth spurts, and social pressures. But on top of that, many students have not been adequately equipped and empowered to communicate their thoughts and feelings. Some teenagers wear all of their thoughts and feelings on their sleeves; some students seem fine and then explode; and others create impenetrable walls thicker than phone books—they'll never make their thoughts and feelings known to anyone.

Here's a familiar scenario. As you know, it's not uncommon for guys and girls to flirt in youth ministry settings. Two students start to hang out together and eventually start to date each other. Soon she has a promise ring on her finger and he pledges his undying love. The two spend hours talking on the phone at night; and during the day, they spend every minute together. Friends, family, and youth workers may not see these two for weeks. Then, suddenly, tragedy strikes and they split up. As the youth worker, you find that this disrupted relationship is creating ever-expanding social allegiances as students take sides within the youth group. It is painfully clear to you that this couple is trying to resolve the situation through manipulation, power plays, and terrible communication skills. It may be time for you to step in.

As young people grow from children into adults, there are many things that youth workers can do to help them develop interpersonal skills and problem-solving skills.

WHEN TO REFER

When trying to determine when to refer based strictly on communication skills or communication barriers, consider the following questions. If the answer to many of these questions is yes, a student may have more difficulties than just poor communication skills. Poor interpersonal skills may be a symptom of other, more significant issues.

- Does the student manipulate situations by using aggressive language, posture, and tone when sharing thoughts and feelings?
- Does the teenager shut down, walk away, or end conversations without offering opportunities for closure?
- Does the student threaten or hint at hurting himself or herself in order to communicate anger, betrayal, sadness, or other emotions?
- Does the student physically abuse himself or herself in any way?
- Is the teenager engaging in activities that are potentially harmful (such as partying, raving, or abusing drugs and alcohol)?
- Does the student seem genuinely depressed or frequently angry?

COUNSELING IDEAS

Here are several ideas to start with when trying to help your students communicate more effectively.

Offer Parents Help and Support

Look for families within your church body that have healthy and dynamic relationships. If families are willing, invite them to co-sponsor a support group for parents of teens. These groups are helpful because parents can see that there are others who share the same joys and frustrations; they can share experiences and suggestions for effective parenting skills; and parents will learn from other parents who communicate well with each other and with their children.

Hold Off Giving Advice

Most youth workers could easily be pegged as problem solvers. Youth workers deal with problems all the time, and it's very easy for youth workers to slip into the "Give me the facts, take this prescription, and call me in the morning" approach. Unfortunately, this alienates the student who came to the youth worker for help. Instead, be slow to give advice. Prematurely giving advice cuts off the opportunity for communication and does not allow the student to experience the process of working through an issue. The best way to avoid this is to not give advice until you are asked. Or when the time is right, ask the student for permission to give advice, then speak accordingly.

Model Appropriate Problem-Solving Techniques

When you're experiencing heavy emotions, share them in a way that's a blessing to those around you. When you're frustrated or angry with a student, confront the person appropriately and in private. When you're sad, share those feelings with your students when the time is right. When you disagree with a student, enter into a conversation that is honoring and respectful, despite your disagreement. Positive interactions become contagious. Students will realize that speaking with you and relating with you, even during conflict, is something they cherish.

Understand and Articulate the Importance of Body Language

Humans are very expressive and relational. Much of what we communicate is nonverbal. When we communicate with another person, especially during intense moments, it's important that our nonverbal communication allows the other person to feel free to be honest and express his or her feelings. The acronym SOLER, coined by Gerard Egan,[1] can help you remember these steps that facilitate positive nonverbal communication:

- **S**it squarely facing the other person.
- **O**pen your posture. Relax your arms, and let your posture communicate that you're open to what the student has to say.
- **L**ean slightly forward, but don't be intrusive.
- **E**ye contact should be maintained, without staring.
- **R**elax—and a relaxed tone will follow.

Express the Importance of Feelings

It may sound like warm and fuzzy psychobabble, but acknowledging our feelings as valid and real is imperative to our self-identity. If students believe that what they think and feel is invalid, they'll grow to believe that they're personally invalid. They will think that their thoughts, opinions, and feelings do not matter and have no bearing on the people or environment around them. This is destructive because we are created to be relational, and self-expression is one of the primary ways we relate to others. Feelings are things that other people can never debate. If you feel sad or happy, the world has to make a choice to deal with you as sad or happy.

Teenagers need to be able to experience their feelings as important and valid. As you work with teenagers, take the risk of sounding like a corny therapist. Instruct your students to use "I feel _____ because _____" statements whenever possible, but especially during intense dialogues. After a while, your students won't even realize that they're using this technique.

Model Active Listening

Active listening is not nodding your head every five seconds and saying, "Uh-huh. I see." Active listening is a skill that is essential in youth ministry. It engages the student, and it decreases the likelihood that you'll give unsolicited advice. Active listening is a ministry of presence. When youth workers are good at active listening, students will experience God with virtually every interaction because they'll know that you have honored, heard, and understood them—though not necessarily agreed with them. Active listening means slowing down your inner speech (so that you're not thinking of your response before the student even has a chance to finish a comment) and helping the student in clarifying his or her point. Active listening includes paraphrasing what you've heard the student say and giving the teenager a chance to agree or disagree with, or tweak, what you've repeated back to him or her. A common formula in using this technique is to begin with, "So what I hear you saying is..." and then add different and more descriptive words to enhance understanding. Here are some examples:

Example 1
Student: "I'm thinking about going to another youth group because this one is too boring."

Interpersonal Communication

Youth worker: "What I hear you saying is that you want to see more activity in some of the things we do. What are some things that you and your friends might like to see here?"

Example 2

Student: "I just feel like a loser when I come here. Everybody wishes I wasn't around."

Youth worker: "It sounds like you really don't like yourself right now because you're feeling rejected. What part of you do you think people don't like?"

Example 3

Student: (tearfully) "I know I'm not supposed to be thinking about hurting myself, but I just can't take this pressure anymore."

Youth worker: "It sounds like the pressure you're feeling right now is unbearable and you feel like you're running out of options."

Deal With Thoughts and Feelings As They Arise

Society often teaches us to let stuff roll off our backs and pretend that negative things never happen. This may be OK sometimes, but eventually all of us need to share our thoughts and feelings. Many of us don't express our feelings, though, because such sharing isn't an accepted norm.

Model and encourage your students to confront you and one another in private, one-on-one, when they are experiencing strong emotions. For example, if a student is talking while the youth leader is trying to speak, the youth leader may jokingly single out the student and tell him or her to shut up. Despite the need to stop the disrespectful actions of the student, the youth leader may have been out of line in singling out the student in an irritated and abrasive way. The student is left feeling damaged and like a loser. He or she may not want to come back and hear about Jesus from that youth ministry again. A thoughtful and aware youth leader would go to the student immediately after the lesson and apologize; the leader would ask the student to share his or her thoughts and feelings and give feedback to the youth worker. A dialogue between the student and youth leader can validate the student's feelings of isolation and embarrassment and clear up the initial disrespect the student showed to the youth leader.

Recommended Resources

Books

- *Controversial Discussion Starters*, Stephen Parolini. Loveland, CO: Group Publishing, Inc., 1992.

- *A Lasting Promise: A Christian Guide to Fighting for Your Marriage*, Scott Stanley, Daniel Trathen, Savanna McCain, and Milt Bryan. San Francisco, CA: Jossey-Bass Publishers, 1998, pp. 59-68.

- *The Skilled Helper: A Problem-Management Approach to Helping*, Fifth Edition, Gerard Egan. Pacific Grove, CA: Brooks/Cole Publishing Company, 1994.

Intentionally Practice Communication Skills in Ministry Settings

Although this may seem difficult and formulaic, make yourself and your students practice communication skills intentionally during appropriate forums. Initially, it will be a distraction, but in time it will become more natural and automatic. For example, small-group meetings, leadership-training meetings, and classroom interactions may be the best times to implement these skills. As you are facilitating conversation, frequently paraphrase what you hear students say. More important, give students the opportunity to paraphrase what they hear you say. Use "I feel" statements, and guide the students in articulating their thoughts and feelings in a way that allows them to own those thoughts and feelings proudly and without embarrassment.

Imitate Christ's Humility

Philippians 2 encourages us to show tenderness, compassion, and love by being like-minded and being one in spirit and purpose. When we consider others better than ourselves and focus on the interests of others, we cannot help but improve on our own interpersonal skills. In turn, our students will learn to model effective communication and positive problem-solving skills.

---

[1] Gerard Egan, *The Skilled Helper: A Problem-Management Approach to Helping,* Fifth Edition (Pacific Grove, CA: Brooks/Cole Publishing Company, 1994), 91-92.

STUDENT PAGE Use the photocopiable worksheet on page 142 to help teenagers practice communicating their thoughts and feelings. Let the teenager complete the student page at home, and at your next meeting, invite the student to share what he or she wrote.

Interpersonal Communication

Express Yourself

Sharing your thoughts and feelings with other people is important because people are relational and important to one another. Letting people into our lives is a gift we can give one another. Complete the following sentences and plan to share your answers with a person you really trust. Don't think of the most appropriate response. Just complete the sentence with whatever comes to mind.

1. I'm most happy with myself when I...

2. I'm disgusted with myself when I...

3. I get most excited when...

4. I feel lonely when...

5. I get angry when...

6. I'm at peace when...

7. I'm afraid of...

8. I don't understand why I...

9. I feel like I need the most help with...

10. When I'm in a large group, I feel...

11. When I'm alone, I feel...

12. I feel safest when...

CHAPTER 20

Courage for Tomorrow—
Facing Disease, Illness, or Handicap

KYLE D. PONTIUS, Ph.D.

THE BASICS

This chapter deals with a very broad topic that can describe a diverse group of students. However, students who are living with disease, illness, or handicap do share similarities with one another that are not experienced by those without such conditions. For example, diseases such as diabetes, HIV infection, and hepatitis require special care in order for the affected student to stay healthy. Chronic illnesses, including AIDS and cancer, require active treatment to control and hopefully bring the illness into remission. Handicapping conditions, such as autism, cerebral palsy, and quadriplegias (paralysis), require support and accommodations that can set affected students apart from their peers.

Throughout this chapter, I will be describing students with chronic diseases, illnesses, or handicaps as being affected by disabilities. Knowledge of disabilities in general is useful for those who are approached to counsel affected students, or those who interact with these students. The discussion in this chapter will be limited to conditions that are chronic and involve moderate to severe impairments. Therefore, this chapter doesn't include injuries such as broken limbs that will soon heal or conditions such as nearsightedness that can be easily corrected with glasses or contacts.

The Disability Experience

For people affected by disabilities, there is a common "disability experience" that they share. It emerges from having to cope with life in a unique way—one that is foreign to those without the limitations imposed by a disability. Among those with disabilities, an "us" versus "them" awareness develops, along with a unique language that's used to communicate the disability experience to those on the outside. The word "normal" is generally avoided. Distinguishing a person with a disability from a "normal" person necessarily implies that the affected person is "abnormal." To avoid this terminology and to affirm the worth of each person, the autism community, for example, characterizes people who are not affected by autism as "neurotypical." Other diagnostically related communities have their own unique ways of distinguishing themselves from others that encourage a positive image of those affected.

Conditions You Can See

People who have visible disabilities feel the disability experience in a very direct way. A student who uses a wheelchair or who has distinctive physical characteristics is initially identified by the outside world by the disability. This creates a barrier between the affected student and others, making it difficult for him or her to be known simply as a person. People with little knowledge of the disabling condition may tend to keep their distance. Youth programs that don't consider their impact on students with disabilities will necessarily come across as unwelcoming to them. Approaching a student with a disability as a *person* first is necessary in establishing a relationship.

Conditions You Can't See

There are some conditions, particularly developmental disabilities, that present other problems. Teenagers with these conditions will initially appear to be like other students. Without the presence of obvious cues, such as a wheelchair, the limitations inherent with "unseen" disabilities are at times ignored or remain unknown because they are not articulated. Affected teenagers often end up being mistreated as a result. These students become victims of the assumption that if a person looks "normal," he or she should act "normal." When what's considered to be normal behavior doesn't happen, the affected student may be labeled as stupid, lazy, uncooperative, or worse, depending on the situation.

Making Your Ministry Accessible

There are a number of other issues involved when dealing with students who are affected by disabilities. A basic consideration involves the ability of affected students simply to *get* to the youth group. Accessibility laws apply to all buildings for public use. Unless the facility that's used by the youth group was built before the laws concerning wheelchair ramps, accessible restroom facilities, and other considerations were put into effect, these physical accessibility issues shouldn't be a problem. However, if the facilities are old or there are a significant number of activities that take place in homes, physical accessibility may be a problem that should be considered.

Some disabilities involve motor development or language problems that need to be considered when programming activities. For example, Bible drills are *not* friendly toward many students who have problems in these areas. Though they are designed to improve students' knowledge of the Bible, Bible drills also require good fine-motor skills to flip pages and gross-motor skills to stand up as soon as the verse is found. Skills in receptive and expressive language are needed to understand the verbal instructions being given and to read the Bible verse aloud. Success in Bible drills doesn't depend solely upon Bible knowledge, and students with difficulties in any of the areas mentioned above would necessarily be at a disadvantage in such a contest. Take a look at some of the games and other activities in your youth ministry. Do any of those activities present barriers to participation? How can your ministry become more accessible to students with physical or mental limitations?

Providing Structure

The need for structure and predictability is felt by many students who are affected by disabilities. This need can be experienced on two levels. First, some students (or their parents) must make extensive plans ahead of time in order to ensure that the students' needs will be taken care of. For these students, spontaneous trips to the beach or to the mountains are out of the question because of the need to make arrangements for transportation, medication, or diet. If your group typically plans activities at the last minute, students who rely on advance notice may not be able to participate.

Second, some students with disabilities experience a significant amount of anxiety when they don't know what to expect in a given situation. A lack of advance notice or lack of structure could be so upsetting to them that their participation in group activities would necessarily be limited. Generally, students affected in this way would be those with developmental or mental disabilities or those whose physical condition is particularly sensitive to stress.

Working With Parents

One aspect of working with affected students is working with their parents. The parents have a lot invested in their children and are frequently much more involved in their children's lives than parents whose children are not affected by disabilities. Most parents are familiar enough with their child's disability to know what is best for their child; stay in close contact with the parents, and view them as a resource to help you understand their child's needs.

Also be sensitive to the fact that families in which a child has a disability may have other problems (such as conflict, misunderstandings, and so on) because of the stress in their lives. In this respect, it's important to remember that the parents of an affected child have many of the same needs as other parents of teenagers.

Overcoming Social Stigmas

There are certain social stigmas that may need to be dealt with on a group level. Autism, mental retardation, and many mental disabilities carry popular myths with them that should be dispelled. Diseases such as hepatitis or HIV infection may elicit moral judgments that can interfere with the full inclusion of affected students. Youth leaders should be aware of the level of knowledge of the group, parents, and others in the church; and they should help provide the information and other resources necessary to ensure that students with disabilities have the opportunity to learn about God, to worship him, to fellowship with other believers, and to be involved in ministry.

People First

The key point for youth leaders to keep in mind is this: Treat students with disabilities as people first. Recognize the inherent problems associated with the disabilities represented in the youth group, and provide accommodations within the youth program so that all students feel welcome to participate.

WHEN TO REFER

Most students who are affected by disabling conditions will come into the youth program knowledgeable about their disabilities. They may also come armed with a treatment team that

Physical Handicap or Disease

includes a counselor for themselves as well as a family therapist. Situations may arise, however, that would make it appropriate to refer the student to a competent Christian professional.

Keeping in mind that a student with a disability is as much a person as anyone else, it is reasonable to expect that he or she may become depressed or anxious or need help in dealing with issues that any teenager might be confronted with. In addition to the challenges of being an adolescent, a student with a disability may experience some problems just because of the disability. For example, there may be increased life stress involved in dealing with the limitations of a disability or in handling the demands made on a student's time or other resources.

It's important to check out anything that seems unusual or problematic in the behavior of the student or in the family situation. In some cases, the issues are already known and are being dealt with in an existing counseling relationship. If not, briefly discussing the problems and offering an appropriate referral can be the best action. A referral is appropriate in the following situations:

- when a referral is requested by the student or parents
- when a student threatens to harm himself or herself or someone else
- when substance abuse is known or suspected
- when a student exhibits emotional or behavioral changes (such as moodiness, anger, or agitation), perhaps due to changes in health status or at the introduction of a new treatment
- when social or interpersonal interactions or issues become a problem

For many affected students, it may be important to refer them to a counselor or psychologist who has experience in dealing with the specific disability. This is particularly true when the issues involved are specifically related to the disabling condition.

COUNSELING IDEAS

Many of the ideas discussed in other chapters are very appropriate when working with students who are affected by disabilities. Many counseling situations will center on issues that are not primarily related to the disability; even situations that do center around the effects of a student's disability require general counseling skills along with specific knowledge of dealing with the emotional or relationship problems that might be associated with the disability.

Recognize the Unique Culture

Beyond the basics, there are a few things to keep in mind when you're counseling a student who is affected by a disability. First, know the unique culture of the disability. The affected student lives as a minority in our society. In counseling a member of any group that's different from your own, the difference in life experience is a potential barrier to any help that could be offered. This is true whether you are counseling a student who is affected by a disability or a student from an ethnic group or culture that's different from your own.

One effective way to challenge this barrier is to ask the affected student about his or her disability. It's likely that the student won't be embarrassed—the teenager knows he or she has a disability—and, in fact, you may find that the teenager is delighted that you care enough to want to learn more. Asking questions does two important things: First, it informs you. Second, and perhaps more important, it empowers the student. Being in a position to teach someone about his or her disability puts the student in the role of the expert, and it can be a real boost to his or her self-esteem.

Look at Relationships

It's important to consider the various relationships that the student is involved in, as well the particular issue being discussed. This is true for all counseling situations, and it's especially important when you are dealing with a student who may be dependent on a number of people (family members and others). These various relationships can at times become an issue themselves. Because of this, it's particularly important to be able to make a connection with the student without forming an alliance with him or her against others in the student's life. Complaints about doctors, therapists, parents, and others can easily be used by a student as a way to align a helpful listener with the student against others. Keeping firm but loving boundaries is important to prevent this from happening. Reflecting feeling statements back to the student is one practical way to handle situations in which there may be pressure to take sides. For example, saying, "You must feel very angry after being treated that way" is much preferred to making a comment such as, "That doctor really violated your trust when he did that."

Take Action

Counseling an affected student imposes additional responsibilities on the youth leader, though these responsibilities may not be obvious. When a youth leader is counseling an affected student, he or she then becomes responsible for making changes within the youth program to accommodate the student's needs. For instance, if a student with a disability says that he or she feels isolated and ignored within the youth group, the leader needs to consider what changes should be made in order to better include students with disabilities in youth activities and in the overall program. It doesn't work to provide a safe environment for the student to vent his or her feelings if you are unwilling to be an advocate for the student in areas that you can influence. However, you should keep in mind issues of confidentiality in these situations. It's also important to consider that if the student perceives you as someone with the power to make changes, and those changes aren't made, legitimate feelings of betrayal could be added to the other issues involved.

Symptoms and Day-to-Day Functioning

There is generally a twofold focus in terms of goals when counseling people who are affected by a disability. The initial focus will be on decreasing the current symptom—such as helping the student feel less depressed, less anxious, less angry, or better able to cope with change. The other focus involves increasing the student's day-to-day functioning in some way. A youth leader who is counseling an affected student will most likely focus on the first goal; however, he or she can also help in the second area, particularly when there are specific functional goals the student is working on with another professional. For instance, many students with developmental disorders participate in social skills training. By being aware of the curriculum that's being used by the student's therapist, the youth leader can create social situations in the youth group where the student can practice learned skills.

See the Whole Person

Viewing teenagers with disabilities, or anyone for that matter, as having physical, psychological, social, and spiritual needs is important in any helping or educational activity. The hurts felt by students with disabilities are felt on all of those levels, even if only one component seems

Physical Handicap or Disease

obvious. Being aware of how the student might be affected on each of those levels helps assure that the *whole* person is being considered. For example, a teenager with cancer is affected by disease on a biological level. He has specific emotional responses to the disease that may or may not be helpful to him. His interpersonal relationships are changed because of the cancer, and his relationship with God is challenged in some way. Each of these areas is related to the others but is distinct as well. The youth leader may be best equipped to deal with spiritual needs, yet he or she must be aware of the student as a whole person.

Recommended Resources

Books

- *Health Psychology: Integrating Mind and Body,* George D. Bishop. Boston, MA: Allyn and Bacon, 1994.

- *Human Disability and the Service of God: Reassessing Religious Practice,* Nancy L. Eiesland and Don E. Saliers, editors. Nashville, TN: Abingdon Press, 1998.

- *No Disabled Souls: How to Welcome People With Disabilities Into Your Life and Church,* Jim Pierson. Cincinnati, OH: Standard Publishing, 1998.

- *Unexpected Guests at God's Banquet: Welcoming People With Disabilities into the Church,* Brett Webb-Mitchell. New York, NY: The Crossroad Publishing Company, 1994.

- *What Psychotherapists Should Know About Disability,* Rhoda Olkin. New York, NY: The Guilford Press, 1999.

Using Scripture to Encourage

Because of the diversity of issues involved in working students who are affected by disabilities, Scriptures on a number of different subjects can be appropriate. Passages dealing with one's concept of God and how God works his plan through his people may be particularly useful. The following verses are good starting points for working with students who might be wrestling with their concept of God, looking to him for comfort, or needing encouragement to keep going.

- Psalms 41; 46; 62; and 121
- Romans 8:28
- 2 Corinthians 12:7-10
- Philippians 3:12-14
- Hebrews 10:19-25

STUDENT PAGE Use the photocopiable worksheet on page 149 to help teenagers process their feelings regarding physical challenges or diseases. Allow the teenager to work on the student page independently, then discuss the exercise with the student during a subsequent meeting.

Facing Pain

At times we're faced with mental, emotional, or physical experiences that are hard to deal with. It may be a relatively short-term problem, such as a time of depression. Or it may be a long-term issue, such as a chronic illness or physical disability. Sometimes it's best to just directly confront the issue that's causing the pain. Use this activity to help you face the pain in your life. Write in a journal or notebook, or simply write on the back of this page.

Begin by using your imagination. Focus on the part of yourself that's the source of your pain, and give it a personality. Imagine that you can have a conversation with it. Start your journal entry by taking on the personality of the pain, and have it address you. Begin with the sentence, "Hello [your name], I am your [pain or problem] and I..."

When you've spent some time writing from the perspective of your pain, switch roles. Be yourself and address your pain. Confront your pain on the issues that concern you. When you've finished, you may be done with the exercise, or it may help to switch roles again. When you're completely finished, write about the experience you just had, including any insights you may have discovered and how you feel after having done the exercise.

CHAPTER 21

Sexual Addiction—
Differentiating Between Curiosity and Obsession

SCOTT GIBSON, M.S.W., L.C.S.W.

THE BASICS

It seemed to be one of those kinds of counseling sessions that I have far too often with teenagers. Rick seemed to be talking a lot about nothing. Sure, he was entertaining and interesting, but inside I kept asking myself, "Why is he here?" Rick was struggling with grades, had some problems with his family, and was fighting with his girlfriend. But for the most part, Rick seemed like a normal seventeen-year-old. So I asked him the question, "What *aren't* you talking about?" I expressed to him my observation that he was talking about some important things, but it seemed to me that there might be other issues that were causing him greater concern. After some more discussion, he said, "Well, I guess I'm really here because I think I'm addicted to sex. I can't go without it. I'm concerned that it's going to ruin my life if I don't figure out what to do about it."

Rick, like many other teenagers, struggled with his newfound sexuality and exploration of sexual behaviors. Many students may not feel that they're addicted, but Rick's struggle with his strong urge to have sexual relations with others is a common experience for many teenagers.

The problem of students struggling with their sexual behaviors is made worse by our culture's mixed messages. Students who are taught abstinence-based sex education at home and at church are bombarded by the media's message that they should express and explore their sexuality to their hearts' content. Easy access to pornography on the Internet and blatant sexual references in music and on television cause many students to struggle with this new biological urge to connect and reproduce. Furthermore, while the secular world may have come a long way, there is still a lot of shame in Christian circles when it comes to discussions about sex. Sex is a subject that many students never talk about with the people who know and love them. And through working with many youth pastors over the years, I've concluded that many youth leaders, too, aren't doing well at dealing with this internal force that God has placed in each one of us.

Young men and women today are looking for examples of godly people who celebrate and enjoy the sexuality that God gave them within the boundaries he provided, without using shame in order to control their sexuality. Most of the teenagers that I've worked with who have sexual concerns are trying to shame the very thing that God created as a good gift. Helping students learn not to attach shame or guilt to their sexuality is important.

The church has also done damage to teenagers by the lack of discourse we provide about sexuality. Teenagers' normal questions about sexuality need answers from concerned, biblically oriented adults who can help students develop healthy views about sexuality.

So if you're going to help students who have sexual addictions, look in the mirror first. Spend some time getting clear on what you believe the Bible has to say about sexuality. Students will sense the shame and guilt if those are part of your own sexual self-image.

I have received too many referrals from youth pastors who, after talking with a student about the teenager's sexual struggles, have labeled the student as sexually addicted. This chapter discusses the fundamentals of what constitutes a sexual addiction, guidelines for when counseling is needed, and what you can do to help teenagers who have questions and concerns about their sexuality. This topic has been covered in many books, and this chapter will address only some of the basic aspects of sexual addictions.

Let's get back to Rick's situation. Once I helped Rick talk about his sexual concerns and start to explore the great gift sexuality was meant to be in his life, Rick began to see that his sexual urges were not the enemy. In my work with teenagers, I often find myself telling young men and women that they are *normal*. Students need a place of safety to talk about their sexuality. In Rick's case, his parents were really struggling with what to do regarding their son's normal sexual curiosity. Their fear about his becoming a man who was interested in sexual things produced anxiety in them and led Rick to believe that there was something very wrong with him. As a result, Rick shamed some of these normal feelings, and this shame only gave his sexual urges *more* power. Through talking about these feelings and understanding what was going on inside him, Rick saw his sexuality as a gift from God. As he unburdened himself of the shame, he was able to see God's boundaries as protection for him so that he might enjoy this gift to its full extent.

As youth workers, it's imperative that we help teenagers understand God's perspective on sexuality and walk with them as they have questions or concerns about this issue.

WHEN TO REFER

It will be fairly *uncommon* for you to run across a teenager who truly has a sexual addiction. The majority of students who might feel that they're addicted are *not*. However, to prevent possible problems with addiction in the future, it can be helpful for a student to talk with a professional counselor to work through his or her struggles and to help the student develop a healthy sexual perspective. The following are some statements you may hear students make; let these statements serve as signals for you that it's time to help a teenager connect with a counselor.

- *"I've tried to control my sexual activities, but I just can't seem to stop."* Just as eating is a normal biological urge, our sexual urges will never be stopped. But if a student's sexual activities seem to be escalating in frequency despite negative consequences or attempts to establish normal boundaries, he or she could benefit from talking to someone. It may just be the student's perception, but counseling can help a teenager see himself or herself in a less critical, less judgmental manner.

- *"I feel like I'm leading a double life."* Sexual activity is something that most people don't talk about, but if a student is hiding his or her activity from those who are close to him or her, it is important for the teenager to talk to someone who can help.

- *"I regularly masturbate through use of Web sites, pornography, or phone sex."* It's normal for teenagers to feel curious about their sexuality and their bodies. With easy access to the Internet, sadly many students will check out pornographic Web sites. However, repetitive and continued use of pornography, which can cause serious damage to a person's relationships with others and with God, should be addressed.

- *"I frequently masturbate to calm myself down."* Some students use masturbation to deal with emotional problems or stress. Orgasm does cause a biological release that relieves anxiety, but the potential risk is that a student can develop a pattern of relying on his or her sexual activity for relief instead of dealing directly with the feelings and thoughts he or she is struggling with.

- *"My sexual activities are becoming more and more dangerous."* Teenagers who are involved with sexual activities like prostitution, unprotected sex, or public sex are putting their futures in serious danger. If there is risk or potential harm in a student's activities, it is important for the teenager to work with a professional counselor to look more closely at what might be going on in the student's life.

- *"I feel like I can't connect with God anymore because of my sexual activities."* A common concern that students struggle with is their perception of how God views their sexual urges. Having teenagers talk to a Christian counselor can help them connect with a God who is open and available to be involved in *all* areas of their lives.

- *"My sexual activities are getting in the way of my normal responsibilities or relationships."* If a student's sexual activities are having an impact on financial obligations, job responsibilities, or relationships at home, this is a sign that he or she may be sexually addicted.

COUNSELING IDEAS

The label of sexual addiction often carries with it much shame and guilt. When working with students, it's *very important* to be extremely cautious in labeling a teenager's sexual activity as an addiction. You should always let a professional counselor make that determination. However, it's important for you to understand what an addiction is and how you can help students who may be struggling with a sexual addiction.

An addiction is a behavior that a person cannot manage. It impacts his or her life and causes negative consequences. Outlined below are four key elements of addiction: compulsive behaviors, negative consequences, obsession with sexual thoughts, and tolerance.

Compulsive Behaviors

There is a compulsive nature to sexual addiction that is exhibited when a person continues the behavior despite repeated efforts to stop. One aspect of sexual addiction that's tricky is the fact that stopping sexual behavior does not mean the desire for sex will stop. Just like eating, our bodies are designed by God to have sexual urges that seek some type of satisfaction. Young adolescent males begin experiencing nocturnal emissions, or wet dreams; this is one way that God designed our bodies to process some of these natural, normal desires.

Negative Consequences

A second aspect of sexual addiction is that an individual continues the behaviors despite negative consequences. A teenager's grades might suffer because the student is spending more and more time involved in sexual activities. Or a student could be impacted financially; a person struggling with sexual addiction may run up large credit card bills by renting pornographic movies or by calling 1-900 numbers. Since many teenagers don't have access to credit cards, though, financial consequences for students may not be as common as they are with adults who are sexually addicted.

Obsession With Sexual Thoughts

A third aspect of addiction is a preoccupation or obsession with sexual thoughts. What's challenging in dealing with students is distinguishing what is normal and what is a sign of addiction. Today's teenagers are growing up in a society that sexualizes many things, and many students regularly think about sex. One way to understand how occupied a teenager is with sex is to talk through the teenager's daily activities. If the student spends a significant portion of his or her unstructured time thinking about sex, this may be a sign of a potential problem.

Tolerance

A final trait of a sexual addiction is tolerance. Tolerance means that the individual must keep escalating his or her behaviors to obtain the same "high" that he or she once received. This is usually evidenced in an escalation of intensity, frequency, or attempts with more risky behaviors. At first a teenager might start by visiting a pornographic Web site or experimenting sexually with a peer. If a student is becoming addicted, he or she will need to do more and more risky activities to achieve the same satisfaction. The teenager may increase the frequency of visits to Web sites or engage in unprotected, risky sexual behaviors such as frequent visits to seventeen-and-older strip clubs or unprotected sexual encounters with strangers. These behaviors are highly risky and signal that the addiction may be in full force.

Normal Curiosity vs. Sexual Addiction

It can be challenging to discern whether a teenager is sexually addicted or whether he or she is just exploring the newfound sexual desires that are a result of passing through puberty. Many of the students I work with express concerns about their sexuality. In helping teenagers develop healthy, God-honoring boundaries in their sexuality, it can be beneficial to help them look inside and figure out what's going on with their sexual struggle. I often challenge students to think of their personal identity as made up of many parts. I ask students to consider this question: "When it comes to sexual behaviors, what parts (thoughts or behaviors) come to mind?" I have found that there are some parts that are common in students who are struggling with addictive sexual behaviors.

Managing Sexual Urges Through Shame and Guilt

The first part that I often deal with is the part of a student's personality that is trying to manage his or her newfound sexuality. The intent of this part is to help the person not ruin his or her life by allowing sexual urges to take control. This is a good thing. There are boundaries that God gives us to maintain sexual purity. These boundaries are for our protection and long-term health. The concern about this aspect of an individual's personality is not what it is seeking to do, but *how* it is seeking to manage those sexual urges. Often people manage their sexuality through shame or guilt.

One individual I worked with came to see me because he had begun an inappropriate sexual relationship after thirty-eight years of sexual abstinence. This experience was devastating to him, but when we started to talk about the part of his personality that helped him remain abstinent, he realized that he had managed his sexual urges in an incorrect way; whenever he had a sexual thought or urge, he immediately shamed himself. He'd then begin the process of confession and become stricter with himself. He basically had an internal tyrant that whipped the sexuality right out of him. This part of his personality caged his sexuality instead of giving it healthy, God-honoring boundaries.

This part of his identity took a lot of pride in managing his sexuality, but it left him very alone. When he talked to those close to him about his sexual fall, they expressed how differently they felt about him now; prior to this, they felt as if he couldn't relate to them because he never seemed to struggle. People often try to manage their sexual struggles all by themselves. You can help students realize that they don't have to be alone as they figure out their sexuality.

Motivation to Action

The second part that's common to the sexual addict is the part of his or her personality that actually motivates the person to do the sexual behaviors. This is not necessarily a bad part of the person—usually the intent is to do good for the individual. For example, one student I worked with noticed that she initiated sexual relations with her boyfriend whenever she felt very alone. She valued saving sexual intercourse for marriage, but when she started to feel lonely, a part of her wanted to squelch the loneliness by initiating sex with her boyfriend. We worked on discovering other, healthier ways to deal with feelings of loneliness, and eventually she began to feel less of a need to initiate sexual activity with her boyfriend. She learned to identify the relationships in her life that would help her not feel so alone.

Exiled Sexuality

The last part that I often see in people who have sexual struggles is the part that has been cast out. Young women are often given the message that their sexual desires and feelings are dangerous or abnormal; adolescent girls who are dealing with sexual thoughts and behaviors often feel very isolated and alone because they think of it as purely a guy's struggle. When you talk to your youth group, make sure you clearly present the message that young women also struggle with the issue of sexuality and that, if a young woman does struggle with this issue, she is not some anomaly that should be shipped off the planet. Teenage guys, too, often exile the sexual parts of their personality. Our society presents a message that a normal man's desires should be hyper-sexually charged. If a student isn't that way, he may feel abnormal.

These aspects of a person's identity often get exiled in childhood. Parents often give children the

Sexual Addiction

message that the body is something to be ashamed of. I remember working with one family whose mom had caught her five-year-old son with his hands in his underwear. She scolded him for this behavior and brought him in because she was concerned that he might become a sexual addict. I first assured the mother that her child was not going to become an addict, but that he was just displaying normal five-year-old curiosity about his body. I explained to her that my greater concern was the message that she might be giving to her son out of her fear; I helped to educate her about normal sexual curiosity, and she learned different ways to deal with her fear. This mom did a great service to her son by helping him learn that his body was a gift from God and his normal interest was not a bad thing.

Masturbation

One subject that is going to come up when you counsel a student who has sexual struggles is the issue of masturbation. A good way to approach this is to have the student do a search through the Bible to discover what God says about this topic. The student will soon discover that there is no reference in the Bible to masturbation, though the Bible is clear about impure thoughts and lust. If the Bible is silent about this activity, we need to help individuals not feel such guilt and shame when they engage in this activity. I often challenge a person who is struggling with this issue to keep a masturbation journal, and I ask the person to evaluate what's going on in his or her life before and afterward. The point is to get to the root of the problem—to get the focus off the masturbation and to find out what's going on inside of the individual.

Sexual Urges and Self-Image

Teenagers often believe that they are bad because they have sexual thoughts. Yet, as you look at Jesus' interactions with people, his reaction to sexual impurity is one of love and grace. When he spoke with the Samaritan woman in John 4, he offered forgiveness. I often use this example with students, because sometimes when they experience their brokenness or humanity, they tend to go after it like Jesus went after the money changers in the Temple. Jesus spoke with truth and power to those people who were deceived and self-righteous. But when we approach Jesus with an attitude of brokenness and humility, there is grace abounding!

Identify Problem Behaviors

Make sure you prompt the student to be specific about his or her activities. Identify the specific behaviors that concern the student and how often he or she is practicing the behaviors. Your own comfort level of talking about these specific behaviors will come into play here, because teenagers will sense your apprehension as you talk. If you don't feel comfortable talking about these sexual issues with your students, that's OK. I've been in situations where I've felt that I couldn't really help a person because the thoughts and feelings inside me were too loud. In this case, it's OK to refer a student to a counselor—you are serving the teenager and yourself in the long run. But consider getting additional training or finding someone to help you work through these issues so that you can learn and grow as well.

Involve Parents

Involving parents is important, but it can be tricky. In a counseling setting, you must consider the student's expectation of confidentiality (except in life-threatening situations). A good place to start is by asking a student if he or she has talked to Mom and Dad about these sexual struggles. Explore why a teenager has or has not discussed the issue with his or her parents. The information you get will help you understand the student's concerns.

In my church, I do a parent education seminar about sexual issues as well as other concerns of adolescence. One way to help your students is by educating and working with their parents. You may not be the one to run a seminar, but you may have Christian counselors in your church who could help you. When you team up with the parents, you can make an impact in the parents' lives and ultimately in the lives of your students.

Understand Your Own Sexual Struggles

Finally, I'd recommend that, as a youth worker, you get intentional about working through some of the issues related to your own sexual activity. I have worked with *too many* youth workers who are living a double life. The most important person that God has given you to impact is *you*. Don't neglect what might be going on in your life as you try to help others.

Recommended Resources

Books

• *Don't Call It Love: Recovery from Sexual Addiction,* Patrick Carnes. New York, NY: Bantam Books, 1992.

• *Every Man's Battle: Winning the War on Sexual Temptation One Victory at a Time,* Stephen Arterburn and Fred Stoeker, with Mike Yorkey. Colorado Springs, CO: WaterBrook Press, 2000.

• *Faithful and True: Sexual Integrity in a Fallen World,* Mark Laaser. Grand Rapids, MI: Zondervan Publishing House, 1996.

• *False Intimacy: Understanding the Struggle of Sexual Addiction,* Harry W. Schaumburg. Colorado Springs, CO: NavPress, 1997.

STUDENT PAGE Use the photocopiable worksheet on page 157 to help teenagers think through their sexual behaviors. Have the student take the page home to work on, and discuss the exercise with the student in a subsequent counseling session.

My Sexual Struggles

Take your Bible, a pen, and this page to a private place. While this page is designed for you, you may want to talk about it afterward with someone you trust, such as a parent, your youth leader, or a counselor.

The specific behaviors that are causing me concern are...

I do these behaviors when...

Before I participate in these behaviors, I'm feeling... (What do I need when I'm feeling like this?)

After participating in these behaviors, I feel...

Study 1 Thessalonians 4:3-7, and consider what God says about sexual activity. Then answer the following questions.

How can I control my sexual desires in a way that is "holy and honorable"?

Who in my life can I share my struggle with for support, encouragement, and accountability?

CHAPTER 22

Facing Temptation–
Equipping Students to Make Wise Sexual Choices

SCOTT GIBSON, M.S.W., L.C.S.W.

THE BASICS

Each year schools all across America run abstinence-based sexual education programs to help students make wise sexual decisions. More resources are available to help students make these important decisions than ever before. Many parents are beginning to talk with their children about the subject of sex. Many church youth ministries are trying to tackle the issue head-on. Current statistics show important declines in the rate of teenage pregnancy. According to a Kids Count special report, "Since 1991, the percentages of American teenagers getting pregnant, giving birth, or having abortions have all fallen. Teen pregnancies have declined 14 percent since 1990, reaching the lowest annual rate in more than 20 years. Similarly, the rate of births to teens is down 12 percent from the beginning of the decade. These welcome declines occurred in every state and the District of Columbia and across all racial groups."[1]

This is good news, but the reality is we still have a long way to go. The report goes on to say, "In 1996, more than half a million American teens gave birth. Most of these adolescents were unmarried, and many were not ready for the responsibilities and demands of parenthood."[2] Teenage pregnancies threaten these new mothers' schooling and increase the likelihood that these young women will be poor and dependent as adults. The children born to teenage mothers are also at risk for future challenges. (For more information on unplanned pregnancies, see Chapter 9.)

What students need is strong leadership to help them with the sexual decisions that they will make. I believe that the church plays a *crucial* role in challenging students to reach a higher standard. I've worked with too many Christ-following teenagers who have made sexual decisions against their personal values of abstaining until marriage. The resulting emotional pain of these decisions can be devastating.

The students I have counseled have taught me a lot about why they make the sexual decisions that they do. As youth workers, we have a tremendous opportunity to walk alongside students and support them in these decisions.

While there has been a lot written about ways to approach this topic, we will be looking at the *emotional* dynamics that often exist when students make decisions to be sexually active. So often when the subject of sex arises, the whole discussion becomes all about sex and sexual drives. But it's important not to be fooled by this; in many cases, sexual decisions have little to do with sex and are instead driven by emotional needs.

Furthermore, while it's God's desire for each person to remain sexually pure until marriage, there will always be students who choose to experiment sexually. We often learn from our mistakes. I have known many strong Christian adults who experimented sexually during adolescence. There are consequences that they've faced, but their life isn't over. The biggest help that we can be for students who make mistakes is to walk with them and help them evaluate their sexual decisions.

WHEN TO REFER

Many of the students you will have discussions with about their sexual decisions will not need referrals to Christian counselors. When a student is talking with an adult about what he or she is feeling about sexual choices, this is a *good* thing. I have far less concern about these students than those who *aren't* talking about it. When you are really listening to a student talk about his or her questions and concerns regarding sexual activity, you are meeting an important emotional need for that student to be heard and understood.

The students that you will want to refer for further counseling are those in the following situations:

- students who are living a "double life"
- students who are facing an unplanned pregnancy
- teenagers who are struggling with their sexual identity or sexual preference issues
- students who are dealing with previous abortions
- teenagers who are involved in promiscuous sexual activity
- students who are involved in sexual prostitution or other aspects of the sex industry
- individuals who are involved in sexually abusive relationships
- students who are overwhelmed with guilt and shame about their sexual activities
- teenagers who are involved in emotionally hurtful relationships in which they are also sexually active

There may be situations in which students feel uncomfortable talking to you as their youth leader about their sexual activity. I worked with one student whose parents were close friends of his youth pastor, so he didn't feel safe talking to the youth pastor about his struggles. In a case like this, make an attempt to push past this and assure the student of confidentiality; but always encourage the student to talk to someone, even if it isn't you.

COUNSELING IDEAS

In this section, I will focus on three areas: the impact of the media, normal sexual curiosity, and the emotional-sexual link. Understanding how these issues impact sexual decision making will help you serve your students more effectively. As you discuss these issues with teenagers, remember that you can learn from your students. In my counseling practice, I always ask questions of teenagers, not only to understand them better, but also to better understand the culture that they're a part of.

The Impact of the Media

The first element to keep in mind is the impact that the media has on students with regard to sexual choices. Students are constantly bombarded with sexual messages. The more I learn about these messages, the more sense it makes how confused many teenagers are in their decision making. For example, in the fall of 2000, I sat down with my sixteen- and fourteen-year-old sons and watched the MTV Video Music Awards. If you saw the event, you may remember a popular young female singer stripping down to nude-colored clothing so that she looked as if she were naked. I had an interesting discussion with my sons about this. The message they got loud and clear was that sex is really important and sells lots of music CDs.

Take some popular music CDs and look at the lyrics; it's likely that many of the songs promote free expression of sexuality without responsibility. One practical way to help teenagers think through these issues is to have them bring in their CDs and talk about the songs in their small group. Together, consider what the songs are communicating about values, and discuss what the Bible has to say on this subject. We don't need to isolate students from the world; we need to prepare them by helping them see and evaluate the messages they're exposed to.

Consider coming up with some youth group activities that center around discussing the messages from movies or songs. Plan a night when you can all watch or listen to something together. Make you sure you include parents in this activity as well. First, have an open discussion about the pros and cons of the messages in the movie or song. Then have the students look up and discuss Scripture passages that address such issues. Make sure that you set aside some time for students to process any decisions they might make regarding their media consumption. Consider including parents in a debriefing session so that they can better help their children make wise choices.

Normal Sexual Curiosity

The second aspect you'll want to address is teenagers' natural, normal curiosity about their sexuality. In the past, and sadly even now, students' normal curiosity gets classified as shamefully perverse. Parents often react with a "not my little Johnny!" approach that gives Johnny a skewed perspective, as if there were something perverse about his interest in his body and sexuality.

One parent I worked with had walked into the den and found his teenage son with his hands down his pants. The parent freaked out and told the son how disgusting that was. The student was embarrassed for being caught and felt ashamed, though he had just been watching sports on television and had no sexual intent with his behavior. The parent had a distorted view of his own sexuality, and when he saw his son exploring his body, he passed on his own shame to his son. I worked with the parent and helped him talk to his son about appropriate times and places to explore his body, but also helped them both see the great gift that God has given each of us in our physical sexuality. There are clear boundaries in Scripture about expression of this gift, but we often make the playing field much narrower than the Bible does.

I recommend that you dedicate a youth meeting to the topic "What the Bible says about sex (and what it doesn't)." Prior to that meeting, invite parents to a separate forum so that they'll understand what you'll be communicating, as well as how they can help their teenagers have healthy, God-honoring relationships.

Adolescents need to figure out what to do with this new aspect of their life. When something is new to any of us, we often become very curious. Students will be naturally curious about new things, sex included. When students have the opportunity to explore, discuss, and learn about their sexuality in safe ways, they will be better equipped to honor God in their sexual decisions. Instead of viewing it as opening Pandora's box, remember that discussing sexuality with students helps them begin thinking, praying, and figuring out just how they believe God wants them to behave.

The Emotional-Sexual Link

The last element to remember when counseling teenagers about their sexual decisions is the link that often gets established between people's emotional needs and their sexual needs. As we're growing up, we all have various experiences in which some of our emotional needs are unmet. Parents and adults aren't perfect, and when children's needs don't get met, children can do amazing things to survive those hurts and injuries. Kids will often take those emotional needs and bury them deep within, so that they are no longer aware of the needs and learn to do without them. Through several years of these types of experiences, a child often develops an "inner room" of needs and feelings that aren't being acknowledged. Then along comes puberty, and the child becomes aware of his or her sexuality.

Suddenly this newfound sexuality offers a method for meeting those hidden inner needs. Some time ago, I worked with a young woman who was sixteen years old and pregnant with her third child. Despite previous attempts to help guide her into making different decisions, she continued to make decisions to become pregnant. Her previous counselors had given her helpful information about birth control and advice for making different decisions, but they missed delving into and understanding the emotional-sexual link.

I decided that if I was truly going to help this young woman, I would need to understand the part of her identity that was driving her to get pregnant. I asked her to tell me about what she felt when she was pregnant and what she thought about that experience. I asked her to tell me the story about the first time she was pregnant at the age of thirteen. She told me about the horrific experience of being raped by an uncle and the loneliness she felt in her living situation. The aunt who was her caretaker was abusing drugs and gave her little attention. But when she was pregnant, for one of the first times in her life she felt a wonderful feeling of being needed and loved by someone. As she read and learned about the baby growing inside of her, she began to feel as if her life had purpose and meaning. She told me about the day she had her first child and was able to hold the baby and see what a wonderful thing she had done by bringing this new person into the world.

Then she described how she went home from the hospital and the overwhelming loneliness began to take over her life again. She became depressed and felt like ending her life. As we talked about it more, it became clear to her that pregnancy was the avenue she'd used to help herself feel better. This was her emotional-sexual link. We then began to work to help her understand her emotional needs and empower her to meet those needs in other, healthier ways.

In working with students who have made poor sexual decisions, I've found that many students have made these decisions while trying to meet some emotional need. What often happens in counseling about sexual choices is that these needs never get addressed. And when the counseling doesn't address these emotional issues, students' decisions don't change.

Students will often make choices that in the short term will help them feel better, even though

Recommended Resources

Books

- *Hold On to Your Heart: Making the Most of the Gift God Gave You* (booklet in the Dare 2 Dig Deeper series), Amy Stephens. Colorado Springs, CO: Focus on the Family, 2000.

- *Passport to Purity*, Dennis and Barbara Rainey. Little Rock, AR: FamilyLife, 1999.

- *Why Wait?: What You Need to Know About the Teen Sexuality Crisis*, Josh McDowell and Dick Day. Nashville, TN: Thomas Nelson Publishers, 1988.

Video Resources

- *Good Sex: A Whole-Person Approach to Teenage Sexuality and God*, Jim Hancock and Kara Eckmann Powell. Grand Rapids, MI: Zondervan Publishing House, 2001.

- *Parenting Teenagers for Positive Results: An Interactive Video Course for Small Groups and Sunday Schools* (Session 4: Navigating Sexuality), Jim Burns. Loveland, CO: Group Publishing, Inc., 2001.

in the long run the decisions might hurt them. One way to approach this is to have students think about their needs and write them down so that the needs can be addressed intentionally. It is also important to help the students involve God and others in their lives to meet these needs.

---

[1]   Foreword to When Teens Have Sex: Issues and Trends—Kids Count Special Report, Revised Edition (Baltimore, MD: The Annie E. Casey Foundation, 1998).

[2]   Foreword to When Teens have Sex: Issues and Trends—Kids Count Special Report.

STUDENT PAGES Use the photocopiable worksheets on pages 163 and 164 to help teenagers think about their sexual boundaries. Let the student work on either of these pages as homework. At your next meeting, invite the student to share his or her thoughts about the exercise.

How Far Should I Go?

_____
_____
_____
_____
_____
_____
_____
_____
_____
_____

An important decision when you date someone is "how far you should go." In the column on the left, make a list of the sexual or romantic activities that people take part in (like holding hands, talking, kissing, or having sex). When you're done, number them in order, from least risky to most risky.

Decide where you will draw the line. Where do most teenagers draw the line? Where do your close friends draw the line? Where do you think God would want you to draw the line?

If you stay true to the line you've decided on, what are some of the feelings that you might have when you go against the flow?

What can you do with these feelings?

Sexual-Emotional Links

In the space below, write down as many of your emotional needs or wants as you can think of.

Which of those needs might also be met through being involved in sexual activities?

What might be the danger of meeting those emotional needs primarily through sexual activities?

What are some God-honoring activities that would help you meet these needs?

CHAPTER 23

Perfectly Imperfect—
Dealing With Shame and Guilt

TREVOR SIMPSON, M.A.

THE BASICS

At some point, all trusted youth workers find themselves counseling students who have really screwed up. Humanity has fallen and it can't get up! Teenagers come to you and confess the poor choices that they've made and the messes they've gotten themselves into. It's the youth worker's job to find a proper balance of trust, parent-student allegiance, grace, justice, and redemption for those who have made poor choices and are experiencing a deep sense of shame.

People of all ages have sex outside of marriage; abuse drugs, alcohol, girlfriends or boyfriends, and others; and sometimes do things that are much worse. The youth worker's task in process-ing these situations with teenagers may be more challenging and more important than the work of those who are counseling people of other ages. Because of their developmental stage, when adolescents make poor choices, they're simultaneously dealing with the consequences of their actions *and* forming who they're going to become. How they experience the consequences and (hopefully) redemption of their mishaps can imprint upon them and their children negatively or positively for generations to come. In Christ, we have the opportunity and privilege to be a part of this redemptive process and to help lift our students out of the bondage of shame.

Ever experienced a situation like this one? Andrew has been active in the youth group for three years and has clear gifts in leadership and a vibrant relationship with Christ. He is a kind, intelligent, and well-spoken junior in high school. As his youth pastor, you have developed a healthy and honest relationship with Andrew. He is one of the youth group's main student leaders. Recently, Andrew has been absent from youth ministry activities, and you feel that he has been avoiding you. After you've unsuccessfully tried to set up a meeting with Andrew to see how he's doing, he suddenly shows up unannounced. He shares with you that his girlfriend, Kara (another student who's active in the youth ministry), is pregnant, and they don't know what to do. He is clearly regretful and shaken, and he's frozen at the prospect of telling his parents and Kara's parents about the pregnancy.

In this situation, it may seem easy to tell Andrew that he should get out of student leadership, tell his parents, tell the church, have the baby, put it up for adoption or get married, and live happily ever after. That may or may not be what needs to happen in a situation like this one. During these times, however, our initial focus should be more on the individual than on the *results* of intervention. The results of intervention will happen naturally and are a part of the redemptive process. If we proceed with only the final goal in mind, intervention may feel hurried and callous, and damage could be done. These are deep holes that have been dug, and Andrew, his girlfriend, and countless others like them need the body of Christ to help them get out.

Often, poor choices equal a crisis, and virtually every crisis provides an opportunity for the individuals involved to grow. I will not specifically address crisis intervention in this chapter; instead, I will begin to explore the youth worker's role in the redemptive process for students who are experiencing debilitating shame.

WHEN TO REFER

Referrals can be tricky in these situations because the teenager has most likely confided in you and desires anonymity. As the student's youth worker, it is critical that you don't *ever* make a promise not to refer or not to tell others. The student should know ahead of time the guidelines that you've set about breaching confidentiality. A general rule is to tell students that you'll go to others if their confessions suggest that they may hurt themselves or hurt others. You may need to define specifically what "hurting yourself or others" means to you. (For example, a student may believe that smoking marijuana is not dangerous to himself or to other people. You may disagree and should clarify this with the student before the subject comes up in discussion.)

Prior to referral or consultation, it's important to notify the student that you are going to seek additional guidance. When dealing with issues surrounding guilt, shame, and forgiveness, here are some guidelines you can use. If you answer yes to any of the following questions, you may want to consider referring the student or seeking additional counsel:

- Have these issues brought harm to the student or to anybody else? Do these issues put this person or any other person in danger?
- Does this problem make you feel clueless and inadequate as a counselor?
- Do these issues cloud your objectivity and limit your ability to love this person?
- Does personal involvement with these issues, either now or in the past, limit your ability to give fair and excellent counsel? Just because you may share a common experience, it doesn't automatically mean that you are the right person for the job. For example, a youth worker who was wounded by his or her parents' divorce and is still harboring bitterness may not be the appropriate person to counsel a student on extending grace to parents through their divorce. Or a youth pastor who struggles with pornography or lust is *not* the best person to counsel a teenager about premarital sex.
- Do these issues typically need specific clinical expertise? Examples of such issues include eating disorders, drug or alcohol dependence, sexual addiction, clinical depression, or psychotic episodes.
- Are there significant legal questions that you or your church need to consider if you are involved in this intervention?

COUNSELING IDEAS

Here are a few things to keep in mind when a student tells you about sinful behavior or issues of shame.

God Is Bigger Than You Are or Ever Will Be

Remember that the Holy Spirit lives in you and ministers through you to other people. That may mean saying to a student, "I don't know how to help." Or it may mean keeping your mouth shut and listening. Regardless, pray for your own motivations and ideas to take a backseat as you focus on being attentive to the needs of the student sitting across from you. Trust that God can use you in many different ways and will use you if you let him.

Stay Calm and Love People

It is imperative that you love the people you counsel, though you may not love their actions. Fake it if you have to, and communicate to people that they're important and that it's important that they're there with you. Communicate your appreciation that they trust you, and reassure them that confessing to you was the right choice. For example, a student may tell you that he or she got drunk at a party and had sex with several peers. Typical internal emotions might be anger, disgust, bitterness, and even hatred toward the student. However, as a youth worker, you must initially curtail the external manifestations of those severe feelings. Instead, communicate unconditional love, support, and appreciation that the student trusts you with the information. There will be a time for you to share your feelings, but that time should come only after the confessing teenager is able to embrace the fact that he or she is in a safe and inviting environment and that you accept him or her.

Don't Give Advice Until It's Asked For

When a student confesses something to you, listen first. Put your inclination to give advice on hold. If you fly off the handle or go off on a mini-sermon, you communicate that your words are more important than the student's thoughts and feelings. The teenager is already experiencing shame and guilt and is feeling bad about what happened. He or she probably already knows what should have been done or what should be done now. The reason the student is meeting with you is to feel loved and validated as a person.

Be Aware of How a Student's Behavior Is Affecting You

There are many disturbing behaviors out there that may really make your skin crawl. If you find yourself in a situation where your concentration is lost, or you experience strong internal hatred toward the student, it is probably best to remove yourself from the situation after finding additional help and support for the student.

Err on the Side of Grace

Shame-filled people most likely know that they've disappointed and hurt others. There will be a time and a need for you to communicate your thoughts and feelings on the matter and to instill justice and restitution. However, as stated earlier, the initial intervention should focus on the needs of the student and not necessarily on the outcome. After the weight of the confession is brought into the open and Christlike love has been communicated (and hopefully embraced), it is appropriate to begin discussions with those involved about consequences and justice.

Imagine this scenario: Phil and Terry come to you feeling guilty and confess that they turned off the power at their neighbors' house right after their neighbors left for a two-week vacation. It was just a joke, but their neighbors came home to a house that smelled of rancid food. The neighbors lost hundreds of dollars' worth of food and suffered some other damages because of the lack of power. You know these neighbors and know that they're skeptical of Christians, but they've recently shown an interest in the Christian faith.

It would be easy to launch into a lecture about evangelism, heaven and hell, the body of Christ, and "Love thy neighbor!"—but Phil and Terry don't need to hear that just yet. Instead, you should initially respond to the needs of the confessors. The teenagers will eventually get the points of justice and consequences as this situation plays out.

Help Students Understand How Their Behavior Has Affected You

After a student has had an opportunity to share the problem and you have communicated acceptance, share your honest thoughts and feelings with the student. As the teenager hears your words and experiences your acceptance, he or she will understand how his or her behavior has hurt you or others, but that in your eyes he or she is still accepted.

Be an Advocate for All

When you're working with a student who is experiencing shame and guilt, it's important that you act as an advocate for the student and all others who will be affected by the student's behavior. In the first example, Andrew and Kara made poor choices, and as a result Kara has become pregnant. Their choices will impact not only them, but will also have a dramatic impact on their families, friends, youth group, and church body. The youth worker represents all of these people in some capacity and should think about how these individuals need to be involved in this process.

Guide Students in Creating a Plan

The initial confession is generally not the only needed confession. Come up with ways to appropriately involve all of the people who are affected by the situation. In Andrew's case, it would be prudent to inform his parents and his girlfriend's parents. The teenagers may also need help finding resources regarding adoption. They may need additional wise counsel regarding the negative spiritual, physical, and emotional consequences of abortion. They'll eventually need to tell the other students in the youth group. In other words, they'll need you as their trusted youth worker to be with them as much as they will allow you to be. The youth worker is not functioning as a spokesperson or bail bondsman; instead, the youth worker should serve as a foundational rock of love and acceptance.

Communicate That Forgiveness Is a Process

Teenagers' poor choices often hurt others, and it may take those people time to get to a point of forgiveness or reconciliation. A student may immediately want everything to be as it was, but that is not usually possible. Help the student understand that finite, fallen humans can get to a place of genuine forgiveness, but it takes time. God forgives us immediately, and we can rest assured in his love. Parents, friends, and others may need the freedom to be angry for quite some time before fully forgiving the student.

Recommended Resources

Books

- *In the Grip of Grace: You Can't Fall Beyond His Love,* Max Lucado. Nashville, TN: W Publishing Group, 1996.

- *The Ragamuffin Gospel: Embracing the Unconditional Love of God,* Brennan Manning. Sisters, OR: Multnomah Publishers, Inc., 1990.

STUDENT PAGE Use the photocopiable worksheet on page 170 to help teenagers who are processing mistakes they've made begin to understand their choices and consequences. Use the student page during a counseling session, allowing the teenagers involved to complete the worksheet together. Then discuss their responses with them.

Beginning to Pick Up the Pieces

There is not one perfect person living today. The entire world is filled with people who sometimes screw things up. Use this page to help you begin the *process of growing* through your mistake. Answer each question honestly, then talk through your responses with your youth worker, a friend, or another person you trust—someone you know will help you through this tough time.

Think back and write down what choices and events led up to this mistake.

As you made this decision, what feelings did you have at that time that made it seem OK?

Who are the people that this choice is going to affect? How will it affect them?

If you could look into the future and paint a perfect ending to this situation (where everybody is happy), what would it look like?

What steps would have to happen to make this scenario come true?

In the aftermath of the mistake, what parts of this growing process are you responsible for? What parts of this process are out of your control?

CHAPTER 24

S.O.S!–
Ministering to Stressed-Out Students

SCOTT GIBSON, M.S.W., L.C.S.W.

THE BASICS

Every one of us experiences stress. Stress results from the normal ups and downs of life as well as from the crises that most of us hope never happen to us. Stress often results from external sources, but it can be generated by internal sources as well. In our fast-paced society, many people are impacted by stress, and the symptoms that result can affect our physical, emotional, and mental health.

Stress is important in helping us do our best. Prior to taking final exams, many students experience anxiety that helps them get ready for the challenge ahead. They may experience nervousness in their stomach, sweaty palms, increased heart rate, and increased blood pressure. These natural reactions prepare a student's body and mind for the upcoming challenge and can help the person do his or her best.

While short-term stress can help us prepare to be at our very best, staying in a state of stress can be physically and psychologically damaging. When stress is not handled or is handled poorly, it can lead to problems such as high blood pressure, ulcers, or other conditions. If stress is unchecked, over time it can contribute to heart disease and weaken other bodily functions.

The challenge that many teenagers face today is that they encounter stress from several sources. Their bodies are rapidly changing. Our culture has placed unhealthy pressure on teenage girls, communicating that their bodies should look like those of female supermodels. Young men also feel pressure to make their bodies fit the "perfect male" standard set by the culture. School also causes stress, as it challenges students to achieve the best possible grades in order to secure the brightest future. Relationships with other students also bring stress. Adolescents are learning to form intimate relationships with people outside of their families. Students often begin and end relationships rapidly as they learn from their experiences. Family relationships are another cause of stress for teenagers. Some parents tend to "freak out" about things their teenagers do, and add additional pressures by attempting to force their children to conform to their expectations.

In this chapter, I'll address some of the signs of stress and ways in which you as a youth worker can effectively help students live a more peaceful existence in this stressed-out world. When working with a teenager who is experiencing stress, the goal will be to support the student, help him or her relax, and help the student make positive choices for his or her life.

WHEN TO REFER

The following signs and symptoms may indicate that a student is experiencing too much stress and should be referred to a professional counselor:

- The student has severe mood swings.
- The student is very withdrawn from peers.
- The individual has either lost or gained a lot of weight recently.
- The teenager is very dependent on a parent.
- The student is involved in "delinquent" or disobedient behaviors.
- The student is having trouble going to sleep, staying asleep, or getting up in the morning.
- The teenager is having trouble in school.
- The student stares into space for long periods of time.
- The student gets into many conflicts or fights.
- The individual has experienced panic attacks.
- The teenager has expressed suicidal thoughts.
- The student loses interest in things that he or she used to enjoy.
- The student cries easily and often.
- The teenager performs compulsive behaviors such as hair pulling, face picking, nail biting, excessive hand washing, or other ritual behaviors.

When you are considering referring a student to a professional therapist, talk to the student's parents about your concerns, and get their feedback about what they see going on with their son or daughter. Often parents miss certain things because they are just too close and involved. Your perspective as someone outside of the family is important.

COUNSELING IDEAS

Take Care of Yourself

The first person to take care of when counseling a stressed-out student is you! Ministering to others *is* stressful. Burnout in the helping professions due to stress is very common, so don't forget to pay attention to your own needs. Each week I spend approximately twenty-five hours listening to and being with people who are under stress. Some people's problems are potentially life-threatening, and most are very important issues that will impact the person's future. I am well aware of the weight of what happens in my office. I have found several things that help me avoid the negative impacts of stress and maintain my spiritual, physical, and personal relational health.

- The first thing I do each day is connect with God. This daily connection keeps me grounded. It also reminds me of who really is responsible for things. I have changed the format of these connections through the years, but reminding myself of God's presence in my life is vital.

Stress

- Another element that's important is taking care of myself physically. Daily exercise and healthy eating habits help me maintain the energy and stamina that this work sometimes takes. It also helps me relieve stress and get the most out of the days that I have here on earth.
- I also pay attention to my personal relational world. Since my days are full of relational giving, I work at creating relationships in my life where I get to receive as well. My family has become a safe place for me to be me, and I have a good friend who I meet with weekly where the agenda covers both his and my needs. Professionally, I also see a therapist on a regular basis. I have issues just as everyone else does, and I need a place where I can "dump" and figure out what God is doing in my life. If you don't have a supervisor or someone who will just listen, consider seeing a professional to help you with this. I believe that God has called me into ministry primarily to do his work with me, and secondarily so that I can benefit others. I want to understand what God is doing and make sure that I'm not distracted by others' stress.

Identify the Source

When you're with a student who is under stress, the first thing you'll want to do is identify where the stress is coming from. As the student tells you what's going on, the source of stress might be obvious, but it's important to help the teenager identify the source for himself or herself. This will greatly aid the student in problem solving and dealing with the stress in the future. To simplify this process, I will often help an individual identify whether the stress is from an internal source or an external source. In most cases, it's a combination of both.

External Stressors

Oftentimes there will be an external event that creates stress in a student's life. Some external sources of stress can be changed, and others can't be changed. I've worked with many students who are still wishing that their mom and dad would remarry. When a teenager is focusing on trying to change the unchangeable, I might ask, "What would it be like if you could have your mom and dad back together again?" or "If that happened, how would you feel?" I also attempt to uncover any beliefs that the individual might have concerning his or her role in the external event. I might ask a question such as, "Since your parents did that, what do you feel they are saying about their feelings toward you?" Students often carry burdens that are based on their underlying beliefs about situations.

I remember one student who still constantly wished that her parents were together—ten years after her parents had divorced. This student had started to act out in school and do things that she had never done before. Her parents were concerned and got involved in family counseling sessions to support her. During one session, I got the sense that this young woman was pleased with the meeting. I asked her about how she felt during the session with both of her parents there. She loved having them in the same room and was glad that her school problems were doing such "wonderful" things. But as we explored why she felt this way, we discovered an underlying feeling that she had about the divorce. She felt that if she had been more lovable, her parents would have stayed together. In this case, the external event of the divorce affected her internal beliefs. I worked with the family and the student to help them understand the truth about the divorce and to help the student understand how her parents felt about her. Once she understood that the divorce had little to do with her, her grades and behavior began to improve.

There are some external sources of stress that the student *can* do something about. I tell students that they are the ones who are responsible for managing and taking care of their lives. If they can figure out a different way to manage an external stressor, then so much the better. The big temptation you will have is to want to solve students' problems for them. Unfortunately that approach usually just creates more problems.

For example, I once worked with a student who was extremely stressed-out about his relationship with his girlfriend. They were sexually active (which was contrary to his personal beliefs), and they were fighting more than they were getting along. As I heard about all of the stress this relationship was creating, I thought, "It might be best to just dump the girlfriend and move on." I didn't say it quite that bluntly, but I might as well have. My opinion became obvious to him. What followed were sessions in which he defended the relationship and tried to prove to me why the relationship was so good for him. That's right—open mouth, insert foot.

The best thing to do is ask questions that will help the teenager figure out what he or she needs to do to respond to external sources of stress. When I'm not trying to fix the student's problems, I might say something such as, "Wow, you're under a lot of stress. It seems that if there was a way to do it differently, that would be nice for you. What do you think?" The student usually agrees, and then we talk about the things that he or she has tried so far that haven't worked. It's important to remind students that it can take time to figure things out and that each failed attempt will get them closer to a solution.

Life Management

In these situations of stress, a youth worker's role is to empower a student to take an active part in managing his or her life differently. Resist the desire to solve the problem for the student or to give him or her a quick fix. In the short term you might help, but in the long term you'll keep getting calls from the student. When the next stressful situation comes along, the teenager will not have learned how to manage the stress in his or her life.

Once a student has developed a plan of action, I'll often suggest that the student experiment with the ideas. Then as we run field tests, we'll learn together what works and what doesn't. I've worked with many teenagers who struggle with falling asleep or staying asleep at night. Since sleep is important to our mental health, I see this as one symptom we could work on that would help the student. After the student has a list of potential solutions, I have him or her write down in a journal what was tried and what the results were. Through these students, I have learned things that have helped in my work with others, too.

Family Stress

If the stress that a teenager is experiencing is largely related to family concerns, you will need to get the family involved in the process. Doing so can help the student feel less stressed since the problem is no longer his or hers alone to figure out. In a first counseling session with the teenager, I usually have one or both of the parents present. In front of the student I will tell

Stress

the parents, "I don't believe that this problem is all with your son or daughter. For you to be most helpful to your child, we will work on you, too, and look at ways you contribute to this." Some parents don't like to hear it, but it's true.

I remember one couple who came in because they had concerns about their daughter. They decided to come in initially without her, and so we started to work on the daughter's problems. After a few months of working with this couple, their daughter's symptoms disappeared and she began doing much better. We never had a single session with her. As the parents worked on *their* parts of the problem, the daughter was able to manage her stress as they made the appropriate shifts. At their last session, they remarked, "We came in to work on our daughter's issues. She never came. We worked on *us*, and she's doing great now." She was lucky to have such parents. I believe that if you are going to help students today, you must also work with parents and families. It might be your forte to hang out with teenagers, but if you ignore the family system that's central to your students' lives, you'll miss some valuable information and opportunities to have an impact.

Internal Stressors

Other sources of stress are internal ones. Internal stressors relate to how we think and feel about the everyday events in our lives. Beliefs such as "I'll do horribly at this activity," "people won't understand," or "nothing will help" all create greater stress when dealing with everyday problems. And when extraordinary problems come, good luck! The good news about these internal stressors is that they can *always* be changed.

This can be a challenging concept for some teenagers to understand. An important tool in helping students become aware of internal stressors is to have them journal. I often require teenagers to journal once a day right before bedtime. I've found that many stressed-out students have difficulty sleeping because of all the thoughts going through their heads. Often when they see their own thoughts and feelings on paper, they see how normal they are, and they can rest easy. This also helps them understand and begin to master their internal world.

God Is Sovereign

After Jesus addressed his disciples' concerns about his future, he said in John 16:33, "In this world you will have trouble. But take heart! I have overcome the world." Obviously, the fact that Jesus has overcome the world does not mean that there's any less trouble. Christians often believe that because of grace our lives should go easier. This just isn't true. What Jesus is telling us in this passage is that we should take comfort because he is in charge.

Remind students of God's sovereignty. The fact that he is in charge is true regardless of whether a student feels it or not. Dr. Herbert

Recommended Resources

Books

- *Disappointment With God,* Philip Yancey. Grand Rapids, MI: Zondervan Publishing House,1997.

- *Life Strategies for Teens,* Jay McGraw. New York, NY: Fireside 2000.

- *The Prayer of Jabez for Teens,* Bruce Wilkinson. Sisters, OR: Multnomah Publishers, Inc., 2001.

- *When Life Hurts: Understanding God's Place in Your Pain,* Philip Yancey. Sisters, OR: Multnomah Publishers, Inc., 1999.

Benson has documented on MRI brain scans that changes take place in the body when someone prays or meditates. The activity of prayer produces relaxation, and the body's activities become more evenly regulated.[1] Prayer helps us relax, like an infant being held and rocked. Through prayer, the body generates similar feelings of being held during stressful times.

Each week I spend time praying for each of my students. I have seen miraculous answers to prayers in people's lives—and I have also seen the work in my heart. Make sure you close each counseling session with prayer. Rally any or all prayer intercessors in your congregation to support you in this work (while maintaining students' confidentiality).

---

[1] Jeanie Davis, "Can Prayer Heal?" (July 23, 2001) at http://my.webmd.com.

STUDENT PAGE Use the photocopiable worksheet on page 177 to help teenagers understand what the Bible has to say about stress and worry. Allow a teenager to work on the student page at home, then discuss the exercise with the student in a subsequent counseling session.

Dealing With Stress

Take your Bible, a pen, and a notebook to a quiet spot. Spend some time reading the following passages and answering the questions. After you've answered the questions, share some of the things you wrote with a parent, your youth leader, or a counselor.

Read Matthew 6:25-34.

What are the things in your life that produce worry or concern?

How do you feel about these things?

Of the things that you're worried about, what are the things that you can't do anything about?
Make a prayer list for those things:

What can you do to help you worry less about those things?
Journal some of your thoughts:

CHAPTER 25

I Can't Go On—
Intervention in the Life of a Suicidal Student

SALLY SCHWER CANNING, Ph.D.

THE BASICS

Suicide, or taking one's own life, is a tragic reality for some teenagers and their families and communities. As disturbing as the thought is for adults who care about young people, suicide is one of the leading causes of death for teenagers in the United States, and rates appear to be increasing.[1] In addition to those teenagers who die as a result of their actions (completed suicides), there are other young people who have made one or more suicide attempts, and those who quietly suffer with thoughts to end their lives. Each year, young people who have run out of hope use firearms, poisons (pills, medications, carbon monoxide, and other toxic substances), hanging, and other means to this end. While it is never possible to fully guarantee the safety of another human being, this chapter includes important information that could help you recognize when a person may be in danger of taking his or her own life and help you assist that person in getting the necessary treatment. (Other life-threatening behaviors such as eating disorders and substance abuse are discussed in the specific chapters that deal with those issues.)

Signs of Suicide Risk

Unfortunately, it is impossible to predict with absolute certainty who will attempt suicide or commit suicide. Still it is important to carefully consider a number of factors in a student's past and present, family, and environment that put the teenager at risk.

Present factors:
- The student desires to be dead.
- The teenager thinks about or talks about killing or harming himself or herself.
- The student has developed a plan for killing himself or herself.
- He or she expresses hopelessness or a sense that things will not or cannot get better.
- The teenager has an inability to see a future for himself or herself.
- The student experiences an overwhelming sense of guilt or shame.

- He or she exhibits a significant change in behavior or personality (such as a quiet teenager who begins to act recklessly, or an outgoing teenager who becomes withdrawn).
- The teenager gives away valued possessions or in other ways seems to be saying goodbye.
- The student is involved in substance abuse.
- He or she exhibits impulsivity as part of a personality or conduct disorder.
- The teenager hears voices urging him or her to commit suicide (rare).

Factors in the student's past:

- The student has had suicidal thoughts or made previous suicide attempts.
- The student has a history of depression.
- There is a history of suicide in the teenager's family.

Factors in the student's circumstances or environment:

- A friend or peer has committed suicide.
- There has been media coverage, especially sensational coverage, of the suicide of someone (such as a famous person) that the student may identify with.
- There are firearms in the student's home.
- The teenager has experienced a significant loss, such as the death of a family member or friend, separation from a parent, or breakup of a significant relationship. (It is important to think of "significance" from the student's perspective. A loss that could seem minor or "just part of growing up" to an adult may be devastating for a teenager.)
- The student has gone through a significant transition (such as a move to a new school or divorce of parents).
- The teenager has a secret stressor (such as pregnancy or ongoing sexual abuse) that is unknown to significant adults.
- Other major stressors are present in the student's life.

WHEN TO REFER

The risk that a teenager will commit suicide exists on a continuum. The unhappy teenager who confides that he or she sometimes wishes to be dead, but who vehemently denies that he or she would ever act upon those feelings, may not be in as much danger as the hopeless student who tells you he plans to kill himself later that day with the gun his father keeps in the bedroom closet. The latter situation is an emergency, and the student should *immediately* be connected with a physician, psychiatrist, or licensed mental health professional who can ensure the student's safety and provide treatment. However, the first student, as well as every teenager along the continuum, should also be taken seriously and would benefit from competent, compassionate counseling or treatment from a professional Christian counselor, psychologist, or psychiatrist. Remember, no suicide risk, threat, or attempt should be taken lightly. Concerns and questions about the level of a student's risk for suicide should be discussed with a trained professional.

A youth worker may also have teenagers in his or her ministry who engage in what are referred to as self-injurious behaviors. Examples include the student who repeatedly cuts or inflicts cigarette burns on his or her arms or legs, although the cuts or burns are not life-threatening. This student also needs skilled, professional help, and a suitable referral should be made as soon as possible.

COUNSELING IDEAS

When there is the possibility or threat of suicide, the situation is so serious that it *always* requires the involvement of a professional. As a youth worker, it is important to understand that the primary responsibility for the treatment of a suicidal person needs to rest with a physician, licensed psychologist, or psychiatrist, and is beyond the training and expertise of most youth workers. At the same time, you will want to do what you can to support the young person and his or her family. So how can you help?

Responding to an Immediate Threat of Suicide

The most important concern when there is a possibility that a student may be suicidal is taking steps to ensure that the student gets the help needed to be safe. If you are concerned that a person is at risk for harming himself or herself, you will want to do the following things:

- Stay calm.
- Say a silent prayer for wisdom and peace for yourself as well as for protection and comfort for the student.
- Ask the student if he or she is thinking about killing himself or herself.
- If the teenager says yes, ask the student whether he or she has thought about how to do this.
- If the student has a plan, ask the teenager whether he or she has access to the means to carry out the plan (such as access to a gun or pills).

If a student answers yes to any of these questions, the student may be in *imminent danger* of killing himself or herself. Many professionals believe that having a suicide plan and having the means to carry out that plan (for example, if a student knows where to get a gun or has a full bottle of antidepressant medication) substantially increases the danger of suicide. If the student has answered yes to the above questions, you will want to take the following steps:

- Thank the student for his or her courage and trust in sharing honest thoughts and feelings with you.
- Make it clear to the person that you care about him or her.
- Show respect for the thoughts and feelings the student has shared with you. A person who is suicidal will likely see things in a distorted way, but it's important to understand that this is his or her present reality.
- Reflect the student's feelings back to him or her to show that you've heard and understood. (Depending on what the student has shared, a possible response might be, "You're very depressed right now and don't see how things will ever feel better.")
- At the same time, make it clear that you know there is help for the teenager and that you believe the student can feel better. Convey this with conviction, but be very careful not to sound too cheery or upbeat or the student may feel that you don't understand the depth of his or her despair and may discount or reject your help.
- Tell the student that you don't view suicide as an acceptable option for him or her. Be gentle and loving in tone to avoid reinforcing the sense of shame that some suicidal individuals feel.
- Make it clear that the student needs help to be safe.
- Seek to obtain a promise from the student that the teenager will not hurt himself or herself and will agree to get help. You may want to take the approach of many professional

counselors and have the student complete a simple "contract" stating this (see the handout on page 184). The added formality of this approach seems to highlight the seriousness of the situation and the need to ensure the student's safety.

- Do not leave the person alone.
- Do not agree to keep the teenager's intention to kill himself or herself a secret.
- Immediately involve the student's parents or guardians, as well as your direct supervisor in your ministry, whenever possible and appropriate. It is helpful to enlist the student's cooperation in informing parents. (Youth workers will need to know the policies of their organization as well as any local, state, or federal laws that apply to confidentiality, parent involvement, and other matters related to dealing with minors.)
- Do whatever is necessary to connect the student with a professional who can help *now*. A person who is suicidal should not be expected to go to an emergency room, doctor, parent, or counselor on his or her own. Waiting a day or two for an appointment may be too late. Because the risk of suicide is so serious and the outcome irreversible, it is better to be too cautious than not cautious enough.
- Make plans with the student and his or her parents about restricting the means to commit suicide; this can be a challenge because there are many ways by which a person might kill himself or herself. It's important to think beyond the familiar methods of suicide to those that may be less recognized, such as engaging in very high-risk behavior. Some injuries and deaths that appear to be accidents (such as a motor vehicle crash or an assault in a dangerous area) actually result from the suicidal person putting himself or herself in harm's way. Some steps in restricting the means of suicide include the following:
    1. Find out if the student has a plan for how he or she would commit suicide.
    2. Decide how to restrict access to the harmful means in that plan (gun, pills, rope, knives, razors, automobile, and so on). Although the person who is truly intent upon ending his or her life can likely find a way to do so, removing guns or pills from the home or restricting access to the car can help save a life.
    3. Even if the student has not mentioned a gun, talk privately with the teenager's parents or guardian to determine if the student has access to one. The presence of a firearm in the home has been shown to significantly increase the risk of suicide. Be sure to have this conversation away from the suicidal person, in the event that the teenager is not aware of the presence of the firearm or he or she had not yet considered using it.
    4. If there is a gun in the home, plan for the gun's removal. Parents can call their local police department to find out how to safely dispose of a firearm.
- Talk with the parents about the urgent need to stay with the teenager until a professional evaluation can be made.
- Arrange to personally accompany the student or have the student accompanied by a parent or other trusted adult to an emergency room, physician, or mental health professional.
- If you won't be going with the student yourself, arrange for follow-up with the accompanying adult to ensure that the plan was carried through.
- Offer to act as an ongoing support person to the student and the student's family.

How to Respond After the Student Has Accessed Professional Help

- Continue to watch the student carefully, being sensitive to clues about how the student is doing.
- Follow up with the student regularly. Agree to meet with the teenager individually or with the family.
- Act as a support person, encouraging the work the student is doing to get better.
- Agree to be an accountability partner to support the student's involvement in treatment. Indicate your concern, and ask the teenager about his or her treatment: When does he or she go? How often? How open and honest is he or she being with the counselor?

  People who are experiencing serious problems do not always feel hopeful or positive about their treatment or their counselor. The counseling relationship is a unique one that is difficult to judge from the outside. It involves both comfort and discomfort as the person learns new coping strategies. Be careful about making negative judgments about the treatment or the professional. Urge the student to discuss with the counselor any questions, concerns, or distress he or she may be experiencing related to treatment.
- Do what you can to involve the student as soon as possible in the scheduled activities of your ministry again.
- Work closely with the teenager and his or her family to discuss expectations of confidentiality with respect to others in the ministry.
- Do not assume that everything is OK just because the person appears to be feeling better or says he or she is better. The threat of suicide can be so horrifying that helpers may want to gain relief from their own worry and sadness by being too quickly convinced that the danger is over. Recovering from depression and thoughts of suicide takes time and can include setbacks along the way.

When a Student in Your Ministry Has Committed Suicide

Sometimes, no matter what you've tried, it happens: a student in your youth ministry or in your community commits suicide. How you respond is critical to everyone who is touched by the tragedy. What can you do?

Of course, youth workers will want to offer their emotional support to the teenager's family. Family members may be feeling tremendous shock, sadness, anger, and guilt, and your providing a listening ear can be a comfort to them. In addition, facilitating practical assistance (such as meals or help with funeral arrangements) is often appreciated in the early stages of grieving.

Youth workers should also be aware of a phenomenon called suicide contagion. Suicide contagion refers to the increased risk of suicide for others who have been touched by a person's suicide. While this phenomenon is not fully understood, it appears that in some instances, exposure to suicide increases the risk of suicide in teenagers who were already experiencing problems. Here are some steps to take that may help decrease the risk of suicide contagion:

- Work closely with the student's family to discuss expectations related to how things will be handled, being sensitive to the family's need for privacy during their time of grief.
- Be attuned to what other students in your ministry already know about the situation.
- Be especially alert to the students who may have been distressed prior to the suicide. You

Suicide

can use the list of risk factors provided in this chapter (pp. 178-179) to identify others who may be at risk of harming themselves.

- Be aware that the way in which a suicide is discussed may influence the risk of suicide contagion.[2] Avoid sensationalistic, detailed descriptions of the means of suicide; don't give a simplistic picture of why the person may have committed this act ("because his girlfriend broke up with him"); avoid focusing solely on the positive aspects of the person (a person who has committed suicide has often been struggling with significant problems over time); and don't discuss the person or the event in ways that could glorify the person or the suicidal act.

---

[1]   Statistics related to suicide are available at www.cdc.gov/safeusa/suicide.htm.

[2]   See "Suicide Contagion and the Reporting of Suicide: Recommendations From a National Workshop," The Morbidity and Mortality Weekly Report (vol. 43, no. RR-6, April 22, 1994), 14-17. Information about suicide and suicide contagion is also available from the National Institute of Mental Health's Web site at www.nimh.nih.gov/research/suicidefaq.cfm.

Recommended Resources

Web Resources

- www.cdc.gov (Web site of Centers for Disease Control and Prevention. Click on "Health Topics" and look for "suicide.")

- www.nimh.nih.gov (Web site of National Institute of Mental Health. Information about suicide is available at www.nimh.nih.gov/publicat/depsuicidemenu.cfm.)

- www.suicidology.org (Web site of American Association of Suicidology)

STUDENT PAGE Use the photocopiable contract on page 184 to help in intervention efforts with a suicidal teenager.

Choosing Safety, Choosing Life Contract

I, _____, agree to choose life today. I will not take any

actions to harm myself. I agree to take the following steps to get help:

_____

_____

_____

_____

_____

_____

_____

_____

_____

_____

_____   _____
NAME   **DATE**

_____   _____
WITNESS   **DATE**

COLLEEN J. ALDEN, M.A.—Colleen is the Client Services Director at Alternatives Pregnancy Center in Littleton, Colorado, where she focuses on counseling women and teenagers facing crisis pregnancy issues. Colleen has worked with teenagers in many capacities, including several years of ministry with Young Life. Colleen received her bachelor's degree from Miami University (Ohio) and her M.A. in professional counseling from Colorado Christian University.

ROY E. BARSNESS, Ph.D.—Roy is a licensed clinical psychologist in private practice in Seattle and is an associate professor in the School of Psychology, Family, and Community at Seattle Pacific University. He completed his M.A. in theology at Fuller Theological Seminary and his Ph.D. in clinical psychology at the California School of Professional Psychology, Los Angeles. He has done postgraduate studies in family therapy at the Los Angeles Family Institute and has also studied at the Northwest Center for Psychoanalysis in Seattle. He is the father of two teenage boys who have taught him just a little more than he thought he ever needed to know about adolescence!

SALLY SCHWER CANNING, Ph.D.—Sally is a core faculty member in the doctoral program in clinical psychology at Wheaton College, where she also directs the Urban Partnership Initiative. Sally is a community and licensed clinical psychologist who specializes in community-based interventions with urban, low-income children and families through collaboration with faith-based community organizations. Sally has a bachelor of arts degree in music performance and earned her Ph.D. in counseling psychology from the University of Pennsylvania.

JAMES D. FROST, M.A.—James works as a licensed psychological examiner for AGAPE, Inc., a Christian social services agency in Nashville, Tennessee. Specializing in treating mood and anxiety disorders, James worked in community mental health centers before joining the staff at AGAPE. He earned his B.S. at David Lipscomb University and his M.A. in clinical psychology from Middle Tennessee State University.

SCOTT GIBSON, M.S.W., L.C.S.W.—Scott is a psychotherapist in private practice at Changes Unlimited in Arlington Heights, Illinois. He specializes in adolescent, marital, individual, and group therapy. Scott previously worked with teenagers through a ministry of Campus Crusade for Christ and served on the pastoral staff of Willow Creek Community Church in South Barrington, Illinois, for twelve years. Scott received his B.S. from Purdue University and his M.S.W. from Loyola University, Chicago.

D. PATRICK HOPP, Ph.D.—Patrick is an assistant professor at Seattle Pacific University, where he supervises the clinical work of doctoral students in psychology. As a licensed psychologist in private practice, Patrick specializes in adult and adolescent individual psychotherapy and psychological assessment. Patrick received his B.S. in psychology from the University of Washington and his M.A. in Christian leadership and a Ph.D. in clinical psychology from Fuller Theological Seminary.

CYNTHIA LINDQUIST, M.S.—Cynthia is a veteran public school teacher certified in K-12 special education. Cynthia's specialization is in working with students with learning disabilities and behavior disorders and the educable mentally handicapped. Cynthia earned her B.A. in elementary education from Trinity International University and her M.S. from Northern Illinois University.

LARRY LINDQUIST, Ed.D.—Larry is a faculty member in the departments of Educational Ministry and Youth and Family Ministries at Denver Seminary, and he has nearly two decades of experience as a public educator and pastor to students and families. Larry earned his B.A. from Trinity International University, his M.A. from Trinity Evangelical Divinity School, and his Ed.D. from Northern Illinois University.

JULIE A. ODELL, M.A.—Julie specializes in adolescent issues, including parent-adolescent relationships; women's issues; and issues related to adult children of abusive families and families with addictions. She works as a counselor in private practice and also as a counselor for several ministries and organizations in northern Colorado. Julie received her bachelor's degree in psychology from Colorado State University and her master's degree in counseling from Assemblies of God Theological Seminary.

KYLE D. PONTIUS, Ph.D.—Kyle is a clinical psychologist in practice with Meier New Life Clinics in Orange and San Juan Capistrano, California. Kyle has served on the adjunct faculty of Azusa Pacific University and Concordia University, Irvine, teaching developmental psychology on both the graduate and undergraduate levels. He has also been on the pastoral staffs of three churches serving in the areas of youth, Christian education, and counseling. Kyle holds a B.A. from Seattle Pacific University, an M.A. in Christian education from Talbot Theological Seminary, an M.S. in counseling from California State University, Fullerton, and a Ph.D. in psychology from United States International University, San Diego.

TREVOR SIMPSON, M.A.—Trevor works as a youth pastor at Crossroads Covenant Church in Loveland, Colorado, and is a self-employed therapist specializing in crisis intervention, adolescents and families, and interpersonal communication skills. Trevor has several years of youth ministry experience and has worked as a residential counselor with children and youth. Trevor received his B.A. from Trinity International University and master's degrees in both counseling and youth and family ministry from Denver Seminary.

ROBERT A. WATSON, Psy.D.—Robert is a licensed clinical psychologist and an assistant professor of clinical psychology at Wheaton College. He is a core faculty member of the doctoral program in clinical psychology and is interested in understanding the relationship between psychological development and Christian spiritual formation. In addition to his work at Wheaton, Robert is in private practice and provides counseling, consulting, and supervision services. Robert received his B.A. with honors from Florida State University, his M.A. in clinical psychology from Wheaton College, and his Psy.D. from the Illinois School of Professional Psychology.

TERRI S. WATSON, Psy.D.—Terri is a licensed clinical psychologist and an assistant professor of psychology at Wheaton College, and she coordinates Wheaton's master's program in psychology. Terri has extensive experience in child and family therapy as well as clinical supervision, and she is a member of the American Association for Marriage and Family Therapy and the Christian Association for Psychological Studies. Terri provides supervision and consultation to many Christian agencies and missions organizations. Terri received her B.A. with honors from Indiana University, her M.A. in clinical psychology from Wheaton College, and her Psy.D. from the Illinois School of Professional Psychology.

Group Publishing, Inc.
Attention: Product Development
P.O. Box 481
Loveland, CO 80539
Fax: (970) 679-4370

Evaluation for
The Comprehensive Guide to Youth Ministry Counseling

Please help Group Publishing, Inc., continue to provide innovative and useful resources for ministry. Please take a moment to fill out this evaluation and mail or fax it to us. Thanks!

● ● ●

1. As a whole, this book has been (circle one)
not very helpful   very helpful

1   2   3   4   5   6   7   8   9   10

2. The best things about this book:

3. Ways this book could be improved:

4. Things I will change because of this book:

5. Other books I'd like to see Group publish in the future:

6. Would you be interested in field-testing future Group products and giving us your feedback? If so, please fill in the information below:

Name _____

Church Name _____

Denomination _____ Church Size _____

Church Address _____

City _____ State _____ ZIP _____

Church Phone_____

E-mail _____

Group-Building Resources for Your Youth Ministry

Tough Questions: 500 Bold Discussion Starters
Josh Warren with Foreword by Doug Fields

Introducing the first book by Josh Warren, son of Saddleback Church pastor Rick Warren. Packed with 500 bold discussion starters, *Tough Questions* isn't about trivial questions...it's about things that kids really care about. Scripture. The Heart. Accountability. Relationships. Experiences. Topics that force them to evaluate themselves...their relationships with others...and their relationship with God. With 3 levels of intensity, these discussion starters are perfect for any setting to get kids sharing about things important to their faith.

ISBN 0-7644-2392-4 $9.99

Josh Warren is the son of Rick Warren, pastor of Saddleback Church. Josh wrote these questions as a teenager and used them for powerful discussions with other teens while in high school, and then later as a college student.

Risk in Our Midst:
Empowering Teenagers to Love the Unlovable
Dr. Scott Larson with contributions by Dr. John Hoover

Challenge teenagers to reach out to their peers with Christ's love!

Show youth the power they possess to minister to their hurting peers. With riveting true accounts—and practical tips for training teenagers to reach out—this book will ignite your ministry with Christ's compassion for the spiritually needy. A must-have resource for anyone interested in loving the unloved and teaching young people to do the same.

ISBN 0-7644-2248-0 $15.99

Order today from your local Christian bookstore, online at www.grouppublishing.com, or write:
Group Publishing, P.O. Box 485, Loveland, CO 80539-0485.

The Winning Spirit: Empowering Teenagers Through God's Grace
Chris Hill

This youth ministry veteran details a fresh vision and practical philosophy for youth ministry. It's about loving kids as Jesus loves them. Grace-based youth ministry that gives students a God's-eye view of themselves as winners. In this book, you'll find...

- a new perspective on youth ministry that transforms students' lives through love and grace, set against a backdrop of the biblical story of David—before Goliath.
- a strong foundation for life-changing ministry along with a lot of practical ideas and examples from the author's ministry.
- real-life accounts of young people's lives changed through love and grace.

Be inspired, encouraged, and motivated by a new dream for your youth ministry.

ISBN 0-7644-2396-7 $16.99

Chris Hill is an 18-year youth ministry veteran of successful grace-based youth ministry in both urban and suburban settings. A sought-after speaker and writer, he currently serves as youth and associate pastor of The Potter's House in Dallas, Texas, where Bishop T.D. Jakes serves as senior pastor. It is one of the largest and fastest growing churches in the country.

At Risk: Bringing Hope to Hurting Teenagers
Dr. Scott Larson

Discover how to meet the needs of hurting teenagers with these practical suggestions, honest answers, and tools to help you evaluate your existing programs. Plus, you'll get real-life insights about what it takes to include kids others have left behind.

ISBN 0-7644-2091-7 $15.99

Order today from your local Christian bookstore, online at www.grouppublishing.com, or write:
Group Publishing, P.O. Box 485, Loveland, CO 80539-0485.

Equip and Encourage
Parents of Teenagers

Parenting Teenagers for Positive Results:
An Interactive Video Course for
Small Groups and Sunday Schools
Jim Burns

Help parents develop their skills by comparing notes with youth culture and family expert Jim Burns. The video features 12 segments with insightful teaching and humorous vignettes of "real" family situations. Parents of teens and preteens interact after each session in a guided, small group setting. They'll be equipped to parent their teen, encouraged and affirmed in their role, and able to forge lifeline friendships with other parents—so they can navigate the teen years with joy and confidence! Focus on six key aspects of parenting teens: attitude (yours and theirs), self-image, communication, sexuality issues, media discernment, and how to help teenagers grow spiritually. Includes a 12-segment video, an easy-to-use Leader Guide and six Participant's Guides.

ISBN 0-7644-1304-X $89.99

Jim Burns, Ph.D., serves as President of YouthBuilders, an organization that exists to empower young people and their families to make wise decisions and experience a vital Christian lifestyle. Jim is a frequent guest on TV and radio programs. His daily radio feature program that provides parenting advice is aired on over 500 stations/ outlets, enjoying a daily listening audience of over 1.3 million.